ADRIANOPLE

BLACK SEA

Adrianople

Didimocheion

ntinople

SEA OF MARMARA

Gallipoli

Plampsaka

ASIA MINOR

LESBOS

Mytilene

Germe

Geliana

Phocea

Magnesia

Kula

Smyrna

Philadelphia

CHIOS

Tire

Nicaea Palaiapolis

Ephesus

Anaia

THE CATALAN CHRONICLE
OF FRANCISCO DE MONCADA

Para Ramón José Sender
un noble aragonés

The Catalan Chronicle
of
Francisco de Moncada

Translated by
Frances Hernández

Edited by
JOHN M. SHARP

TEXAS WESTERN PRESS
THE UNIVERSITY OF TEXAS AT EL PASO
1975

COPYRIGHT 1975
TEXAS WESTERN PRESS
THE UNIVERSITY OF TEXAS AT EL PASO

Library of Congress Catalog Card 70-175244
ISBN 0-87404-036-1

Illustrations by
José Cisneros

Designed by
Evan Haywood Antone

ACKNOWLEDGMENTS

Many friends, scholars, and colleagues have aided me over the years in the preparation of this translation. Of these I am most in debt to Dr. Ramón Sender, who first led me to Moncada's chronicle, suggested that I bring it into English, and then tirelessly assisted me with the peculiarities of his native language and the complexities of northern Spanish history. To Dr. John McCarty Sharp I owe deep gratitude for his conscientious, erudite, and often brilliant editing of the work. Staffs of the Zimmerman Library at the University of New Mexico, the Widener Library at Harvard University, and the college library at the University of Texas at El Paso have been unstintingly helpful.

CONTENTS

ILLUSTRATIONS

CHARTS

TRANSLATOR'S PREFACE

I

IN 1620 AN ERUDITE YOUNG ARAGONESE gentleman-scholar, Francisco de Moncada, completed his history of the adventures of a band of northern Spanish mercenaries who fought their way around the Mediterranean in the fourteenth century. Collating the accounts of Ramón Muntaner, a soldier-chronicler on the expedition, with those of other eye-witnesses or contemporary reporters—Desclot, Berenguer de Entenza, Zurita, Pachymeres, Gregoras, Chalcocondyle, and Cantacuzene, he produced a literary chronicle that has become a classic of the genre: *Expedición de los catalanes y aragoneses contra los turcos y griegos.*

Moncada's motives for the work, as he explains in his introduction, were "a natural desire to preserve the country's dying memories that merit eternal existence" and to add luster to his own family's history, although his surname itself does not appear in the narrative. It occurs frequently, however, in the annals of the northeastern provinces, first in the legends of the Reconquest when it began in Catalonia. The earliest known Catalan poet was Ot de Montcada of the eleventh century; other Moncadas are among the medieval aristocracy of France and Italy. Two famous brothers of the name were wept over by their king when they died at an assault on Majorca and were buried at Santes Creus, the second of the great Cistercian monasteries founded by Count Ramón Berenguer IV. Cervantes fought under a Catalan leader named Montcada at the decisive Battle of Lepanto on October 7, 1571, and Lord Byron made his Don Juan a member of the eminent family.

The chronicler's grandfather, another Francisco de Moncada, was named Marquis of Aytona by Felipe II. His father served as viceroy of Aragon and ambassador to Rome, and his mother, also a Moncada, was Catalina, the baroness of Callosa. With such a history, he grew up possessing a detailed knowledge of his forebears and a profound appreciation for the past of Aragon, including the remarkable expedition that began in 1301. Little is known of the childhood and youth of Moncada. He knew European and Near Eastern history and geography, much of which he may have learned at first hand on campaigns with his father against Vienna and Flanders.

Apparently one of the books he studied as a child was *Tirant lo Blanch*, a chivalric tale by the Valencian, Joanot Martorell, which was praised in *Don Quixote*. It is a realistic adventure story based on the exploits of the Almugavars in the East, as they were reported by the chronicler of the Catalan Company, Ramón Muntaner. Along with his rigorous traditional education, Moncada must also have read many of the *libros de caballería* from the troubadors of the time of Alfonso II of Catalonia through the periods of their development into chronicles and then true histories on the classical model. He would, for example, have known Jaime the Conqueror's account, *The Book of Deeds*, in which the flamboyant monarch outlined his campaign plans for Valencia and the Balearic Isles.

When he was twenty-four he married Margarita de Castro y Cervellón, heiress to the barony of La Laguna. Assimilating her land titles to those of his own family, Moncada lived near the king's court until the advent of Felipe IV. Under conditions of leisure and luxury, he began to write, publishing his *Genealogy of the House of Moncada* in Pedro de Marca's *Histoire du Béarn*. His *Antiquities of the Sanctuary of Monserrate* is not extant; the *Life of Boethius* was not published until six years after his death.

His literary activities ceased when he was named ambassador to Germany. A busy political and diplomatic career ensued, making the rest of his life a series of missions and expeditions. In 1622 his sovereign sent him into Catalonia to pacify a group of discontented citizens who were refusing to accept their new viceroy, Bishop Juan Sentís. Moncada skillfully managed the matter to satisfy all. He continued to serve the interests of the crown successfully, though often depressed and anxious about his own affairs. Frequently he lacked funds to carry out his office according to the requirements of Spanish royal dignity, for which King Felipe, struggling against pauperism himself, was slow in sending support. Always he suffered homesickness for Aragon.

Moncada's father died in 1623, compelling the new Marquis of Aytona to return to the lands of his family. But he was soon ordered back to the Low Countries to serve as counsellor to the king's weak-willed aunt, Princess Isabel Clara, who was constantly threatened with attack by the Hollanders and all the enemies of the House of Austria. In spite of Isabel's resentment of her nephew's intrusion into her affairs, she soon found the talented Aragonese indispensable to her court. Although ultimately second in command of all the Spanish forces in the Netherlands, Moncada wrote long, fervent letters to Felipe, asking to be relieved of his charge. But to the ruler who depended upon him so entirely, such a removal in the increasingly turbulent times was out of the question. In 1635 Moncada was killed in battle at Goch in the duchy of Cleves, without realizing his dreams of a peaceful life among his books again. The king expressed his grief to the dead vassal's children, Guillén Ramón and Catalina, mourning the loss of a great man in a period when he was needed most. Thus, the noble Aragonese left behind him as lasting monument not his splendid record in court and diplomatic affairs, his achievements in wide classical learning, nor his considerable personal popularity, but, rather, a charming tale, the *Expedición.*

He could not have picked a historical episode with more lasting appeal for his countrymen. When the ancient tradition of holding literary contests called the Floral Games was reinstituted by the Academy of Belles-Lettres in Barcelona in 1859, the winner of the verse competition, Joaquín Rubió i Ors, walked away in the troubador's velvet cap and silver garland, awarded for his composition on the exploits of the Catalans in Greece from 1311 - 1388. Moncada's version is a meticulously constructed narrative of some 75,000 words, which he dedicated to his uncle, don Juan de Moncada, the archbishop of Tarragona and primate of northeastern Spain. His research required study of fragmentary documents—full of contradictions and discrepancies—in Latin, Greek, and, most often, *llemosí,* the conventional name for the Catalan language. The abrupt sentence structure and archaic vocabulary of the seventy chapters show influence of the Catalan tongue, even though they are written in the fluent Castilian required for publication under Felipe IV of the Hapsburg dynasty. Although the story seems to end logically and neatly with "the adventures of the Catalans and Aragonese in Athens," it is apparent that he did not intend to abandon the work at that point. He closes the chronicle with the comment, "until such time as we have full and accurate records of what happened during the hundred and fifty years they remained in Athens."

II

The Catalan Company began its adventures in a setting of political turmoil that existed throughout Europe in the last years of the thirteenth century. Western Christendom had expanded eastward, with a resulting complex of feudal states in Palestine and Syria, established by crusaders from the northern Mediterranean shores. In England the century ended with the reign of Edward I and the Model Parliament; in France the dynasty of Hugh Capet lost territory to the British, but developed gradually toward the summoning of the States General in 1302. In Germany, Frederick II of Hohenstauffen, born and educated in Italy, became the king of Sicily, the emperor of the Germanys, and the wonder of the world. On the Iberian Peninsula the formative era of the Ramón Berenguers in northeastern Spain was over.

It had been a colorful time when the Counts of Barcelona, whose descendants were among the leaders of the Catalan Company, ruled in Aragon and Catalonia. Ramón Berenguer I (1035-1076), who had inverted the name of his father, Berenguer Ramón I, extracted tribute from the neighboring Moorish kings and supervised the adoption of the Usatges, a form of Magna Carta, that codified the rights and powers between ruler and nobles. The third Berenguer, Ramón the Great, ruled from 1096-1131, and having married a daughter of the legendary Cid, Ruy Díaz de Vivar, acquired with her all but two of the Catalan counties, as well as much of Provence. From this position of increased strength, he was able to establish commercial and diplomatic relations with Genoa and other Italian republics, form alliances with the adjoining provinces of Aragon and Calabria, and finally marry his daughter to Alfonso VII of Castile. When his first son, known as Alfonso, the Warrior of Aragon, died in 1134 without leaving an heir, Ramón III removed his second son, also Ramón, from a monastery and betrothed the youth to Petronilla, the two-year-old child of Ramiro II of Aragon, called the Monk. Soon afterward the domains of Aragon and Catalonia were merged under young Ramón IV, when his father-in-law abdicated the throne to return to his monastic vows. Although ruler of a now vast realm in the Iberian peninsula, the new Ramón refused to call himself a king, pointing out that there were many minor kingdoms in Christendom, but that those of the lineage of Barcelona were the greatest of the counts in the world.

Count Ramón Berenguer IV did not forget his obligations to the Cistercian monks who had educated him; he founded the two great monasteries, Santes Creus and Santa María de Poblet, near Espulga de Francolí, where the kings of Catalonia-Aragon were afterward buried. When he died in 1162, he left Petronilla with a ten-year-old son, Ramón Berenguer V. But as the lad came to the throne, he decided to become a king of Aragon, rather than a Catalan count as his father had been so proud to be: Alfonso I of Aragon-Catalonia. His mother abdicated her claim to the Catalan patrimony two years after her husband's death, leaving the boy to call their domain Aragon, even though most of the territory was Catalan. By the time he had reigned seventeen years, he and Alfonso VIII of Castile divided all of Spain between them. In addition to the House of Aragon, he had established a Mediterranean navy as a permanent institution, using it to make himself known as "the emperor of the Pyrenees," to ally himself with the Italians of Pisa, and to expand his hegemony across southern France from Nice to the Atlantic. The dynasty of the Berenguers, the great counts of Barcelona, passed with the rule of Alfonso I, an institutional innovator as well as a troubador of the deeds of his ancestors.

His son, Pedro II (1196-1213), was called the Catholic because early in his seventeen-year reign he deeded his wide domains to the Pope, who then formally returned them to him as a fief to govern. By this maneuver Pedro was apparently hoping for strong Papal support against his threatening French neighbors to the north. But help was not forthcoming when the anti-Papal Albigenses invaded, led by Simon de Montfort. Pedro lost his rule at the battles of Muret and Provence. His small son, Jaime, came to the throne at five after his father's death, a boy who led a dangerous childhood under the severe control and close surveillance of de Montfort. But, effectively protected by Pope Innocent III, he survived to become Jaime the Conqueror, sending the French home again and adding the Balearic Isles and Valencia to the combined kingdom. A legendary figure, remembered as seven feet tall with blue eyes and red-gold hair, Jaime permitted during his reign the first parliamentary assemblies and even started off with a fleet on a crusade to Palestine, though only a few of his ships managed to get through a fierce storm at sea.

At the end of his flamboyant sixty-three-year reign, Jaime was succeeded by his eldest son, Pedro III, the Great, of Aragon (1276-1285), who continued his father's ambitious foreign policy. To the integrated regions of his patrimony, Pedro eventually added Sicily and Tunis, entering into his alliance with the Hohenstauffens by marrying Constanza, the daughter of Manfred, the German king of the Sicilies. Through this agreement, however, he became involved in the centuries-long struggle between the Pope and the Holy Roman Emperors. The primate of the Roman Church had just won a victory, as part of the spoils for which he claimed southern Italy and Sicily. But King Manfred did not recognize Innocent's authority nor concede his demands. Since the Pope could not muster the power to enforce his claim on the southern island, he offered the region to a stronger and more dependable vassal, Prince Charles of France, who he thought could manage the intractable Sicilians.

Charles of Anjou, the seventh son of Louis VIII, had been given the right to rule Naples and Sicily largely through the influence of Pope Urban IV and later of Clement IV. In 1265 he marched with his army to confront the defiant Manfred at Naples. An Italian nobleman, Buoso da Duera, came out at the head of an army of Ghibelline partisans to oppose the French foreigners. The local soldiers, people from Apulia, were charged to hold the pass at Ceperano against the invaders. But, either under secret pressure from the Pope or the obligation of a bribe from Charles's forces, they allowed the French to ride through near Parma unharmed. In the subsequent, unexpected battle at Benevento, Manfred was killed and Charles took the rule. He held sway uneasily, however, threatened again two years later by Manfred's nephew, Conradin. He defended his claim by concealing the number of his reserve troops from the attackers, using the battle stratagem suggested by Alard de Valéry.

Charles maintained his tyrannical rule until 1282, the day of the fierce and famous uprising of his resentful subjects at Palermo—the Sicilian Vespers. It was a popular, spontaneous, general slaughter of all the Frenchmen on the island. Many contemporaries believed that the rebellion was encouraged by the new Pope, Nicholas III, who had come to the office two years before and apparently did not favor Charles of Anjou as enthusiastically as had his predecessors. It is uncertain what his opposition was to the French prince, but later historians tend to doubt his complicity in the Vespers. Pedro II of Aragon, old ally and son-in-law of Manfred, did take advantage of the political climate, however. He sent up his fleet from Tunis, under the command of his admiral, Roger de Lauria (called Llúria by the Catalans) to help the Sicilians at Messina, where Charles was besieged. The Angevin prince retreated to Calabria, was defeated off Malta, and subsequently died. Manfred's former subjects offered Pedro the crown, which he graciously accepted, with Roger de Lauria, a Sicilian of Constanza's train who had been educated in Catalonia, in attendance. For this effrontery against a Church-appointed ruler, Pope Nicholas excommunicated the Aragonese king—the grandson of Pedro the Catholic. This time his throne was offered to Charles of Valois, the second son of the French king, who promptly invaded the contested realms in 1285. The French almost won, but were driven back by de Lauria and an epidemic of smallpox. Pedro the Great, however, after the long struggle to secure his rights, died the same year. Worried about his soul, still in conflict with the Church, he sent word to the Pope from his death bed that he was willing to return the Sicilians to the power of the Holy See.

But his son, Alfonso III of Aragon, did not intend to abandon Sicily in subjection to his dying father's religious whim. Although a youth of twenty-one himself when he reached the throne, he sent his younger brother, Jaime, to govern the island as a separate kingdom. Alfonso the Liberal's short reign was besieged by turmoil; he was forced to defend the Balearic Isles against his uncle, Jaime, who had joined the French against his father, and he became involved in a long contention with Aragonese and Valencian nobles who had also conspired against him. In 1291 he finally changed his mind about Sicily, and, like his father, renounced his claim, even agreeing to pay back tribute to the Pope. But, after six years as king, he died before he could act upon his treaties of peace with France and the Church. Young Jaime of Sicily succeeded him, and again the Aragonese and Catalan nobles worked to prevent the loss of the Italian land for which they had fought so hard.

When the prince returned to Catalonia as Jaime II of Aragon, he left his younger brother, Fadrique, to rule Sicily. Before many years passed, the beleaguered islanders were for a third time threatened with the unwanted rule of the Church. Their former ruler, King Manfred's grandson, then entered into a business arrangement with the Church to exchange Sicily for the islands of Sardinia and Corsica, which he was to be allowed to hold in fief—after he had conquered them. But the Sicilians had had enough of perfidy; they proclaimed Fadrique their king and rebelled against both Aragon-Catalonia and the Pope in a long war that finally ended in 1302—when Fadrique married Leonora of Anjou, the daughter of one of the rival claimants to the papacy. Once more a young prince of the House of Aragon promised the succession of Sicily to a possible Pope, his father-in-law. It is at this point in the history of Catalonia-Aragon that the action of Moncada's chronicle begins.

III

In 1302 King Fadrique of Sicily had reached a peaceful agreement with his older brother, Jaime II of Aragon, and Pope Boniface VIII regarding the rule of his country. According to their treaty of Caltabellota, Fadrique would remain on the throne for life, after which the crown would revert to the House of Anjou. Sicily, however, remained Catalan in speech and law for centuries.

Fadrique's immediate problem after the exhausting conflict was to get rid of the army that had preserved him. During the medieval period there were no regular standing armies; in time of war the nobles simply outfitted their vassals and peasants for battle. But a class of roving mercenary soldiers did gradually emerge, largely made up of dispossessed men of the gentry who travelled in small bands of national allegiance and offered their services to threatened or ambitious governments. When the young Sicilian ruler found himself against the much stronger forces of Aragon and the Pope, he arranged for the services of the Catalan and Aragonese professionals who had been trained in the generations of turmoil in the northern provinces. They were thoroughly competent, but when their mission was over, they became an expensive and threatening menace to the kingdom. They could not safely return to their homeland, nor to any Christian land under the power of the Pope.

The army called itself the Free Company of Catalans, but they were popularly known as the *almugávers* or "skirmishers" from the Arabic *al-*

mugawar. Most were light-armed infantrymen, veterans of the campaigns of Pedro the Great. Some of the leaders were of the old Catalan nobility, *los señores allodiales,* who had lost their family land holdings through political disaffection. More were from the *emparats* or *homes de paratge,* an intermediate, dependent social class, protégés of the nobles. Barcelona and the surrounding charter towns, such as Tarragona, also provided members from the strong middle class. Of course, a few *colonos* or *paveses,* a a veritable serf class, overburdened with taxes and service obligations, accompanied their masters.

Roger de Flor, a thirty-four-year-old soldier of fortune of German blood, was chief of the Company. Fadrique had given him the rank of vice-admiral on the strength of his experience with the Knights Templar in recent Crusades. Roger's exploits in the battles at Acre were famous, including his killing of an enemy chieftain with a banner staff as a weapon. After the fall of Acre in 1291, the Catalan Templar had enriched himself from the spoils gathered by the Knights, to the extant that the order's grand master had denounced him to Pope Bonifacio as a robber and apostate. Roger was thus, because of his disgrace with the Church, in a position to fight against it for Fadrique.

As an escape from his dilemma, the young king made brilliant arrangements to send his burdensome supporters far away to the Eastern end of the Mediterranean. Andronicus, the older Greek Grand Duke at Constantinople, was threatened by the Turks who had overrun Asia Minor. In 1301 Fadrique was negotiating for good salaries for the men and for their leader the title of Grand Duke and Princess María of Bulgaria as a wife. Through this alliance with the Emperor's niece, both Fadrique and Andronicus hoped for a permanent association. Roger and the Company embarked the following summer from Messina, fifteen hundred horsemen and four thousand soldiers, fitted out by Fadrique with thirty-nine ships to transport them. But the projected relationship lasted only three years.

The Company found the Palaeologus empire—established in 1261 to replace the Latin hegemony of the Fourth Crusade that had moved in more than fifty years before—besieged by Turks on the north and east and menaced by French Angevins and Genoese on the north and west. The Catalans were soon effective against the Emperor's enemies; two years later no serious challenger remained. But trouble began to develop in Constantinople. There were confrontations with Genoese emissaries, the old commercial rivals of trading ports in Catalonia. Then the Emperor's son, Michael Palaeologus, grew fearful of the wealth and honors that members of the Company had acquired with their successes and especially of the increasing number of mercenaries who joined them. As Roger de Flor sensed the rising suspicion among his employers, he sought to clarify his position with demands. He asked that one of his lieutenants, Fernando Aonés, be given the title of Admiral of the Empire and one of the Emperor's female relatives in marriage. Roger himself ascended to the rank of Caesar and established his headquarters at Gallipoli.

Moncada's chronicle describes the intense jealousy that the Byzantine Greek nobles felt for the Catalans, which came to a climax in 1305 when Prince Michael summoned Roger de Flor to Adrianople on pretext of some celebration. His wife, María, the closest members of her family, and the Council of the Company urged Roger not to accept the invitation, but he was determined to go. After ordering Aonés to deliver María to safety in Constantinople, he departed with three hundred mounted attendants and a thousand on foot. They were massacred at the banquet, from which it was reported that only three Catalans escaped.

The three thousand three hundred members of the Company remaining at Gallipoli, many of them women and disabled men, elected the Grand Duke Berenguer d'Entenza to replace Roger and planned their revenge. The new chief, brother-in-law to King Pedro the Great's old admiral, Roger de Lauria, strengthened their large fortress on the strategic juncture of the Sea of Marmara and the Strait of the Dardanelles and, one month after Roger de Flor's death, formally declared war on the Greeks. They soon lost a squadron of ships and Berenguer, who disappeared as a prisoner. Then the former seneschal of the army, Berenguer de Rocafort, succeeded to the command, leading the men in their defense of the fortress for two years, in the burning and sacking of towns within the Greek empire, and to a vengeance against the Palaeologus dynasty that rivaled the ferocity of the Sicilian Vespers. Eventually the Catalans moved out on their depredations into Thrace, Macedonia, and Bulgaria, and then southward to Smyrna and Ephesus, occasionally hiring out their services here and there.

In 1310 a new duke achieved precarious power in the city-state of Athens, inviting the Catalans to help him secure his throne. But this member of the French Brienne family had as much difficulty with his employees as his predecessors had had in Constantinople. Within six months of their alliance, the mercenaries had dispatched the enemies of Duke Gautier, quarreled and fought with the Athenians, and dethroned and executed their patron. The Council of the Company then decided to end their quarter of a century of wandering and settle in the ancient and agreeable duchy on the Attic Peninsula. They sent ambassadors back to King Fadrique in Sicily, asking him for a royal ruler. He promptly designated in 1326 his second son, the young Prince Manfred, represented by his older brother, Alfonso. The boy died, but Alfonso organized the Catalan state of Athens as a formal part of the domains of the kingdom of Aragon-Catalonia, which lasted more than fifty years.

Moncada's chronicle ends with the establishment of the House of Aragon in Athens under Fadrique's son, Alfonso, who stayed on as the formal sucessor to Manfred. The descendants of the Almugavars continued their looting expeditions into Tartary, Persia, and Armenia, followed by other forays against Neopatria and the Morea. In 1353 they sent an expedition to help Venice defeat their old enemies, the Genoese.

When Pedro IV (1335-1387) succeeded his father, Alfonso the Benign, in Aragon, trouble developed in the homeland that called some of the now expatriated Company back to Spain. Pedro, who was known as the Ceremonious because of his hypocrisy and concern for appearances, needed his forces to counter the opposition of recurrently restive nobles in the provinces of Aragon and Valencia. In 1348 he met them in a decisive battle at Epila, where feudal anarchy between sovereign and lords was crushed permanently. Eight years later he entered into a great struggle with Pedro the Cruel of Castile, which taxed his resources severely. In sore need of his countrymen who were off in Greece, he was forced to hire the International Brigade, a band of French mercenaries under Bertrand du Guesclin, sometimes called the last great heroic figure of the Middle Ages. At length he formed an alliance with his enemy's half brother, Henry of Trastamara, in 1363, and with some additional help from England, was secured in his rule in 1367 for another twenty years.

The Catalans maintained their distant enclave throughout the reign of Pedro the Ceremonious, resisting all internal and external attempts to banish them. They resembled the Uskaks, South Slav refugees who settled on the Dalmatian Coast two centuries later, where they remained for generations, fighting off both Turks and Venetians by sea, though there were only two thousand of them. The end for the Company came during the short reign of Pedro's son in Aragon, Juan the Unready. A combined force of the powerful Florentine family, the Acciajuoli, the Anjous of Naples, and Navarrese mercenaries slowly reconquered all of the territory held by the Catalan Company. Remnants of the Almugaver army under Pere de Pau defended themselves at the Acropolis for fifteen months. Their leader sent a desperate call for relief to King Juan in Catalonia, but the answer came that no one was available then to help.

The Catalan rule of Athens was overcome in 1388, at a time when Chaucer was working on the *Canterbury Tales* in England and Bernat Metge, Juan's suave secretary, was opening the classical age of Catalan

literature with a prose translation of Petrarch's *Valter e Griselda*. The survivors escaped to the island of Aegina, where a colony maintained its
identity until about 1450, gradually disappearing thereafter. In 1453 Catalan troops assembled again to fight for Constantinople, but this time it
fell to the Turks. The dynasty of the House of Aragon also came to an
end with the reign of Pedro's son, Martín the Humane (1396-1410). His
son, Martín the Younger, ruled in Sicily until his death, which came before that of King Martín of Aragon.

The lineage was then replaced by the House of Trastamara, beginning
with Fernando. His son, Alfonso the Magnanimous, considered gathering the few remaining Catalan colonies of Greece into a new empire. He
even presented a formal claim to the current Duke of Athens, but the
descendants of the Almugavers had lost the aggressive spirit of the old
Free Company. When Moncada was writing his *Expedición*, memory of
the conquering Catalans was so alive in Athens that the most dire curse
was still "May you suffer the vengeance of the Catalans!" and in an ancient section of the city, the citizens still spoke the *llemosí* dialect. The
word *Katallán-i* means "monster" along the Adriatic coasts, preserving
its sinister connotation yet today.

IV

The genre of the literary chronicle stands between the eyewitness jour-
nals of the men of deeds and the meticulous researches of modern historians. All such narratives of the active events of human history share
a respect for chronology and objectivity, but with widely disparate style,
intent, and technique. As a distinct branch of the story-telling art, the
contemporaneous chronicles have been characterized by a brusquely direct
style, a minimum of external detail, and the strong partisanship of participants in the action they describe. Some, like the work of Bernal Díaz
del Castillo, the non-literary soldier with Hernán Cortés in the New
World, shine with vivid, I-was-there immediacy. Others, such as those of
Jean Froissart, the medieval traveler with English and French royalty in
Normandy, convey a cooler, more detached picture. The *Chronicle of
Henry of Livonia* of 1227 combines the view of the man of action with
the finesse of the clerical scholar in Germany. Sir Thomas Malory and
Raphael Holinshed are chroniclers of the collector variety—assemblers and
shapers of old legends, organizers of materials for Shakespeare, Tenny-
son, and J. R. R. Tolkien to use in their own ways in their own time.

The literary chroniclers are artist-historians who gather records shaped
without critical perspective by on-the-spot observers for composition into
more viable and esthetic form. Moncada's chronicle serves as a kind of

culmination of the long Spanish tradition that had developed through the monastic and military routes. The history of their nation was kept alive during the Middle Ages in the small, poor cloisters of the Peninsula, suppressed by Moslem rule until the end of the ninth century. When the Reconquest surged down out of the Asturian mountains, monks were again encouraged to write down the deeds of their bishops and royalty. Among the first to gather these clerical accounts was Pelayo, the Bishop of Oviedo, who combined them with the histories of Isidore of Seville into the first primitive history of Spain. In the twelfth century it was followed by the comprehensive *España sagrada*, the most complete religious history of Iberia, based on the works of Lucas of Tuy and Rodrigo, the Archbishop of Toledo.

Bridging from the Church-sponsored beginning to later secular records, Alfonso the Wise (1272-1284), ambitious father of the chroniclers, collected the learned men of Spain into his court and directed their efforts toward the encyclopedic works that contained all contemporary Biblical, historical, and scientific knowledge: the *Primera* and *Segunda crónica general*. Then noblemen and the occasional literate men who followed them began to record their campaigns for posterity. Throughout Europe their narratives emerged as the rendition of epic legends into prose; folk poetry was combined with eye-witness details to produce the first historical literature. The heroes—Rodrigo the Goth, Bernardo del Carpio, El Cid, El Conde Fernán González, and the Siete Infantes de Lara — moved out of spoken lines and song into the early manifestations of the military chronicle. These stories were often disjointed, fragmentary, and usually anonymous. They were characterized by the medieval approach to the problems of history: with no curiosity about the background or causes of events, nor speculation about the future; with external action offered with rich narrative technique; with spiritual preoccupation, accepting every human happening as God's will; and with a terse, unadorned style, long antedating the courtly flourishes of secular descendants.

López de Ayala's four chronicles on the kings who preceded Juan II assembled such a mixture of legend and fact. The first personal history, *Chronicle of Don Alvaro de Luna, Constable of the Kings of Castile and Leon*, appeared in the fifteenth century. Producing one of the early works with real literary value in the tradition, the author is unknown, but was apparently an intimate friend or servant of the famous constable. He relates in enthusiastic fashion the court rivalries and intrigues, ending the tale with a heatedly indignant dramatization of the noble Don Alvaro's execution by the order of his ruler, Juan II. The same events are recorded by another contemporary in the *Chronicle of Don Juan II*. The merit of both works is in their biographical sketches of the title characters as real men, rather than the glorified heroes who moved in an aura of mystery and magnificence through the old poems.

Hernando del Pulgar (1436-1493), royal chronicler to Fernando and Isabel, flavored his *Chronicle of the Catholic Kings* with eloquent passages and classical references. His book of 1486, titled *Book of the Great Men of Castile*, a series of biographical sketches of twenty-four eminent contemporaries, is not strictly a chronicle, but a lively picture of the times, which serves as a continuation of *The Backgrounds, Descriptions, and Works* by his predecessor, Fernán Pérez de Guzmán (1376-1460?). Two men of the next century concerned themselves more with style in the historical narrative: Jerónimo Zurita (1512-1580) and Ambrosio de Morales (1518-1591). Zurita was a careful technician who explored the archives and collected original documents for his *Annals of the Crown of Aragon*. Morales, similarly well-organized and impartial, produced *The Antiquities of the Cities of Spain* and the *General Chronicle of Spain*.

Out of the monastic and military branches of the genre grew another branch—the artistic history. In his *Wars of Granada*, Diego Hurtado de Mendoza (1510-1575) presents the story of Moorish rule in southern Spain and the wars of Felipe II with dramatic effect:

They began to climb the mountain, where it was said that the corpses had lain unburied, mournful, miserable view and memory. There were among those who looked upon it the grandsons and descendants of the dead men, and people who knew already by legend this unfortunate place . . .

A century later Francisco Manuel de Melo (1608-1666?) followed the model of the *Wars* with a vivid record called *History of the Movements and Separation of Catalonia*.

Then the scene of the Hispanic tradition shifted to the remarkable conquest and exploration of the New World in the sixteenth century. The chroniclers in North and South America lived and wrote about adventures as striking as those reported by Moncada's sources in the Mediterranean. Here the genre returned to its original virility of expression and simplicity of style—the work of men of action, witnesses of or participants in the events they described. The most famous of these was Hernán Cortés (1485-1547), an extraordinary man in many ways, who wrote the epic story of which he was the protagonist, *Letters and Narratives*, in a series of reports to Carlos V. Though his energy and simplicity are typical of his companions, his more cultured style marks him out among the wielders of both pen and sword. One of his soldiers, Bernal Díaz del Castillo (1492-1581?), was moved to write his *True History of the Conquest of New Spain* in indignation at the *General History of the Indies* that had appeared in 1552. The latter was the work of one Francisco López de Gómara (1512-1557?), a former captain of the Spanish army and ardent admirer of the Mexican conqueror, who attributed the entire enterprise to the genius of its leader, without reserving any praise for the soldiers.

Also among the American chroniclers was Gonzalo Fernández de Oviedo (1498-1587), whose *General History of the Indies*, written with careless style and confused organization, is primarily of documentary importance. The first section of the work was printed in 1535, but the last two remained unpublished until the middle of the nineteenth century. Another Hispanic traveler was Bartolomé de las Casas, whose *History of the Indies*, covering the years from the discovery to 1520, earned him the title of Protector of the Indies because in it he so fervently opposed the persecution and exploitation of the Indian natives of the Caribbean Islands. The first chronicle of social intent, the *History* is full of evangelical fire, albeit somewhat exaggerated to support his purpose. While Moncada was collecting his background materials for the Catalan chronicle, his contemporary, Antonio de Solís y Rivadeneyra (1610-1686) was composing the *History of the Conquest of Mexico*, a literary history of similar value that was printed in 1684. Solís's artistry in depicting what earlier writers had only hinted at—the heroic character of his people, the picturesque quality of indigenous customs and civilizations, the grandeur of New World scenery—is always apparent.

Out of this European, and particularly Hispanic, tradition of the literary chronicle, Moncada emerges with his jewel of the genre, utilizing the typical characteristics of strength, simplicity, and vitality. He gives rebirth to the old epic national feeling, presenting his adventurers not only as conquerors, but also as Catalans, offering their story for the glorification of the homeland. In addition, he pursues his narrative with the attention to detail and concern for accuracy of the modern historian, as well as with the conscious structure and vivid color of the artist.

In this translation I have attempted to preserve the rhythm and structure of the original language, with occasional compression of phrasing in order to achieve the conciseness and clarity that characterize contemporary expression. I have followed Moncada's spelling of Catalan names in Spanish form: thus, Pere becomes Pedro, and Joan is Juan. Occasionally I have transformed his Spanish versions to more familiar English spellings of names and places.

The University of Texas at El Paso   FRANCES HERNÁNDEZ

THE HOUSE OF MONCADA

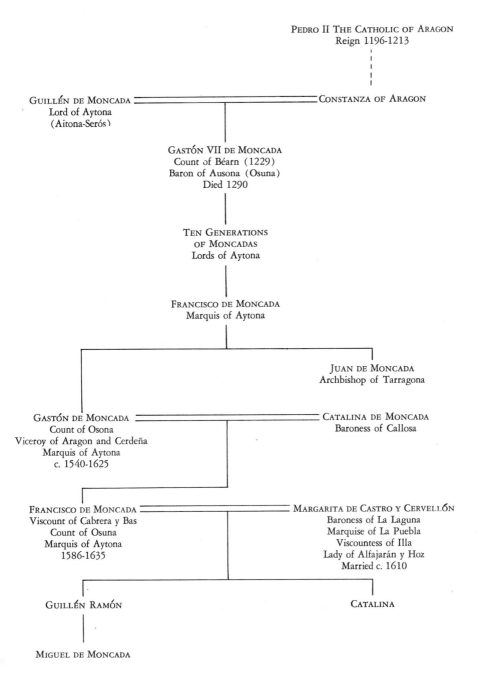

PEDRO II THE CATHOLIC OF ARAGON
Reign 1196-1213

GUILLÉN DE MONCADA
Lord of Aytona
(Aitona-Serós)

CONSTANZA OF ARAGON

GASTÓN VII DE MONCADA
Count of Béarn (1229)
Baron of Ausona (Osuna)
Died 1290

TEN GENERATIONS
OF MONCADAS
Lords of Aytona

FRANCISCO DE MONCADA
Marquis of Aytona

JUAN DE MONCADA
Archbishop of Tarragona

GASTÓN DE MONCADA
Count of Osona
Viceroy of Aragon and Cerdeña
Marquis of Aytona
c. 1540-1625

CATALINA DE MONCADA
Baroness of Callosa

FRANCISCO DE MONCADA
Viscount of Cabrera y Bas
Count of Osuna
Marquis of Aytona
1586-1635

MARGARITA DE CASTRO Y CERVELLÓN
Baroness of La Laguna
Marquise of La Puebla
Viscountess of Illa
Lady of Alfajarán y Hoz
Married c. 1610

GUILLÉN RAMÓN

CATALINA

MIGUEL DE MONCADA

CHART OF THE HOUSE OF ARAGON

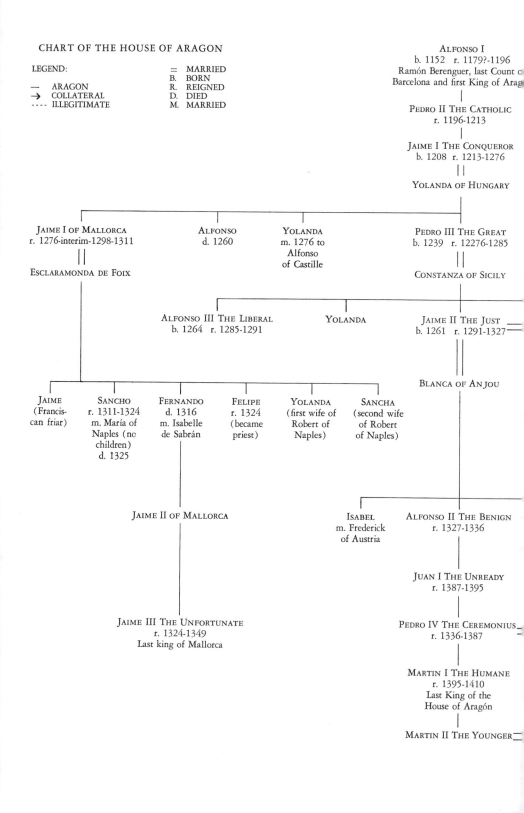

LEGEND:

=	MARRIED
B.	BORN
R.	REIGNED
D.	DIED
M.	MARRIED

— ARAGON
→ COLLATERAL
---- ILLEGITIMATE

ALFONSO I
b. 1152 r. 1179?-1196
Ramón Berenguer, last Count of
Barcelona and first King of Aragon

PEDRO II THE CATHOLIC
r. 1196-1213

JAIME I THE CONQUEROR
b. 1208 r. 1213-1276

YOLANDA OF HUNGARY

JAIME I OF MALLORCA
r. 1276-interim-1298-1311

ESCLARAMONDA DE FOIX

ALFONSO
d. 1260

YOLANDA
m. 1276 to
Alfonso
of Castille

PEDRO III THE GREAT
b. 1239 r. 12276-1285

CONSTANZA OF SICILY

ALFONSO III THE LIBERAL
b. 1264 r. 1285-1291

YOLANDA

JAIME II THE JUST
b. 1261 r. 1291-1327

BLANCA OF ANJOU

JAIME
(Franciscan friar)

SANCHO
r. 1311-1324
m. María of
Naples (no
children)
d. 1325

FERNANDO
d. 1316
m. Isabelle
de Sabrán

FELIPE
r. 1324
(became
priest)

YOLANDA
(first wife of
Robert of
Naples)

SANCHA
(second wife
of Robert
of Naples)

JAIME II OF MALLORCA

ISABEL
m. Frederick
of Austria

ALFONSO II THE BENIGN
r. 1327-1336

JUAN I THE UNREADY
r. 1387-1395

JAIME III THE UNFORTUNATE
r. 1324-1349
Last king of Mallorca

PEDRO IV THE CEREMONIUS
r. 1336-1387

MARTIN I THE HUMANE
r. 1395-1410
Last King of the
House of Aragón

MARTIN II THE YOUNGER

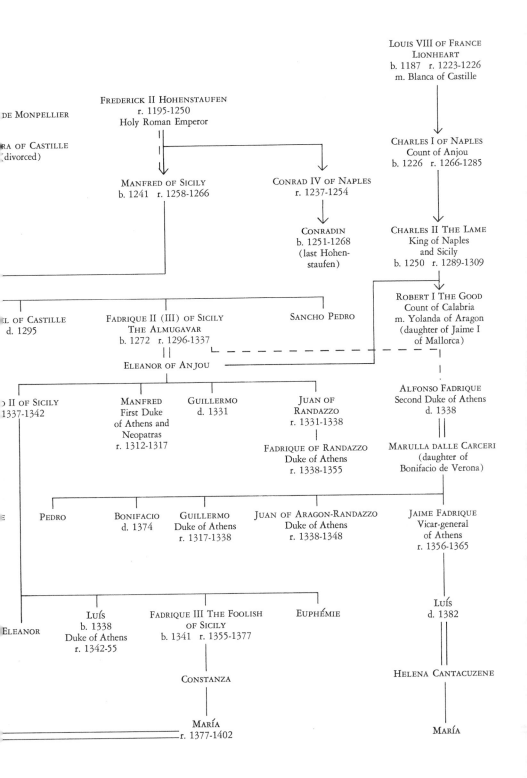

LOUIS VIII OF FRANCE
LIONHEART
b. 1187 r. 1223-1226
m. Blanca of Castille

DE MONPELLIER

RA OF CASTILLE
(divorced)

FREDERICK II HOHENSTAUFEN
r. 1195-1250
Holy Roman Emperor

CHARLES I OF NAPLES
Count of Anjou
b. 1226 r. 1266-1285

MANFRED OF SICILY
b. 1241 r. 1258-1266

CONRAD IV OF NAPLES
r. 1237-1254

CONRADIN
b. 1251-1268
(last Hohen-
staufen)

CHARLES II THE LAME
King of Naples
and Sicily
b. 1250 r. 1289-1309

L OF CASTILLE
d. 1295

FADRIQUE II (III) OF SICILY
THE ALMUGAVAR
b. 1272 r. 1296-1337

SANCHO PEDRO

ROBERT I THE GOOD
Count of Calabria
m. Yolanda of Aragon
(daughter of Jaime I
of Mallorca)

ELEANOR OF ANJOU

O II OF SICILY
1337-1342

MANFRED
First Duke
of Athens and
Neopatras
r. 1312-1317

GUILLERMO
d. 1331

JUAN OF
RANDAZZO
r. 1331-1338

ALFONSO FADRIQUE
Second Duke of Athens
d. 1338

FADRIQUE OF RANDAZZO
Duke of Athens
r. 1338-1355

MARULLA DALLE CARCERI
(daughter of
Bonifacio de Verona)

E

PEDRO

BONIFACIO
d. 1374

GUILLERMO
Duke of Athens
r. 1317-1338

JUAN OF ARAGON-RANDAZZO
Duke of Athens
r. 1338-1348

JAIME FADRIQUE
Vicar-general
of Athens
r. 1356-1365

ELEANOR

LUÍS
b. 1338
Duke of Athens
r. 1342-55

FADRIQUE III THE FOOLISH
OF SICILY
b. 1341 r. 1355-1377

EUPHÉMIE

LUÍS
d. 1382

HELENA CANTACUZENE

CONSTANZA

MARÍA
r. 1377-1402

MARÍA

FRANCISCO DE MONCADA

EXPEDITION OF THE CATALANS AND ARAGONESE
AGAINST THE TURKS AND GREEKS

Dⁿ FRANCISCO D MONCADA

THE CATALAN CHRONICLE
OF FRANCISCO DE MONCADA

TO DON JUAN DE MONCADA, ARCHBISHOP OF TARRAGONA
PRIMATE OF NORTHEASTERN SPAIN, MY LORD AND MY UNCLE

In obedience to Your Honor's† wish, I have organized this short history, which the solitude of a village has placed in my hands, with a natural desire to preserve the country's dying memories that merit eternal existence. I have collected what I could of the ancient papers of Catalonia, and with the aid of its writers and those of the Greeks, I have tried to describe this expedition that our people made to the East. The two terrible threats to this story have been the neglect of the sons of its own heroes and the malice of foreigners who are the enemies of our name and glory; these two factors have vied obstinately for the death of this narrative. I found myself with nothing better to do, and, consequently, remembering my promise to you, I went forth in defense of the tale. I am not sure whether this effort has been enough, because the weapons for the defense are old memoires and the works of ancient authors, both often confused and defective, so that they hinder me rather than provide the help I need. But, although I do not give a full account or even accurately describe the events as they were told to posterity, I have at least replaced the old legends with a longer account than the ancient Catalans left to us. Their neglect seems born of the belief that fame will preserve such illustrious deeds with more care than history does, and that even time cannot obscure them.

God grant long life to Your Honor.

FRANCISCO DE MONCADA
The Count of Osuna

Barcelona, third of November, 1620.

---

†Juan (Joan in Catalan) de Moncada was the brother of Gastón, who was the second Marquis of Aytona and the author's father. Juan occupied the episcopal seat of Barcelona until May, 1612, when he was named Archbishop of Tarragona. Details of his service are recorded in Cabrera de Córdova's *Relación de las cosas sucedidas en la corte de España desde 1599 a 1614*, published in Madrid in 1857, on page 474.

MONCADA'S PROLOGUE

My purpose is to write the story of the memorable expedition that the Catalans and Aragonese made to Eastern provinces at a time when their valor and desire for fortune prompted them to look there for power and fame. Andronicus Palaeologus, the Emperor of Greece, called them to defend his homeland and empire against the Turks, whose forces were so strong that they oppressed his domain and threatened his ruin. But, after our people had succeeded in freeing him from his enemies, he turned upon them, abusing and persecuting them with cruelty and fierce barbarity, until they were driven to look to their own defense and preservation. They applied their invincible forces against the Greeks and the latters' chief, Andronicus, and they were so formidable that all the major princes of Asia and Europe feared and dreaded them; many nations and provinces suffered total ruin by them, and the whole world admired them.

Although this work will be short† because of the neglect of the ancients—who were great for deeds, but poor in recording them—, it will be full of strange, unusual events; of endless wars in distant, remote regions with diverse warlike peoples; of bloody battles and unexpected victories; of dangerous conquests successfully accomplished by a handful of divided Catalans and Aragonese, who were at first the laughing stock of nations, and later the instrument of the punishment that God sent through them.

They conquered the Turks in the first bloom of Ottoman grandeur, dispossessing them of their broad, rich provinces in Asia Minor, and surrounding them in the wild, rough forests of Armenia, with the aid of the intense strength and vigor of their swords. Later, the Turks turned against the Greeks to free themselves from an ignoble death and to revenge the injuries that they could not tolerate without disgrace to their reputation and insult to their names; they joined the Catalans, who were taking towns and cities by force, defeating and breaking up powerful armies; conquering and killing kings and princes on the battlefield; leaving great provinces destroyed and deserted; executing, capturing, or exiling their inhabitants. They poured out vengeance that was more fearful than just, penetrating and trampling Thrace, Macedonia, Thessaly, and Boeotia in spite of all the rulers in the Orient. Finally the Duke of Athens, with all the noblemen of his people, the French, and Greeks, died at their hands; his state was occupied and in it a new dominion founded.

But through all these events there was no lack of treachery, cruelty, plundering, and violence among the Catalans. There was insurrection, the common pestilence not only of an army untrained and weak through the limited power of a supreme chief, but also of great, strong monarchies as well. If the Catalans had succeeded in defeating their ambition and the greed that exceeded the measure of justice as well as they defeated their enemies, and kept themselves united, they would have carried their weapons to the far regions of the Orient; Palestine and Jerusalem would have known crusaders' banners for a second time.

Because the Catalans had valor and military discipline, constancy in adversity, endurance for work, steadfastness in danger, quickness in action, and other warlike virtues to a pronounced degree, they survived so long as anger did not corrupt them; but the same power that God gave them to punish and oppress so many nations became the instrument of their own destruction. With the false pride of success and the vanity of their own prosperity, they became divided against each other over the government. Once divided, they killed each other and kindled a civil war so terrible and cruel that there was no comparison between the deaths and injuries it brought and those that had been caused by foreigners.

---

†Since Moncada apparently intended to write a second part to his history, he placed the title, Book First, above the Prologue, which was repeated in all the editions. The oldest extant, and probably original, manuscript of Barcelona is divided into six books.

BOOK ONE

J. CISNEROS
EL PASO

CONDITIONS OF RULERS AND KINGDOMS OF
THE HOUSE OF ARAGON IN THOSE TIMES

BEFORE WE BEGIN our history, it is important to explain the conditions in which provinces and kings of Aragon found themselves at the time of the story, their armies and weapons, friends and enemies, and the facts necessary to understand the fundamental causes of the expedition.

King Pedro of Aragón, son of Jaime the Conqueror,[1] was called the Great because of his famous deeds. He married Constanza, the daughter of King Manfred of Sicily, who had been killed by Charles of Anjou with the help of the Roman Pontiff, a blood enemy of Emperor Frederick.[2] With Manfred's death, Charles became the king of the two Sicilies. Soon after, the unfortunate Conradin, last king of the House of Suevia, which was broken and destroyed, fell into the hands of Charles and was sentenced to lose his head on a public scaffold — to the eternal memory of a vile revenge and monstrous example of human fickleness.[3] At this time Pedro did not have the strength to satisfy himself for the deaths of Manfred and Conradin, nor later to hold his throne against the civil wars. The Moors of Valencia were rebellious, and the petty lords and noblemen of Catalonia were resentful and discontented. But they were also the declared enemies of Charles, provoked by French and English arms that were formidable for their strategy. The kingdoms of Sicily and Naples were far from theirs, however, and their people were occupied with defending themselves against closer enemies.

All these difficulties checked the king's offended spirit, but they did not lessen the memory of the insult. Occasionally Pedro met with his brother-in-law, King Philippe of France, for interviews to which Charles, the son of the king of Naples, also came to offer the French king his friendship. Pedro always excused himself when Charles arrived, showing in his expression the deep contempt and disgust that left the company uncomfortable and ill at ease. Charles no doubt would have begun to make preparations and to arm himself had he believed the Aragonese king's forces were equal to his spirit and intent. But heaven sent Pedro enough strength to take vengeance for Conradin's innocent blood, which had been shed by such dark means that no one realized what was happening until the execution itself made them public.

The miserable Sicilians, incited by French insolence and outraged by their insult and dishonor, took arms against their oppressors. In the famous revolt called the Sicilian Vespers,[4] they threw off from the people's neck the insufferable yoke of Charles and the French, who had unjustly abused them by leaving them to the discretion and subjection of tyrannical ministers, a cause which most often produces changes in states and miserable ends to their rulers. Then Charles collected a powerful army to punish the daring rebellion of his subjects. Realizing that the door to all pity and clemency was closed, they placed their hope in Pedro, the Aragonese king. Like a true Christian prince, he was in Africa with an army of soldiers and nobility from his kingdom, triumphant against many Berber sheikhs and kings.

Sicilian ambassadors came before the king with enough tears and sorrow to move the heart of not only a king already offended by particular insult, but of any man with human feelings. They pointed out that the Sicilian people, so proud of their name and so anti-French, would help him revenge Manfred's unfortunate death and the outrage of Conradin. Finally, they described to him the dangerous state of their liberty, lives, and property, explaining that if Pedro did not help them, they were threatened by the rigorous punishment of Charles, who was just now above Messina, promising a pitiful end to the whole kingdom.

Moved by the arguments of the Sicilians and his own desire for vengeance, Pedro left Trapani with all his forces and overtook his enemy so quickly that Charles hardly realized he was coming before he saw his men and found himself forced to leave the place and to retreat ignominiously to Calabria.

Charles's friend, the Pontiff, and his relative, the king of France, openly declared their support and took up arms against Pedro. The king of Castile, who should have helped the latter through both relation and friendship, was away from his country — and inclined to side with the greater power. Pedro's brother, Jaime, king of Majorca, also abandoned him, even offering help and passage through his country to Pedro's enemies. He made as excuse for this behavior the weak defenses of his island, unequal to opposition to such a powerful enemy: an excuse that small rulers often use to hide a contemptible deed, blaming necessity for what ambition is responsible. King Pedro found himself without friends, backed only by his own courage, fortune, and desire to satisfy the insult to his house.

At this time when everyone judged him lost, he managed to defeat his enemies on several occasions, coming out each time reinforced by new assistance and alliances. He destroyed and humbled them either on land or at sea, maintained the name of Aragon, and became the first king from Spain to plant his conquering banners in Italian kingdoms, on which foundations the monarchy rests today.

Pedro drove Charles from Sicily and with even greater efforts tried to reduce him to obedience, in the course of which great and memorable events took place. But the House of Aragon always confirmed itself within the kingdom with victories, not only against the power of Charles, but also against all the major rulers of Europe who had helped him.

Both kings died while vying in fury and cruelty in their warfare, and, by right of succession, Charles the King of Naples was followed by his eldest son of the same name, who was at the time a prisoner in Catalonia. Pedro of Aragon was succeeded by his two sons: Alfonso, the elder, in his Spanish kingdoms and Jaime in Sicily. The war continued until Alfonso died, leaving his brother, Jaime, as king, since he had no sons. Jaime returned to Spain, charging his younger brother, Fadrique, in Sicily to govern the land and defend his name. When Jaime was established in Aragon, he sent for some of the forces of his former kingdom and then abandoned Sicily to the Church. His motives for this measure were fear of a combined attack by Castile, France, and the Church, as well as the persuasion of his mother, Constanza, a woman of singular religious fervor who preferred to see her son forfeit his kingdom rather than lose more time in reaching a reconciliation with the Church.

Jaime and Constanza sent ambassadors to Sicily to put the renunciation into effect and to deliver the kingdom to the Roman Pontiff's legates. But the natives and former soldiers were indignant at the ease with which their king was renouncing what they had gained and kept with so much bloody toil and that he was delivering them without concern to their enemies, from whom they could expect servitude and death. To the Sicilians the measure seemed certain peril, and to the Catalans and Aragonese living there it seemed a complete disregard for the honor they had won against their enemies in so many years of fighting — all caused by the resolution of an ill-advised king. Therefore, they took up arms again, resisted the legates, and persuaded Fadrique as the true successor of his father and brother to proclaim himself king and take charge of the common defense.

It was not difficult to convince this high-spirited ruler in the flower of his youth, who could not hope to rise from his position as a vassal subject to his brother's laws, a sufficient cause, even had it not been righteous, to thrust a few years onto Fadrique's youth. He named himself king and as such was accepted and crowned. Prepared with good soldiers and loyal people who were quick to defend him in the cruel war that threatened, Fadrique became the second liberator of his country. He opposed his worst and nearest enemy, Charles; the Pope, who was defending his claim; and his brother, Jaime, who had become his declared enemy. Jaime collected forces, attacked, and defeated him in a naval battle, with which the war was considered over and Fadrique finished. But, through the hidden disposition of divine providence, which sometimes changes events beyond common hopes so that we may realize that only it governs and directs, Fadrique held on to his kingdom, to the universal happiness of the good, the astonishment and fear of his enemies, and the glory of his name.

A little later Jaime of Aragon destroyed the alliance by separating from it, a decision which caused considerable regret and resentment among the other kings, who believed that without the strength of Aragon it would be a fatal and impossible task to conquer another king of the same house. Experience confirmed this, for once Jaime had left the alliance, Fadrique's enemies were always defeated. The young Aragonese continued to gain victories until his opponents were forced to sue for peace, leaving him with his kingdom — the mere thought of which they found annoying. Finally, after some disagreements, a firm peace was established with Fadrique's marriage to Leonora, the daughter of Charles. With this arrangement, Sicily was free from the fear of returning to ancient servitude, and King Fadrique became the peaceful lord of the country he had defended with so much courage.

His brother, King Jaime, maintained the kingdoms of Aragon, Catalonia, and Valencia in the greatest peace and distinction, beloved by his subjects, feared by infidels, and served by great chieftains. He was powerful on the sea and watched every opportunity to magnify his crown in imitation of his ancestors. The king of Majorca, youngest ruler of the House of Aragon, peacefully reigned over the dominion of Montpellier and the counties of Roussillon, Cerdagne, and Coblentz. These lands were difficult to defend because of their scattered locations and the strength of their neighbors, among whom the lesser kings were always wavering. But during this time Jaime of Majorca ruled with the same high reputation and fortune as that of the other kings of his house.[5]

REFERENCES

1. Jaime I the Conqueror (1208-1276) was one of the greatest Spanish kings and most flamboyant medieval rulers of Europe. He came to the throne at the age of five, following his parents, Pedro II the Catholic (reign, 1196-1213) and Marie de Montpellier, and ruled for sixty-three years. He had a dangerous childhood under the control of Simon de Montfort of a rival French family, but he was protected by Pope Innocent III, who put him under the care of the Order of Templars at Saragossa.

He grew to be a huge man of immense strength, astute and patient. According to legend, he was seven feet tall with blue eyes and red-gold hair. At thirteen he married Leonora, the daughter of King Alfonso VIII of Castile, but later divorced her on the grounds of consanguinity. Then he married Yolanda, the daughter of Andrew II of Hungary. He was soon entangled in wars with the Albigenses, members of a Catharistic religious sect of southern France, and with Montfort over his inheritance in Provence. He achieved the conquest of the Balearic Isles in four years, took Valencia from the Moslems, and signed a treaty with Louis IX of France for the surrender of French claims to Catalonia. He started to Palestine, but his fleet was wrecked, though a few ships reached their goal. He instituted the first parliamentary assemblies during his reign, and established Catalan as the official language of the Aragonese kingdoms. He also wrote one of the four most famous Catalan chronicles, *Llibre del feyts del rey En Jacme,* or *Book of the Deeds of the King, Don Jaime.* At his death he gave his son Pedro his Spanish possessions, and to Jaime, Majorca and Montpellier.

2. The Pontiff was Pope Clement IV (1265-1268).

3. Conradin, the nephew of King Manfred of Sicily, was the legitimate heir of Emperor Frederick II Hohenstaufen (1194-1250) of the Holy Roman Empire. Two years after Manfred was killed in battle, by Charles of Anjou, seventh son of King Louis VIII of France, the young commander was defeated by the same forces, who used Alard de Valéry's strategy of concealment of reserve troops to overcome him. His public execution in the manner of a common criminal was an outrageous insult. It was revenged finally by King Pedro III the Great of Aragon, who was married to Conradin's cousin, Constanza of Sicily.

4. The mass rebellion of the Sicilian people against their Frankish rulers of the House of Anjou broke out on Easter Tuesday, March 31, 1282. The uprising began spontaneously in a church near Palermo at the evening service, hence the name, "Vespers," when a French soldier insulted an island woman, and it spread rapidly through the kingdom. Thousands of Frenchmen were slaughtered, the rulers driven out, and a republic proclaimed. Charles II of Anjou, the King of Naples, collected a fleet to besiege Messina, but he was challenged and defeated by another king eager to rule the Sicilians: Pedro the Great. His claim rested on the fact that his wife, Constanza, was the daughter of the former king, Manfred. Thus, instead of maintaining the right they had won to their free communes, the rebels of the Sicilian Vespers found themselves again forced to submit to royal authority and a feudal social system.

5. Jaime II the Unfortunate of Majorca (reign, 1324-1349) came to the throne when his childless uncle, King Sancho I, died. Jaime was the last independent king of the island. He fell in a battle in which his kingdom was attacked by his cousin, Pedro IV the Ceremonious of Aragon.

Second Chapter

THE CHOICE OF A COMMANDER

SUCH WAS THE STATE of the kings of Aragon, Majorca, and Sicily when the old soldiers and chosen captains who had served under Pedro the Great, his son Jaime, and finally the younger son, Fadrique, deemed that the war was over at last in Sicily, now that peace was strengthened by the marriage of Leonora to their king: a bond of friendship between major powers, so long as selfishness and ambition neither dissolved nor diminished it; and, once dissolved, a cause of the most burning enmity and implacable hatred. When they could no longer look forward to a rift and war again in Sicily, they decided to plan a new expedition against the infidels and enemies of Christianity in remote, isolated provinces. It was the strength and courage of these fighting men, as well as their desire for more glory and triumph, that had helped them spread their influence on Sicilian battlefields, and now they were determined to look for tougher opportunities and more dangerous risks in order to increase their fame and fortune.

Two motives, both concerning their self-preservation, helped them to arrive at this decision. The first was that they had little security in returning to Spain, their homeland, and living there with comfortable reputation, because they had defended Fadrique with such obstinacy against Jaime, their king and natural lord. Jaime was not a ruler of a vengeful nature; he had not consented to hold them traitors during the war against his brother and was even less willing to punish in cold blood what he could have but would not while they were offending him by following Fadrique's banners against his own. But, although the insulted majesty of a ruler may offer forgiveness, the memory of an offense continues to stay with him. It might not be strong enough to injure them, but it would certainly prevent their serving in the offices that their qualifications merited, as noblemen and administrators either in peace or war.

The second and most powerful motive that forced them to leave Sicily was the fact that Fadrique was no longer able to support them with the same generosity as before, since much of the royal holdings had been spent or destroyed by twenty years of war. They were accustomed to squandering foreign property as well as their own, and when they needed anything, they plundered the towns and cities that they had conquered to get it. Since both sources of income had been cut off now that peace had been made and the war was finished, they decided that it was impossible to reduce themselves to living with moderation.

Like his father and brother, King Fadrique was a shrewd observer of the industry and valor of his subjects, noting their usefulness in war while witnessing their deeds, and he was rarely deceived in distributing his favors. He gave more credit to his eyes than to his ears, and always distributed his awards according to service and not to personal sympathy. Because of this attitude, there were few complainers and malcontents in his kingdom; his subjects realized that he could not distribute estates and households to everyone who deserved them and that some were necessarily left with less compensation than their services merited. When their people saw the kings of the House of Aragon giving what they legally could with lavish liberality and grandeur to the distinguished captains, they suppressed their dissatisfaction, attributing the selections to the incomparable virtue and valor of those who were preferred and finding themselves inferior.

These were the causes that moved the Spaniards in Sicily to attempt to advance themselves in new undertakings and conquests. There were four outstanding leaders who encouraged and strengthened the rest of the group that served under their standards: Roger de Flor, vice-admiral of Sicily;[1] Berenguer de Entenza and Fernán Jiménez de Arenós, both noblemen; and Berenguer de Rocafort, all well known and highly regarded among their men as soldiers of great prowess.

They spoke about their plans to their retainers and friends, finding them well disposed and ready to follow them on whatever campaign they might resolve to take as most profitable and honorable. To make final agreements, they met in secrecy where they decided to choose a chief before planning the expedition. They realized that without a leader who could and would command determination and wise counsel were useless. By common acclaim of all those who were present, Roger de Flor, powerful Vice-Admiral of the Sea, was named chief. He was a valiant, distinguished soldier, fortunate sailor, and possessor of more wealth and money than all the other captains, a condition that was the principal cause of his election.

REFERENCES

1. Rutger von Blum, son of a German official of lower status in the retinue of Emperor Frederick II Hohenstaufen. Roger, as his name was translated, was described by the historian, Pachymeres, as "a man in prime of life, with fierce eyes, quick reactions, and hot after adventure." (Kenneth M. Setton, *Catalan Domination of Athens 1311-1388, p. 3.*) In 1302 he was thirty-four.

Third Chapter

WHO WAS ROGER DE FLOR?

ROGER DE FLOR, he who was elected by the Catalans as their general and supreme chief, was born in Brindisi, the son of noble parents. His father was a German named Richard de Flor, who served as retainer for Emperor Frederick; his mother, an Italian woman, native of Brindisi. Richard died in the battle between Charles of Anjou and Conradin, whom he supported because he was the grandson of Frederick, Richard's king and lord.

When Charles, insolent with victory, had cut off Conradin's head, he confiscated the lands of all those who had helped the unfortunate ruler. With this loss, Roger and his mother were left in poverty, a condition under which the boy was raised until he was fifteen. At that age a French gentleman named Vassaill, member of the Order of Templars,[1] took a fancy to young Roger and offered him in Brindisi the opportunity of working on the *Alcon*, a Templar ship of which Vassaill was captain. Roger sailed with him for several years, managing to make such a good impression in his employment that the Order received him among its members and gave him the rank of Sergeant Friar, which was almost equal to that of Knight in those times.

In this capacity Roger began to be known and feared in all the Eastern sea. When the city of Ptolemais, also called Acre, surrendered to the forces of Melech Taseraf, the Sultan of Egypt, Roger, according to the historian, Pachymeres,[2] was one of the men present there in a monastery of the Templars. He realized that the city could not be defended, succeeded in collecting in a ship a crowd of Christians with the property they were able to carry off, and escaped from the cruel fury of the barbarians.

Roger did not lack enemies among the men of his own Order; many were jealous of his prowess. They made trouble between him and his Grand Master, accusing him of acquiring profit by means not becoming to his profession, of abusing the common privileges, and of making off with the spoils he had taken from Acre. By now this famous brotherhood had reached the last degree of its old age and was nearing the end; its members had become weak with the vices of age and time. Their hearts were full of envy, avarice, and ambition in place of the ancient valor, brotherly attachment, and Christian piety that had once made them admired and venerated in all the provinces.

The Grand Master planned to seize Roger when he heard the first accusation, but the wily youth learned of these intentions. He knew the greed of his chief and the baseness of his brothers. Without staying longer at Marseilles, where he happened to be at the time, he rushed off to a more secure place and waited for the false, malicious accusations to blow over.

He retired to Genoa, where, aided by his friends, including one Ticin da Oria, he fitted out a galley. In this craft he sailed to

Naples to offer his services to Robert, Duke of Calabria,[3] who was preparing for the war with Fadrique. Robert paid little attention to this proposal, judging Roger quickly by his small crew of men. This lack of estimation annoyed Roger so much that he went to serve Robert's enemy, who received him with gratitude and open arms. The king's appreciation was not only an expression of his generous nature and comradely ease with soldiers, but also of the force of necessity produced by the impending war. It would not have been prudent for the Sicilian prince to decline services voluntarily offered in such pressing times, when his life and liberty were in danger and when friends and people who were obligated to him were abandoning him. The man who comes to be a friend in danger, when the ruler he offers to assist is threatened by more powerful forces, who has no natural obligation and owes no fidelity as a subject, should be admitted and honored, even though he comes for his own interests or because the enemy has injured or insulted him. For, the more offended such a man is, the more useful and dependable will be his service.

The war raged between Robert and Fadrique, during which Roger credited himself with several distinguished feats. He often helped in places hard-pressed by the enemy, and with a small fleet took it upon himself to impede the free navigation of the Neapolitan seas and coasts. He thus became a vice-admiral; in less than three years' time he performed services so remarkable that he was one of the main causes for Fadrique's remaining in Sicily. His name became immortal, and he collected more wealth than a vassal is wont to. This was the situation in which Roger de Flor found himself when the Catalans and Aragonese chose him their chief for the undertaking they were planning.

REFERENCES

1. The Poor Knights of Christ of the Temple of Solomon became one of the great military brotherhoods of the twelfth century, founded at Jerusalem in 1119 by eight French knights. Unlike the Hospitallers and the Teutonic Knights, the order was military from its founding by crusaders. A Burgundian knight, Hugues de Payns, and a northern Frank, Godoffroi de St. Omer, undertook to protect pilgrims to the Holy Land after the crusade, and were soon joined by six others on their mission.

By 1300 the group had grown to about 20,000 with great wealth and power. The rule of order drawn up by Bernard de Clairvaux in 1128 had been replaced by general license and corruption. On October 13, 1307, all members were imprisoned by the Inquisition; the Grand Master, James de Molay, and the provisional head, Guy of Normandy, were burned at the stake in Paris. Their property was confiscated by the Brothers of St. John of the Hospital and King Philippe.

2. George Pachymeres (1242-c. 1310), greatest Byzantine scholar of the thirteenth century, covers the period, 1255-1308, with the most detailed and only contemporary historical picture of the reigns of Michael VIII and Andronicus II Palaeologus. He was strongly concerned about Eastern Orthodoxy and against the Roman Catholic Church or any of its representatives, who were then exploring the possibility of reunion of the two branches of Christianity. Rubió i Lluch calls his history, in Pachymeres's *Andronicus Palaeologus, sive historia rerum ab Andronico seniore in imperio gestarum* (Rome, 1669), the most complete and exact account of the Catalan expedition, ending with the discussion of the divisions among the chieftains of the Company. Setton (p. 263) says: "In his very extensive account of the Catalans in the Levant, Pachymeres is fairly accurate, and makes some show of impartiality as a historian in dealing with the unpopular Latins (cf. *De Michaele Palaeologo*, V, 23, ed. Bonn, I, 401). He is, nevertheless, very prejudiced against the Catalans."

3. In spite of this early misjudgment, about twenty years later the Duke became King Robert I the Wise of Naples (reign, 1309-1343) upon the death of his father, Charles II the Lame (1285-1309).

Fourth Chapter

THE LEADERS PLAN THEIR JOURNEY AND ASK
PERMISSION OF THE KING

WITH THEIR NEW GENERAL, the leaders discussed what undertaking would be most suitable and advantageous for them. Finally, they resolved by common consent to offer themselves to the Emperor of the Greeks, Andronicus Palaeologus,[1] who was being hard pressed by the Turkish forces. The Greek ruler was looking for help from foreign nations; he was doubtful of his own and he was a ruler who had a limited relationship with the Pope. This situation appealed to Roger because he feared the Pope's wrath at his having mistreated some of the provinces of the Church during time of war, and he still lived in apprehension that the Pontiff would demand of Fadrique that he hand over the former Templar to the justice of his Order and Grand Master, as an effective way of gaining vengeance against him.

Although such an ugly deed could not be expected of Fadrique's grandeur, still, kings have a way of placing their fame and reputation above other interests and they forget with ease their subjects' services when it is convenient. Moreover, if Fadrique did refuse to deliver up Roger, it might be the occasion for a break and war, which the king could not well afford at this point. Roger wanted neither to involve his king in new difficulties, nor to place his own liberty in the danger it risked in Sicily.

Pachymeres says in the thirteenth chapter of his second book that the Pope did ask Fadrique for the delivery of Roger. But the king, who felt how unjust it would be to turn over a man who had served him so well, offered instead to write to Andronicus and ask him to accept Roger's service. In this way he could allow the young adventurer to leave his land honorably without giving the Pope pretext for complaining that he was helping the escape of a fugitive from a religious order. But Pachymeres is apparently uncertain on this point, because he assures his readers that if he is mistaken about this it is not his fault, but instead that of the people who spread the story. And he adds that he heard it from the Greeks, who were never very accurate when it came to rumors about the Catalans and Aragonese. He and the historian, Muntaner, differ here because the former states definitely that the Pope asked Fadrique for the person of Roger, while Muntaner claims that this was feared but never actually did happen; and thus it is not surprising that rumor in such a far-off place should have added the rest.[2]

When all plans for the campaign had been decided and several days spent in making arrangements for their execution, the men gave Roger the charge of speaking to Fadrique, explaining their proposal to him, and asking him on behalf of the whole expedition for his approval, since they did not consider it fitting to make such an attempt publicly without his consent and pleasure. The king was at Messina just concluding the celebrations of his marriage to Charles's daughter, Leonora. Roger went there and spoke to him in secret. He explained that the Catalans and Aragonese wanted to leave Sicily and go East, not so much for their own advantage, but because it would free the kingdom of the rather heavy and bothersome burden of their presence during peacetime. He assured the king that his men remained devoted to their ruler and that they would come to serve him from the ends of the earth if he ever needed them. But in the meantime they would appreciate the exercise of his strength and authority in their behalf: a recompense that their service well deserved.

The king answered that he wanted them to make known their resolve to leave Sicily because, although it would better their maintenance, it might damage his reputation. People might believe that he had ordered their departure so as to free himself of his obligations to the Spaniards, and he did not want anyone to think him so ungrateful. He told Roger that if they were called by the hope of new acquisitions and enterprises and were resolved to go, he would aid and assist them to the limit of his powers, provided that they would bear witness to this and make it publicly known. He would rather risk his kingdom and life than fail to fulfill his obligation to them for their outstanding services, but he regretted his inability, because of the poverty of the times imposed by the long war, to reward Roger's men as he wished.

The answer was worthy of a ruler so noble, and was particularly admirable because the virtues of reasonableness and gratitude are so rare among kings, who do not worry about the rewarding of great services beyond the bestowing of ordinary favors. Roger thanked him in the name of all for his favor and the honor he did them and left Fadrique to return to his men with an account of the interview. When the adventurers heard the story, they applauded and praised the king.

Fadrique was one of the most distinguished rulers of his age. Through the grandeur of his spirit and the glory of his deeds, he met and broke the forces of Italy, France, and Spain, who were united for his ruin. In spite of all his competitors, he retained the kingdom of Sicily for himself and his posterity, with whom it is happily preserved today. Nothing more useful for the peace and security of his new kingdom could have happened than the departure of the guests whose quartering and expenses were a real trial for his people. When the war banished peace and kin, in order to wage it, they generously offered their land and possessions to the foreign soldiers who were defending them and aiding them against Charles, whom they feared. But when peace came, the duress left, and they began to fear the uncomfortable closeness of the outsiders. Quarrels and annoyances arose that might have caused grave dangers if the plans for the new expedition had not appeared to intercept them.

REFERENCES

1. Andronicus II (reign, 1282-1328) was the second in the long dynasty of the Palaeologi that began when his father, Michael VIII, usurped the throne from the boy Emperor, John IV Lascaris, for whom he was serving as regent. A cultured man, more interested in theology and the protection of the Greek Orthodox Church than in affairs of state, Andronicus allowed his father's great fleet to fall into decay. The Empire then became too weak to resist the demands of the rival powers of Venice and Genoa or the threats of the Bulgars and Turks on all sides.

2. Professor Antoni Rubió y Lluch of the University of Barcelona (1855-1937), the most distinguished modern scholar of the history of the Catalan Company, discusses the disagreement between the views of these two historians in a brief monograph, *Memóries: Paquimeres i Muntaner* (Institut d'Estudis Catalans, Secció Histórico-Arqueológica), pp. 33ff.

Fifth Chapter

THE DELEGATION FROM THE COMPANY TO THE
EMPEROR ANDRONICUS AND HIS ANSWER

ROGER AND THE OTHER principal chiefs of the army decided that they would send two ambassadors to the Emperor, Andronicus, to offer their service. Ramón Muntaner,[1] one of the important historians of the expedition, who always offered his counsel and assistance, helped give the ambassadors their instructions. The two knights, whose names are wrapped in the darkness

of time and neglect, left for Constantinople to deliver the message
for their whole nation. They arrived in a few days on a galley
furnished by Roger. Knowing of their coming and something of
the message they brought, Andronicus received them with gra-
cious consideration.

The elder of the two ambassadors explained their mission. He
told Andronicus that the Catalans and Aragonese, after peace had
been made between Charles, king of Naples, and King Fadrique
of Sicily, whom they served, were determined not to look for rest
in their homeland but instead to increase their military reputation,
acquired in the past wars, by new deeds. They had for this undertaking forces sufficient in valor and strength: soldiers trained in a
long, dangerous war and officers known for their victories and
noble blood. The ambassadors offered their aid against the Turks
in the name of all with particular fervor because those of the
House of Aragon had been left with the House of Palaeologus as
their only friend when their other allies abandoned them, and because they looked forward to increasing their empire and ridding
it of the enemies of the Christian name, which they wished with
great valor and pride to reestablish in the provinces wrested from
the Greek Empire.

The Emperors were pleased with the unexpected delegation and
its offer from the Catalans, who seemed to be of special value to
the Greeks, since they understood that these were the men who
with fearful valor had managed to sustain the kingdom of Sicily
against all Italy. They were impressed by the grand way in which
the whole group proposed to serve them and received them accordingly.

Andronicus began to discuss the conditions under which the
Westerners would wage war. Following their instructions, the ambassadors asked for a fixed wage for the soldiers and for Roger the
title of Grand Duke[2] and a wife from among the Emperor's grand-
daughters. With such pledges, the Spanish chief planned to secure
his position in the service. Andronicus conceded everything they
asked without alteration; he did not even make an observation
concerning the obvious difference between the state and quality of
Roger and that of his granddaughter.[3] Apparently, the Greek

realized that Roger's inequality was made up for by the general worth of the people he governed, particularly in this hour of need when the Emperor was so hard pressed by the Turks and so uncertain of the loyalty of his own people.

John Lascaris,[4] the legitimate successor to the empire, was living blind and exiled in a country town of Bithynia. Although he was useless as a future ruler, he remained nevertheless a constant reminder of Andronicus's tyranny, and the malcontents of the government considered him sufficient justification to take arms against the present ruler. This situation made the Emperor fearful and suspicious; he was forced to avail himself of foreign aid. He had already received into his service ten thousand Alans,[5] a barbaric people more Christian in their faith than in their actions. Coming from the other side of the Danube, they were recognized as masters by the Scythians of Europe. They had been first to send their ambassadors to the Emperor, offering their assistance. Nicephorus Gregoras,[6] a contemporary Greek writer, records that Andronicus was so grateful for the offer that "it seemed as agreeable to the Emperor as if it had come from heaven." He said that his own people had become so suspicious and antagonistic toward him that he was continually making friendships and alliances among foreigners; would that he had not!

He had also taken into his army several companies of Christian Turks: men with Greek mothers who had left the Sultan, Asen, and been baptized.[7] All these allies Andronicus considered formidable, but Roger's band was beyond any words that the Greek had to praise them, for they were men so superior to the others in his service and so feared in those days. Andronicus sent the two ambassadors back to their chief with the insignia of Grand Duke, which was equal to the General of the Sea and of high dignity (although not the greatest), and went about making the arrangements for the wedding.

REFERENCES

1. Ramón Muntaner, whose name is written as Montaner by Moncada, was the Catalan historian who figures actively in the story of the expedition. He devotes Chapters 194-243 to the Catalan Company in his long account, *Chrónica, o descripció dels*

fets e hazanyes del Inclyt Rey Don Jaume Primer Rey Daragó, de Mallorques é de Valencia: Compte de Barcelona é de Muntpesller: é de molts de sos descendents (Valencia: Viuda de Juan Mey, 1558; Barcelona, Casa de Jaume Cortey, 1562; Stuttgart, 1844; Barcelona, A. Bofarull, 1860 and 1886; Naples, 1878), or *Chronicle or Description of the Feats and Deeds of the King, Don Jaime, First King of Aragon, Majorca, and Valencia, Count of Barcelona and Montpellier, and of Many of His Descendants.*

2. *Megas dux* was the title borne by the highest admiral who commanded the entire naval forces of the Byzantine Empire. The rank was established for the supreme chief of the Navy by the time of Emperor Alexius I Comnenus (1081-1118). Muntaner suggests that the power of the Grand Duke probably was not limited to the Navy.

3. María Asen was in fact the niece of Andronicus, an inaccuracy that Moncada repeats in a few subsequent passages, an error or oversight that Rosell takes as an indication that the work was published uncorrected. María's father, Ivan III Asen, who ruled only one year (1279-80) before taking refuge in Constantinople, was the czar of Bulgaria. Her mother was Irene Palaeologina, Andronicus's sister. Roger, on the other hand, was the son of a German falconer in the service of Frederick II Hohenstafen in the Sicilian kingdom.

4. John IV Lascaris, the last of the Lascarid dynasty of Emperors, was fifty-two when the Catalans reached Constantinople. He was, however, a victim of Andronicus's father, Michael VIII, who had blinded the boy in 1261 when his own son was only three. John had come to the imperial throne at the age of seven when his father, Theodore II, died of the family's hereditary epilepsy at thirty-six. Theodore left his friend, George Muzalon, as regent. But Muzalon, a commoner, was killed by the enraged nobles at the commemoration service for Theodore only nine days after his death. One of them, Michael Palaeologus, then assumed the regency, rising as Grand Duke, Despot, and finally co-Emperor at the turn of the year 1258-59. After Michael VIII had retaken Constantinople from the Franks in 1261, he felt strong enough to eliminate his co-Emperor altogether, replacing the ten-year-old child with his own son, Andronicus. (George Ostrogorsky, *History of the Byzantine State*, p. 400.)

5. The Massagetes or Alans were the wild, warlike tribes of central Asia above the east end of the Black Sea, roaming north of the Syr River and the lake called the Aral Sea. The name included most of the nomad peoples of the Caspian Sea area. They killed almost everyone who tried to overcome them, including Cyrus the Great, founder of the Persian Empire and conqueror of all Asia Minor. Around 1300 Andronicus II had arranged with one group of Alans to give them permission to settle within Byzantine territory in return for their service against the Turks. Ten thousand arrived with families, but were defeated in their first encounter with the Seljuks and turned to pillaging the Greek villages. See Ostrogorsky, pp. 438-40.

6. Gregoras (1290-1360), another of Moncada's sources that were contemporary to the events of his narrative, was a Byzantine historian and encyclopedic scholar whose *Roman History* in thirty-seven books covered the period of the Empire when it was centered in the city of Nicaea and its restoration to the old capital of Constantinople, from 1204 to 1359. A close advisor and collaborator with Andronicus, he wrote on all aspects of economic, constitutional, and administrative questions. In describing Andronicus's financial difficulties, Gregoras compares his payments to powerful

neighbors in tribute for peace to that of a man "who attempts to purchase the friendship of wolves by opening the veins in various parts of his body and allowing them to drain his blood until they are satisfied." (Ostrogorsky, p. 432.)

7. Moncada's word for this group of warriors is *turcoples*. The term originally meant the sons of Turkish fathers and Greek mothers, and later indicated light-armored soldiers. Moncada uses the word for converted Turks.

Sixth Chapter

THE EMPEROR GRANTS A SALARY TO THE FIGHTING MEN AND MANY HONORS AND PRIVILEGES TO THE OFFICERS

ANDRONICUS GRANTED WAGES to Roger's men according to their skill at arms and their occupation. He gave four ounces of silver each month to the men-at-arms and two to the light horsemen and the pilots and mariners who handled the fleet. To the infantrymen he gave one ounce, with the stipulation that they would receive four months' wages when they arrived at the coast of some province of the Empire, and would be provided for two months when they wanted to go back to their homes, either alone or together.

George Pachymeres, the Greek author whose observations have often shed light on this story in spite of his being a great enemy of the Catalans, writes that their wages were twice as good as those of the Turkish Greeks or the Alans, a statement that illustrates clearly the reputation that the Catalan and Aragonese militia had acquired to make such a difference in their preferment among those who served the Empire. On the wages, accommodations, and perquisites that he offered to the nobles and captains, the historians do not record the particulars, only the office and dignity of Grand Duke to Roger and of Seneschal to Corbarán de Alet.[1] Hence, I suspect that their own judgment was what limited their wages and salary, since, as we shall see farther on, the generals asked for money at will, merely signifying the amount, without any obligation to render account to the comptrollers and ministers of Andronicus's treasury.

The ambassadors returned to Italy where they found Roger in Licata, keeping his post and waiting for their message. When he heard the good word that they brought, he set out to see his king and make a report of the honorable reception Andronicus had given his ambassadors and the conditions that he had offered them. The campaign was announced publicly, and the officers collected their men at Messina where the fleet was being prepared for navigation in a few days.

The fleet consisted of thirty-six sailing vessels, among them eighteen galleys and four heavy ships, most of them fitted out with money from the king and from Roger, who spent the estate that he had acquired in the past wars and twenty thousand Genoese ducats drawn in Emperor Andronicus's name to prepare for this expedition. The people were far fewer than expected, because the two Berenguers, of Entenza and Rocafort, could neither join Roger nor follow him, postponing their departure for the following year. Berenguer de Entenza was waiting for new companies of men from Catalonia to increase his forces and depart with greater reputation. Berenguer de Rocafort was detained over some castles in Calabria, which he refused to deliver to King Charles of Naples until the debt for his salary was entirely satisfied. Although the lack of the two captains gave him just cause for delay since they made up the principal part of his army, Roger was determined to leave, embarking on the appointed day. The king, in addition to the ships and galleys he had given them for their voyage, ordered the provision of their food and supplies, and the money that this prince whose reign had known only fatigues and dangers could afford.

This was the reward that was offered to the most invincible and victorious militia of the age, which had served twenty long years under three kings, Pedro, Jaime, and Fadrique, winning from their enemies five naval and three land victories, in addition to other notable encounters and the storming of great, strong cities, as well as their defense of others with laudable obstinacy and incredible valor. Such was the moderation of the times — quite different from today, when we see soldiers who, scarcely have they faced the enemy, than they demand to be repaid with greater rewards.

REFERENCES

1. Zurita calls the Seneschal by the surname of Corbarán de Lehet, but Moncada follows Muntaner's version of the name.

Seventh Chapter

DEPARTURE OF THE FLEET FROM SICILY;
THE ALMUGAVARS

THE CATALANS sailed from the port of Messina, but before they left the lighthouse, they were joined by a throng of Almugavars, fifteen hundred men to serve on shipboard, not counting the officers, and four thousand infantrymen, according to Muntaner. Nicephorus Gregoras, an author who is not entirely trustworthy on many occasions, says that Roger left Greece with only one thousand men, but here George Pachymeres agrees with the Catalan chronicler that there were eight thousand. This seems a more logical number, since it is certain that he arrived with sixty-five hundred wage soldiers who were probably increased to eight thousand with the servants and families of the nobles. Although Nicephorus and Pachymeres do not agree, the former is usually doubtful. I cannot convince myself that Andronicus would have made Roger a Grand Duke and married him to his granddaughter if he had been chief of only a thousand men upon entering his service.

It does not seem outside our story to say something of the Almugavars, since the infantry was composed of them. Antiquity, the mother of forgetfulness, which has lost many brilliant deeds and shining memories and left others confused, also holds the origin of the Almugavars. From what I have been able to find, they were among the barbaric nations that destroyed the Roman Empire in Spain and set up their own in its place. This was preserved in splendor and majesty until the Saracens overran them in less than two years, forcing the remnants of their people into the most rugged mountains, where they hunted wild animals to provide themselves with food and clothing. There the ancient strength and endurance of the race that had been buried in comfort and luxury during their domination was restored by the life of labor and fatigue. They left the forests, taking with them to use against the Moors the weapons wielded before against animals.

They took up their old wandering habits, never building houses or staking out properties. They lived in the fields and on enemy frontiers, sustaining themselves and their families with plunder from the Saracens, for which they continually sacrificed their lives, developing no other craft or occupation than service for wages in war. When kings did not hire them, they followed their own chiefs to raid the frontiers, until the name "Almugavar" became synonymous with plundering among the ancients.

They took with them their women and children, witnesses of their glory or defeat, and, like Germans of all ages, dressed in animal skins with sandals and leggings of the same hide. Their weapons included an iron network worn on the head like a helmet, a sword, a pointed staff somewhat like those used today in companies of harquebus fighters, and usually three or four throwing darts. They handled these darts with such speed and violence that they challenged armed men and horses, a feat that would seem improbable if it had not been recorded by both Bernat Desclot[1] and Muntaner, serious authors of our history who relate the deeds of our people as comparable to those of the most distinguished Greeks and Romans.

Once when Charles, king of Naples, called into his presence some Almugavar prisoners, he marveled at the poverty of their clothing and weapons, apparently useless against the bodies of armed and mounted men, and asked scornfully if these were the men with whom the king of Aragon planned to wage war. One of the soldiers, with characteristic freedom to defend his reputation, replied, "Sir, if we seem so unfit to you and you estimate our power so little, select one of the distinguished knights of your army, with the offensive and defensive weapons of his choice, and I will challenge him on the field with only my sword and darts." Thinking to punish the Almugavar's insolence, Charles accepted the challenge and went out to watch the battle. A Frenchman appeared, completely armed and mounted with his lance, sword, and mace. And there was the Almugavar alone with his sword and dart. But scarcely had he entered the stockade before he had killed the horse and was preparing to do the same for its master, when the king's voice stopped him, proclaiming him victor and free.

During the same war, another Almugavar was attacked by twenty armed men on the banks of a river and managed to kill five of them before he died. Many other instances could be cited, enough for a separate history. Only their name is doubtful — whether it originally belonged to an army or a tribe. I am sure that they were a tribe, and, to back my opinion, Pachymeres called the Almugavars descendants of the Avars, comrades of the Huns and Goths. Although no author contradicts this belief, several of the laws of the *Partidas* clearly refer to them as an army. This situation does not refute the first opinion, however, because both statements may be true.

In the beginning, Pachymeres says, they were a tribe, but as time went on and they developed no art or profession, the name, "Almugavar," came to mean any man who served for wages in the army, in the same way that arts and sciences often take the names of their inventors. But I doubt greatly if many people who were not of their own tribe joined the Almugavars for a life of fatigue and dangers. Unless natural inclination made them follow the profession of their fathers, few men would choose such a living that had been discomfort and continual labor from its beginning. Nicephorus states that "Almugavar" is the name that the Latins — for so the Greeks called all Westerners — gave to their infantry soldiers. But there is no object in presenting argument to such a manifest error, especially against an author so little versed in our affairs as is Nicephorus.

The fleet left Messina and arrived with good sailing at Monemvasia, the port of Morea, where they were affably received and of-

fered provisions according to the Emperor's order. Before embarking again, Roger received orders to speed the voyage. The people
left, cheered by their entertainment, and a few days later during
the month of January they docked at Constantinople,[2] where, according to the thirteenth chapter of Pachymeres's second book,
they were welcomed with universal rejoicing in the city that recognized them as forces for their aid and defense. The Emperors
Andronicus and Michael and all the Greek nobility received and
honored them with much cordiality and display of the greatest
gratitude. Andronicus ordered everyone to disembark and take
lodging in the quarter of the city called Blachernae.[3] The following day wages for four months were distributed, as had been
agreed.

REFERENCES

1. The work of the Catalan historian is *Chrónicas ó conquestas de Catalunya, com-
postes é ordenades per en Bernat de Sclot*, or *Chronicles of the Conquests of Catalonia, Compiled and Arranged by Don Bernat Desclot*. It was translated into Spanish
under the title, *Of the Histories of Some Counts of Barcelona and Kings of Aragon*
by Rafael Cervera, and published in quarto edition by Sebastian de Cormellas in
Barcelona in 1616.

2. Actually, late in the year 1303.

3. The Blachernae section of Constantinople was the ancient area on the Golden
Horn in the north, largely built during the days of Emperor Justinian II (685-695)
and the eighth century. The great Blachernae palace was ruined during the thir-
teenth-century Frankish domination, but gradually rebuilt after the Greeks returned.

Eighth Chapter

ROGER IS MARRIED AND

THE CATALANS AND GENOESE FIGHT IN CONSTANTINOPLE

THE EMPEROR realized that it was to his credit and security
to make it known that the promises he had given to our people
were being punctually fulfilled, and, in order to show this by deeds,
he began with what seemed the most difficult: the marriage of his

niece, María, to Roger. With that, all were pleased, deeming the remaining favors as lesser and more easily conferred.

The ceremony was held with all the solemnity of royalty, since Roger's valor could equal his wife's nobility. María was the daughter of Prince Asen of the Bulgars and of Irene, sister of Andronicus. She was fifteen years old, beautiful, and extremely intelligent.

While the grand wedding feast was going on, a quarrel and then a riot broke out between the Catalans and the Genoese that almost became a bloody battle and was started, as is often the case, from some trivial cause. Pachymeres says that the disagreement was over the twenty thousand ducats that had been lent to Roger before he left Sicily, which the Emperor, in order to restore peace, now offered to repay. But the most evident cause of the fracas was an Almugavar, roaming through the city, whose garb and figure caused the laughter and ridicule of two Genoese who saw that he was alone. The Almugavar's belligerent spirit was irritated by the wit and condescending remarks and, being more expressive with his hands than his tongue, he started the fight by rushing his tormentors with his sword.

Friends and onlookers arrived to take one side or the other, and since the two nations had been mutually suspicious and antagonistic, they now met each other, intent on complete destruction. The Genoese pulled out their banner or emblem and attacked the barracks to which the Almugavars had been assigned in the Blachernae section. Our knights, realizing the danger to their Almugavars, divided into squads and closed in on the disorganized Genoese. While this was taking place, the Almugavars came out of their quarters and joined in to take satisfaction against those who had so unjustly mistreated them. Both sides fought obstinately until the Genoese captain, Roseo da Final, was killed and his men retreated with several casualties and much damage.

Andronicus watched the fight with enthusiasm from his palace windows, expressing his disgust with the Genoese when he saw them being pushed around and even killed. But when he realized that the Almugavars, with their customary fervor, were massacring everyone who got in their way, he began to fear that all the

Genoese in Constantinople might die that day, which would be an uncomfortable situation for his own protection, because the peace of his empire depended upon Genoa. It seemed true that Andronicus would have liked to be free of the Genoese yoke, if he could have managed it safely. But this was difficult, since their power was now so distributed that it could not be overcome at a single blow. If he permitted the Genoese in Constantinople to die, he would anger their other forces that remained whole. And so, with prayers and promises, he begged the Catalan captains to assemble and retire their people. George Pachymeres reports that Andronicus sent his chief of fleet,[1] Esteban Marzala, to quiet the tumult and pacify both sides, but the unfortunate admiral was killed and torn to pieces in the savage uproar. Finally the presence and authority of Roger and the other captains were able to force obedience, and their men retreated reluctantly, for they had hoisted their banners and were ready to attack and plunder Pera, animated by both greed and the desire for vengeance.

The Genoese town was separated from the city of Constantinople by a narrow stretch of sea known as the Horn of Byzantium to the ancients, and is Galata to the Turks and Greeks of today. When our people had retreated and calmed down, the Emperor ordered that wages be delivered to them in recognition of their punctual obedience. They had left about three thousand of the Genoese in the city dead, which, although they were then victors, was the beginning of much future grief for them. They had insulted a powerful rival nation, whose friendship was necessary to keep our army in that empire, for Genoese strength was great and feared everywhere in the East. They were arbitrators in peace and war; owners of illustrious colonies and citadels in Greece, Pontus, and Palestine; admirals of powerful fleets; possessors of vast riches amassed by their courage and industry; and absolute masters of European trade, for which they maintained forces equal to those of the major kings and republics. Through these accomplishments they came to be near masters of the Greek Empire.

When the Catalans arrived in Constantinople, the Genoese had surveyed the forces they brought with them and had realized that the newcomers were dangerous to have in the vicinity of their own forces. And so began the dislike and implacable enmity between the two nations that lasted many years until both of them finally lost their strength and the dominion over the sea. Not until then did the rivalry end that had caused them to fight often, with varying outcome.

REFERENCES

1. Moncada uses the term, *drungarius,* title for the rank in the Byzantine hierarchy that followed the *megas dux,* or Grand Duke, and corresponded to admiral as chief of all the fleet. Around 1300 the *drungarius* also performed the duties of secretary of state for the naval forces.

Ninth Chapter

THE FLEET MOVES TO ANATOLIA
AND SENDS THE PEOPLE TO THE CAPE OF ARTACE

AFTER THE DAMAGING QUARREL between the Catalans and the Genoese, Andronicus realized what could happen with several different armed and offended nations within the city: that there would undoubtedly be a break and on less occasion than there had been the first time. He called in the Catalan officers and explained how happy he would be to have them helping his miserable Christian subjects then being oppressed by the Turks in Asia, and at the same time averting the possibility of more disorder at home. Roger and his captains agreed to embark with their people immediately, but they asked one concession to their peace of mind and the satisfaction of their people. They asked him to name an officer of their own nation to be in charge of their relief and reinforcement. They felt that they could depend on such a man with more security, for they considered it a dangerous practice to leave such a charge as their support in time of need in the hands of a foreign people. They were afraid that Andronicus would appoint a man among the Greeks or Genoese, and that it would be dangerous to their security to have to depend for aid upon foreigners, with whom there is always rivalry and competition, causes of serious quarrels and mischief, particularly as regards aid sent by sea, so subject to weather conditions. A base or malicious general could delay help and afterwards find reasons for excusing or supporting the evil deed, blaming his treachery on the weather and imaginary danger.

Andronicus completely satisfied this request, giving the charge to Fernando de Aonés,[1] making him a general of the fleet with title of Admiral. Fernando, a knight of known blood and personal gallantry, was also offered marriage to a relative of the Emperor, in order that the new relationship should give more authority to his charge. The title of Admiral in that empire was not as supreme as in our times; he was subject to the Grand Duke from whom he received his orders. The Emperor sent a Romanic[2] insignia captain named Marulli, a man of 'birth and position, to join Roger's people, and also George[3] of the Alans and most of his men. The army embarked in ships and galleys of the fleet, crossing the Sea of Propontis, which is called Marmara today. They made land at the Cape of Artace, a little more than a hundred miles from Constantinople at a place they found suitable for the disembarkation of the knights. This cape, called Artaqui by Muntaner and Artacio by the ancients, lies not far from the ruins of the famous city of Cyzicus.[4]

When Roger arrived with the fleet, he learned that on that very day the Turks had tried to take a rampart or wall half a mile in length that was built where the cape joins the mainland. They had given up the assault, more because of the strength of the place than the valor of those who were defending it. This cape extended some miles from their battlement out into the sea; on it are many towns, abundant valleys, and fertile hills. In ancient times it was an island, but since then accumulating sands have attached it to the mainland.

When Roger had definite information that the Turks had attacked the cape rampart, he realized that they could not be far off and hastily unloaded his men, sending spies to scout the enemy camps. In a few hours they found out that the Turks were lodged six miles away between two streams with their women, children, and households. At that time they had not yet abandoned the customs of the Scythians, from whom they claim descent, living mostly as warlike tribes in tents and sheds in the field, moving with the change of season and produce of the land. Their main strength was in their horsemen, who were governed by captains and princes, men of courage rather than blood, obeyed through respect more than obligation. They waged perpetual war without military order against their neighbors, like the Arabians who now possess Africa. They had pursued this kind of life since leaving the banks of the Volga River and entering Asia Minor, where they won credit and reputation from the cowardly Greek and Asian nations. The same happens to monarchies and nations as it does to men; they are born, grow, and die. Greece sprang up when it defended itself from Xerxes, when its valor unmade the power of his numerous armies and forced the barbaric monarch to retreat vanquished in a small boat across the straits of the Hellespont, which he had humbled with a bridge a short time before as a haughty conqueror.[5] It had grown when Alexander's forces passed beyond the Ganges, until the vast limits and borders of nature itself were not larger than his ambition. Its death came when savage hordes, through the weakness of Greek princes and the lack of loyalty among their officers, were able to place it in hard servitude.

During the time that Andronicus occupied the Eastern empire, the Turks were divided by civil wars among themselves. But through the advice and authority of Orthogules, they were pacified and decided to settle their disputes by casting lots. Gregoras and Chalcocondyles[6] record that the provinces went to seven captains, each of whom aspired to the universal government. To Karaman's lot fell the Mediterranean section of the province of Phrygia from Cilicia to Philadelphia; one author, however, claims that he was not one of the seven and that he reigned only in Caria. Karkan received the part of Phrygia that extended to Smyrna; to Kalami and his son went Carasi, Lydia as far as Mysia, Bithynia, and the remaining provinces near Mount Olympus fell into the lot of Ottoman, who was beginning to inspire awe at that period. Soon after receiving his monarchy, he rose up, conquered, and subjugated the tyrants of the other provinces named, until he was left absolute lord of them all. Paphlagonia and the remaining lands of the Black Sea area were occupied by the sons of Amurat. In this condition the Catalans found Asia split among its Turkish lords, making the land with its divided forces vulnerable to our people's victories.

REFERENCES

1. Moncada uses both Haones and Aonés as forms of this surname. Muntaner calls the Admiral Ferrán Daunes, and Zurita refers to him as Fernando de Ahones, which is probably the correct version.

2. The Romanics were the people of various European backgrounds who were descended from those who lived under the rule of the Roman Empire. *Romanos* or *romanaioi* were the remnants of the Latin crusaders in the Greek area.

3. Gircon, in his own language.

4. The Cape of Artace is the southwest shore of the Sea of Marmara, lying along the west side of the Cyzicus peninsula. The seaport town of Artace was built there.

5. The Persian emperor, Xerxes, invaded the Attican peninsula in 490 B.C. with a vast following, but was defeated by the Greek citizens defending their homeland. When he crossed the Hellespont, "sea of Hellas," or the Straits of the Dardanelles, he passed over the boundary between Asia and Europe, a fifty-mile channel that varies from six to two miles at the upper and lower ends.

6. Laonicus Chalcocondyles, an Athenian who spent many years at the court of the Despot of the Morea, or Peleponnesus, wrote the most important account of the collapse of the Byzantine Empire from 1297 to 1493. Taking the classics of Herodotus and Thucydides as his models, he describes concisely the history of the known world from Assyria to the beginning of the Ottoman kingdom in *De origine et rebus gestis turcorum*. See William Miller, *The Last Athenian Historian: Laonikos Chalkondyles* (1922).

Tenth Chapter

THE CATALANS AND ARAGONESE CONQUER THE TURKS

SINCE ROGER KNEW how near the Turks were and did not wish to lose the opportunity of striking before the enemy learned of their arrival, allowing them time to arm or retreat, he called the camp together. In a brief talk he explained to them how he planned to take the enemy camp next day, which could be done easily because it was unguarded. He pointed out the glory that would be theirs if they won, and that through their first encounter would come the fear or confidence on which their reputation depended. He ordered them to spare the lives of none but children, because they would thus inspire more terror among the barbarians, and because they themselves were fighting with no expectation of life if they were beaten. He gave the order in which they would march, and thus ended his speech. His men listened to him with enthusiasm and that same night left the camp in order to attack at dawn.

Roger and Marulli led the vanguard of horsemen, bearing only two standards: one with the arms of Andronicus and one with their own. The infantry followed in a single squadron, commanded by Corbarán de Alet, Seneschal of the Army. He, too, carried only two banners, contrary to the common usage of our times, which were borne at the head of the line, instead of back in the center in a stronger and better defended position. One banner bore the arms of Jaime of Aragon and the other, those of Fadrique, King of Sicily, for one of the conditions of service that the Catalans had demanded of the Emperor was the right to carry the emblems of their native rulers.

The soldiers meant to take with them the memory and authority of their kings, because they believed the weapons of Aragon were invincible. From this desire could be seen the affection and veneration that their rulers inspired in the Catalans and Aragonese, since they preserved their memory and fought supported by it even under foreign rulers in distant provinces. Although this fidelity was remarkable, instead of being rare, it was always the case with them. We Catalans never abandoned a ruler; no matter how cruel or wicked he was, we preferred to suffer his rigor and severity rather than submit to a new master. We did not consider the Sicilian ruler a bastard brother, nor did we exclude the rightful king from our affections. We did not prefer the second brother to the first,[1] but accepted them in the order that nature and heaven had disposed, without altering the situation by particular dislike or regard, when scarcely a kingdom was seen that was not rife with such changes and substitutions.

At midnight the Catalans moved on to the rampart that divided the cape from the mainland, and at dawn they came upon the Turks. The enemy was camped in a secure area that they supposed far from attackers; they accordingly had no sentinels and were sleeping carefree in their tents. Roger and Marulli closed in with the horsemen and tore through tents and thin defenses with great spirit. The Almugavars followed them in the same spirit, furnishing a bloody and fortunate beginning to the new war. Those Turks who were not immediately overcome by the furious rigor of Company swords while they slept woke up to the noise of weapons and voices, terrified and confused by the sudden assault. They snatched their weapons to defend themselves, but they were few, divided, and unarmed. Their resistance was futile and luckless against the strength and daring of their attackers, who were everywhere at once. But they fought desperately, watching the dismemberment and beheading of their dear ones by a people whose name they did not even know.

The Catalans came out completely victorious, leaving the camp strewn with three thousand dead Turkish horsemen and ten thousand men. The few who were left alive were those who had realized in time, amid all the disorder and loss, that the Catalans were impervious to their short lance blows, and escaped. Others who tried to do the same later only met their deaths the faster, because they were so occupied in hurrying away their women and children that they left off defending themselves.

The booty was great, with many captive children. Nicephorus, a native of Greece and our declared enemy, describes in these words the fear and terror that this first attack caused the Turks: "When the Turks saw the fierce impetuosity of the Latins [as he called the Catalans], their valor, their military discipline, and their powerful, gleaming weapons, they fled terrified and aghast, not only far from the city of Constantinople, but way into the depths of their former empire." Our people continued the pursuit but a little way, not knowing the country, and they returned to the cape the same night, having examined and secured their camp.

REFERENCES

1. King Fadrique's birth was legitimate. The comment is apparently in metaphorical reference to his war against his brother, Jaime II of Aragon, over his assumption of independent rule of the Sicilian kingdom, which Fadrique had inherited from Jaime as a vassal state to Aragon.

Eleventh Chapter

THE ARMY RETREATS TO SPEND THE WINTER

IN THE CAMP ON THE CAPE OF ARTACE

W ITH FOUR GALLEYS full of rich presents for both Andronicus and Michael, the Catalans sent word of their victory to the rulers. The most precious lot of the capture was sent to María, the wife of the Grand Duke, Roger, in the name of the soldiers. The quickness with which the foreigners had won such a remarkable victory caused widespread admiration among the Greeks, who began to sing the praises of their champions. They were free at last from fear of the Turks, who, insolent with their victories over the Greeks on the other side of the Bosphorus, had been threatening the city with their naked scimitars. But most of the nobility, instead of showing their gratitude for the benefits derived, as would have been just, were filled with ill-concealed envy of the foreigners' luck. Andronicus's confidants and some of the more prominent persons of his nation began to fear our forces, realizing that they were superior to their own and that so much power in the hands of the strangers within the realm was a dangerous mat-

ter. These opinions and remarks were encouraged by Michael, the
Emperor, who was goaded by a hidden resentment that the victory
had implanted in his soul.

A few months before, he had crossed the straits with a powerful army, but either through fear of the Turks or lack of confidence in his own men, he had come home very embarrassed, without attempting even a small skirmish with the enemy. And when
he saw the Catalans who were so few in number conquering those
he had not even dared to attack with his huge army, his annoyance
began to develop into hatred and active desire for Catalan ruin.
Princes greatly resent anyone who outdoes them in courage, or
even is more clever at making wise remarks, because power does
not suffer virtue and talent in foreigners, especially when this
ability betters theirs. If a trifling competition against an envious
prince in composing poetry could cause the death of Lucan,[1] how
much more would have been at stake if fortune and valor had
been pitted in competition? And thus, a wise captain will never
undertake an enterprise in which his superior has failed — unless
he wishes to compete with him for the throne.

In spite of their success, the Catalans did not press their victory
or attempt to move forward, a stand that damaged their reputation
and caused them to commit deeds in that region that gravely irritated the natives and Greeks. They planned to march inland, but
the first day of November brought such rigorously cold winter
wind and water that they stopped. The rivers were so high they
could not be forded; the sterile countryside was full of enemies;
and the roads over which they would have to travel to aid Philadelphia were so impassable that they decided to put off all enterprise.
With the cognizance and counsel of his captains, Roger resolved to
winter at Cyzicus,[2] a comfortable location because of the strength
of the place and its abundance of food. They also chose this as a
strategic position for embarkation from Greece the following year,
when the task of loading and unloading so many horsemen would
be formidable.

They sent the Emperor word of their decision, which he heartily approved because it suited him to have the army camped between him and the enemy and away from Constantinople and the rest of the Greeks, who were grumbling and discontented because the hired soldiers had been camped for nearly three months in Asia, draining the area of heavy contributions. Andronicus promptly ordered that all types of food not available on the cape be shipped to Roger's men, so that our people passed the winter comfortably. The Grand Duke, Roger, sent four galleys for his wife, María.

Orders were circulated in the quarters to prevent quarrels between the soldiers and their hosts. The soldiers named six of their own people and the natives had an equal number of representatives to agree on what price to put on food. Overcharging would have worked an unjust hardship on the Catalans; low payment would injure their hosts, in addition to the fact that they would be cut off from their usual active commerce with other towns of the area. The Admiral, Fernando de Aonés, was ordered to winter with the fleet on the Isle of Chios, which had a secure port and was near the enemy coastline. This island is the most remarkable one in the Aegean Sea, for it is the only place in the world where the mastic tree grows.[3]

REFERENCES

1. Lucan, the Roman poet born at Córdova in Spain in 39, was the son of Annaeus Mella and the nephew of Seneca, the philosopher. While a young man in Rome, he composed the heroic poem, *Pharsalia,* in ten books that describe the struggle between Caesar and Pompey, but end abruptly in the middle of the Alexandrian War. He was forced to kill himself at the age of twenty-six, ostensibly for involvement in a conspiracy against Nero, but, according to legend, actually because of the Emperor's jealousy of his talents.

2. Since Cyzicus is located on a peninsula off the Mysian shore of the Sea of Marmara, it was almost directly south of Rhodestos on the opposite side. One of the most ancient and powerful cities in Asia Minor, it was originally built on an island connected to the mainland by two bridges. Later a causeway was constructed, which eventually accumulated into a considerable isthmus. Hadrian, the Spanish-born Emperor of Rome, began a magnificent temple there that was finally finished by his relative, Marcus Aurelius.

3. The *almastec* or *almáciga* [mastic] produces a valuable gum or resin.

Twelfth Chapter

FERNAN JIMENEZ DE ARENOS LEAVES THE COMPANY

Because of General Agreement in the disposition of affairs on both sea and land, the winter passed in peace and harmony. But then Roger's forces began to be weakened by internal discord. Fernán Jiménez de Arenós, a knight of noble background and a good soldier, had a disagreement with Roger over the government of his men. Apparently feeling unequal to the competition, he left the army with his people and headed back to Sicily.

On the way home he stopped at Athens, where he was honorably received by the Duke[1] and stayed on in his service. He was offered some military responsibility and remained in the duke's employ until his former comrades needed him on Gallipoli, where he joined them, venturing his life and liberty in their cause like a true knight. Pachymeres says that Roger and Fernán parted because the Grand Duke had frequently warned his captain to reprimand or punish his men for infractions of discipline. Since Fernán did not wish to obey, he separated from the Company with those of his men who wished to follow him. Strong wills were revealed here, when the troops, just out of danger from foreign arms, began to flame up with rivalries and civil wars among themselves!

When the new season came in, Roger and María returned to Constantinople with four galleys to speak to the Emperor about the next expedition and to ask him for money to pay their men before the army went out into the field again. Michael was in Constantinople; Roger wished to visit him and explain his plans for the coming year, but he was not received. Pachymeres says this was due to his being offended by Roger's ill treatment of the Emperor's vassals at Cyzicus. The fact is that Roger collected money from Andronicus with such largesse that he was able to give his men double pay: noble liberality if the ruler possesses enough property and funds to afford it.

Generosity is to be deemed a heroic virtue in a ruler if it has two qualifications: first, if the king has the money to give, and, second, if he gives it to men who deserve it. If one of these two conditions is lacking, there is no virtue, but injustice. Andronicus satisfied the second quality of liberality by conferring gifts on people of merit, but by the first quality he made a grave mistake. His national treasury and the commerce of the empire were so depleted that he could not make payment on other pressing obligations of his government. There is nothing so dangerous as the squandering of money claimed for the common defense, for when the situation really does tighten up and there is serious need for new taxes and assessments, there is also just cause for complaint and rebellion against the former excesses. Such impositions are to be condoned when there is pressing need for the money, but when a ruler uses up the possessions and resources of his land in gifts or useless wastefulness, there is no justification for his lack of organization and care.

Roger and the Emperor discussed the administration of the war that year, in which Andronicus charged him only with aid to Philadelphia. The rest of the campaign he left up to the judgment of Roger and his officers, since he realized that wise orders cannot be made in advance to suit the situation that might arise, especially in the uncertainty of wartime.

Roger left his wife, María, in Constantinople and sailed around the cape with his four galleys on the first day of March in 1303. Shortly after his return to the Company, he took over the business of paying the accounts run up by his soldiers with the natives during the winter, and when the general accounts were checked, he discovered that in the four months they had wintered, some of his men had spent wages for eight months, and others for as much as a year. He was disgusted by the excess and disorder of the army; as a wise and prudent captain, he realized the folly of their ways. But he also knew that his own authority rested on the decision of the soldiers, and he decided not to risk it by applying the remedy to the situation that he thought suitable. A commander is hard put to it to maintain punctual and strict discipline in an army if the power and authority by which he is to impose it are given him by his troops: from such a situation is born insolence and license.

Roger, aware of the progress of the season, paid off the creditors in full for what they had spent in maintaining the soldiers. But since he did not wish to subtract these debts from their wages, he distributed to his men their full four months' pay. Then he took the books in which were recorded the accounts of the rations and excesses of his army and burned them in the public square of Cyzicus, thereby leaving them all obligated and grateful for his generosity.

Greek authors claim that Cyzicus and all the surrounding region was ruined by Catalan cruelty and robbery, and that Andronicus, afraid that Roger would loiter in taking his badly disciplined army off to war, sent his daughter,[2] mother of María, around the last of March to advise her son-in-law to leave with his army because the season and conditions were favorable for war. Since they had just been paid, the soldiers would go enthusiastically.

REFERENCES

1. Guy de la Roche, Frankish nobleman who died five years later. When he and his successor, Gautier de Brienne, were dead, the Burgundian rule of Athens that began with the crusaders in 1205 came to an end.

2. Moncada obviously means the sister of Andronicus, Irene Palaeologina, the wife of Ivan Asen III of Bulgaria. He correctly identifies her relationship in subsequent passages.

Thirteenth Chapter

THE ARMY LEAVES TO HELP PHILADELPHIA AND CONQUERS
KARAMAN, THE TURKISH LORD OF THE PEOPLE
BESIEGED THERE

ROGER'S DESIRE to get into the field, aided by his mother-in-law's persuasion, speeded preparations for the departure, which

was scheduled for the ninth of April. While all were busily stow-
ing supplies for the voyage, two Massagetes or Alans were waiting
at a mill for wheat to be ground, when some Almugavars arrived
and began to insult a woman who was separating the meal within.
The Alans came out to defend her, and in the ensuing argument
complained against Roger, their captain, claiming that given the
opportunity they would deal with him as they had done with the
Grand Domestic.[1] This was Alexios Raúl, whom they had treacherously killed with a dart at a military festival. The Almugavars reported what they had heard to Roger, and, that same night, either
by his order or consent, they fell upon the Alans of the Company
and would have cut the throats of all of them if they had not been
protected by the darkness of the night and the alertness of their
neighbors. As it was, many of them died, including a valiant lad,
the son of George, head of the Alans. In the morning they fought
again, and the Catalans came out on top, having killed more than
three hundred Alans. If the citizens of Cyzicus, angered by repeated bad treatment, had not taken weapons and fought on the
side of the Alans, there would probably have been none left.

Because of this incident most of the Alans left Roger's army.
Promises and pleas persuaded only about a thousand of them to
remain. Roger tried to compensate George for the death of his son
with money, but the father scorned the gift and the insult of the
offer was added to his outrage at his son's death. The barbarian
was filled with resentment, but he hid his feelings and waited for
an opportunity for vengeance.

The quarrel postponed departure until the first of May, when
six thousand who were called Catalans, a thousand Alans, and
the Romanic companies under Marulli embarked, all subject to
Roger's command. Nastago, the chief steward, also went with
them. With these forces they arrived at Anchialus,[2] and from there
with great courage and confidence, according to Pachymeres, they
went out to lay siege to Germe, a fortified place held by the Turks.
But their fame traveled before them, so that when the Turks
realized their intention, they left the location and retreated. But
they did not get away in time to avoid grave danger to their rearguard.

From there they went to a place that Pachymeres's history does not record; he says only that in connection with its defense, Sausi Crisanislao, famous soldier and captain of the Bulgars, was ordered hanged with twelve of his best men. The reason for this execution is not certain. It is only assumed that the prisoners had done a bad job of defending some position that was their responsibility, or surrendered some fortress. Sausi had argued with Roger, attempting to excuse himself, and in the course of the discussion drew his sword and wounded the Grand Duke, an offense for which he was surrendered to the hangmen. The Greek captains delayed the execution and persuaded Roger to pardon the man, because they knew how Andronicus disapproved of punishing a man of so much quality and ability without sufficient cause. Crisanislao had been among the Bulgar captains captured by Andronicus's father, Michael, in the war of the Chana, kept in prison for a long time, and finally freed by the Emperor, who honored him with military and governmental charges in the provinces. For this reason he was in Phrygia, occupied in the service of Andronicus.

Then the army moved on to Geliana on the road to Philadelphia, where word reached Roger from the subjected people in Turkish strongholds, complaining of the servitude they suffered and beseeching his help, since they were Romanics who had for the moment succumbed to superior force and ready to rise against the enemy. Roger sent reply to them to be of good cheer for he would help them. With this in mind he pressed forward to succor Philadelphia, which was his principal objective. Karaman Alisurius, who was besieging it, and whose government extended through the province, raised the siege with most of his army when he heard the Catalans were coming and went out to meet them, seeking revenge for the rout his companions had suffered the year before at their hands. It seemed to him more suitable not to defend Philadelphia, a great city with an armed populace which, encouraged by the approach of a friendly army, would sally forth to fight. He left some in some of the forts, believing that thus those in the city would not try to sally forth. But at dawn from a distance of two miles they sighted one another, and made ready to fight. The Turkish army approached eight thousand horses and twelve thousand soldiers, all Karamanians, the most valiant and fearless of the nation.[3] They were superior to our men in numbers, but quite inferior in courage, discipline, military organization, and offensive and defensive weapons; the only equality was in spirit and desire to fight.

Roger divided his horsemen into three groups: Alans, Romanics, and Catalans. Corbarán de Alet, whose charge was the infantry, divided it into squadrons. When the signal was given for the attack, both armies rushed in with gallant spirit. The battle was soon a bloody one for the Turks, because the Catalans, more practiced in striking and more sure of their offensive weapons, inflicted much damage on the enemy with very little for their own.

The fiercest onslaught was out near the city conduits. The valiant, daring Turks left no means untried to harass our people and make the victory doubtful; until noon it was still uncertain. But the customary valor of the Catalans declared itself for their side, with notable damage to the Turks. They began to run for it, with up to a thousand of the original eight thousand horsemen and only five hundred foot-soldiers managing to escape. Karaman Alisurius retreated wounded. Of the Spaniards, eighty horsemen and one hundred foot-soldiers perished. After the battle, the squadrons formed again and advanced toward Philadelphia, slowly following the enemy, fearful of a major ambush by his copious army. The Turks who had been manning forts abandoned them and followed their defeated leader when they heard of the rout. According to Muntaner, the captives and what was gained in this battle were considerable.

With this victory, the cities of Asia[4] began to raise their heads, cheered by the liberation that the Catalans had begun against the oppressive Turks. This oppression had reached such an extreme that their women and children were being taken for instruction in the foreign religion. The ancient temples and monasteries, where the bodies of so many saints were buried and the memory of our primitive Church[5] that had flourished so greatly in those provinces was preserved, were being profaned. False, abominable adoration of the Prophet was replacing true religion. But since the just decision of God was now ordaining the destruction and servitude of all that empire and nation, it seemed to be of small advantage for our people to bring them liberty, for their decline was apparently predetermined. For when powerful remedies do not cure the disease for which they are administered, death is almost certain. The captains of our people stopped before entering Philadelphia to inspect outlying towns where the Turks might have retreated to reorganize. But they were all found free of the oppressor, who had been frightened far, far away.

REFERENCES

1. The Greek title of *megas domesticus* seems to have had the same relation to the land militia that the *megas dux,* or Grand Duke, had to the navy. It was the highest grade in the army command, and, consequently, one of the first dignities of the imperial house. (Cayetano Rosell y López, *Biblioteca de autores españoles desde la formación del lenguaje hasta nuestros días,* I, p. 13.)

2. This Anchialus is not to be confused with other towns of the same name in the region. It is neither the Bulgarian seaport on the Black Sea a few miles south of Mesembria, nor the ancient Cilician city in southeastern Asia Minor that, according to legend, was built by Sardanapalus, the Assyrian king who drove the Ethiopians out of Egypt and conquered Tyre.

3. Dr. John McCarty Sharp points out that the Karamanians are men from the present-day Turkish province of Karamania, named for this fourteenth-century leader, Karaman.

4. Asia here is not used in the modern sense of the massive continent, but is restricted to the ancient meaning of the provinces of Asia Minor, almost entirely encompassed by modern Turkey.

5. Dr. Sharp indicates that Moncada's *iglesia primitiva* refers to the original group of first-century churches in the Asia Minor territory that is now Turkey, founded by Saint Paul and his fellow missionaries.

Fourteenth Chapter

THE VICTORIOUS COMPANY ENTERS PHILADELPHIA,
TAKES SOME STRONGHOLDS HELD BY THE ENEMY NEAR THE
CITY, AND DEFEATS THE TURKS AGAIN NEAR TIRE

T HE PEOPLE of Philadelphia, freed by the valor of Catalan arms from the siege that had so distressed them, went out to meet the army. Their administrators and Theoleptus, their bishop, a

man of rare sanctity, whose prayers had done more to defend the
city than had the arms of the people who guarded it, headed their
people. The troops of horsemen entered first, waving the conquered banners taken from the Turks. After them came the carri-
ages filled with enemy plunder and then a crowd of captive women and children and some boys spared for the triumphal entrance. The companies of infantry marched in last, bearing in their
midst their banners, followed by the distinguished officers, who
were gleaming with a display such as the peoples of Asia had never
seen; they stood watching in wondering admiration.

Not a soldier entered who was not dressed in silk or scarlet
cloth, although the Turks did not dress in rich clothing in those
times. But they had taken quantities of fine cloth and linen from
the Greeks, and these spoils were recovered in the victory.

The Catalans stayed fifteen days in the city, entertained with
feasting and celebrations and treated with affection and respect by
the citizens, who were grateful to them for their lives and liberty,
since they had risked their own for the Greek cause. Need is always grateful, but, like the benefits it receives, the gratitude also
ends.

Roger left Philadelphia[1] to liberate some towns in the power
of the Turks, Kula among others, some miles east of the city. But
when the Turks heard of their army's flight, they also retreated.
The natives greeted their rescuers with open gates, as people who
had just been freed from servitude. With this gesture, they hoped
to attain pardon for having surrendered so easily to the Turks before. Roger forgave the multitude of the people, but punished
some of them severely. He cut off the governor's head and condemned the principal officer of the regiment to the gallows. When
he hung for a while without dying, the people who were watching
believed it a miracle, cut the rope, and freed the condemned officer.

The Company went back to Philadelphia, where, Pachymeres
says, Roger gathered many ducats and levied heavier taxes than he
should have, since the city was now feeling the pinch for food, as
it was very populous of itself, and the army was stationed there,
too, after the food supply had been so tight during the siege that
an ass's head sold for an incredible price. Nastago, duke and im-

perial steward who had been assigned to Roger's army, left for Constantinople, because as a Greek himself, he could not stand to see the abuses and excesses caused by Roger's presence among the Philadelphians. He tried to get a hearing with the Emperor, but was prevented by María's relatives and friends. From what I understand, he finally went to the old patriarch and through him Andronicus heard the complaints he filed against Roger. As a result, a loud disagreement flared up in the palace between the Archduke's friends and his rivals.

The officers of the Company decided it would be more suitable to drive the enemy out of the coastal provinces first, in order that the hostile power would not be left at their backs and that their own fleet's proximity could provide strength and security. With this plan they left Philadelphia for Nicaea, a city of Lysia, and from there on to Magnesia on the banks of the Maeander River.[2] Roger had scarcely arrived there when two Tirian citizens came to ask his help, telling him that their town was not strong enough to defend itself against the terrible blows of the enemy and would certainly be lost if help were delayed. They told him that the Turks could be caught with little trouble while they were scattered out on the lowland plains. The army could take some booty and add to its honor and the advantage of the natives by tackling the marauders, who retired into the forest at night but came out with the sun again to waste and destroy the country. Roger hastily collected his lightest and fastest men and rushed off toward Tire in order to enter it before daylight. He arrived in good time, traveling thirty-six miles in seventeen hours, with the Turks neither seeing or hearing him.

Morning came and the Turks started down the plains toward the city. They were approaching the gates for their usual attacks when Corbarán de Alet, the Seneschal, with two hundred horsemen and a thousand soldiers, rushed upon them. He charged them fiercely, breaking up and cutting the throats of most of the raiders, except those who recognized their attackers and made off for the mountain fastnesses. Corbarán followed with some of his horsemen, but since the Turks' horses were light laden and ours were heavily burdened with arms, they all arrived at the foothills at about the same time. The Turks, terrified and concerned only for their lives, had left their horses and improved their positions by taking to the heights, whence they could defend themselves and hinder their enemies' climb.

The Seneschal, with more enthusiasm than judgment, ordered his men to dismount as he did himself, and go after the Turks again. But they were stationed on the heights with some protection, defending the summit with stones and arrows, and delivering telling blows to the men who took the greatest risks. Corbarán, as a brave and sturdy knight, was among those who more closely pressed them. In order to climb lightly and more freely, he rid himself of his weapons and then his helmet, which was the act that caused his death. They shot him in the head with an arrow and he died, after which his companions retreated.

The death of such a captain changed the victory of the day to sorrow; the loss of a good chief is often the cause of trouble and damage more considerable than the advantage of the victory won at the cost of his death. Roger grieved deeply; he had planned to marry one of his daughters to the young captain and had placed his hope in his person. Corbarán died more honorably than did some of the other captains; he went down with his sword in his hand and himself in victory, instead of at the hands of traitors, as some of his companions had. Human intelligence is so limited that it often views as a great misfortune what should be counted as one of life's prosperous events. Corbarán's honorable death avoided for him a cruel and disgraceful one, since he ran, one must believe, the same risks as did the other captains. They buried him in a church two leagues from Tire, where Muntaner says the body of Saint George lies. Ten Christians from the Company, who were the only ones to die in the encounter, accompanied their leader to the grave, over which their comrades raised a marble sepulchre, honoring him with solemn funeral rites, for they remained eight days at that place to keep his memory.

From Tire the Company sent an order to the fleet, harbored at
the Isle of Chios, commanding them to move at top speed to the
mainland of Asia and wait at Anaia for the second order.

REFERENCES

1. In 1304.

2. Nicaea was the capital of the Byzantine State during the fifty-seven years (1204-
1261) that Constantinople was occupied by Latin conquerors. In church history, it
was the Bithyian location of the Oecumenical Council called by Emperor Constantine in 325 to settle the Arian controversy, which produced the Nicene Creed. The
Maeander River, proverbial for its wandering, rises in the south of Phrygia, forms
the boundary between Lydia and Caria, and empties into the Icarian Sea between
Mycis and Priene.

BOOK TWO

BERENGUER DE ROCAFORT ARRIVES IN CONSTANTINOPLE
WITH HIS PEOPLE AND JOINS ROGER AT EPHESUS
BY THE GENERAL'S ORDER

BY THIS TIME Berenguer de Rocafort had arrived from Sicily, coming from Constantinople with two hundred horsemen and a thousand Almugavars on two galleys and a few ships. They had finally managed to collect from Charles the money he owed them and had restored to their rightful owners those castles in Calabria that had been in his power. Andronicus ordered him to sail for Asia to join forces with Roger. Thus, he arrived at Chios without wasting time, found Fernando de Aonés preparing to leave, and went with him to Asia. There they sent two fast riders out to find Roger and tell him of Rocafort's coming. The news reached him before he left Tire and caused great rejoicing in the camp. Not only were the men Rocafort brought many and good, but also their leader was famed as a valiant captain. Roger sent Ramón Muntaner to him with orders to leave Anaia and come to Ephesus, also called Alterlocus.[1]

Muntaner left with a troop of about twenty riders and some civilians to guide them over back roads on which they would probably avoid the Turks, who habitually roamed the countryside and attacked the best-traveled highways. This foresight and preparation did not turn out to be of much value to Muntaner, who had to open his way through the road with his sword several times, but finally got to Anaia safely. He welcomed Rocafort on behalf of his people and gave him Roger's orders concerning their departure. Rocafort obeyed, leaving a garrison of five hundred Almugavars with the fleet, and with the rest of his people took the road to Ephesus, where they arrived in two days, accompanied by Muntaner.

The city is one of the most renowned in all Asia for its famous temple to the goddess, Diana, worshipped not only by the Romans, but also by the Persians and Macedonians who were there before the time of the Empire. They had all preserved their rights and immunities, without these being changed when the rulers of the Empire changed, so great was the respect of the ancients for things that they were persuaded held something of divinity and religion. But the best claim to fame for the city was that the apostle and evangelist, Saint John, had established there the first fundamentals of the faith. I will record what Muntaner says of this man, since the story bears some relation to our history.

They say that the tomb of Saint John is in this city of Ephesus, where he was buried when he left the realm of mortals. Shortly after his funeral, a great cloud that looked like fire rose over the place. The people believed that his body was carried off in it, because they could not find it afterwards. There is no other basis for the truth of this story than the traditions of the locality that Muntaner has written down. On the eve before Saint John's Day, "manna" appears in the nine depressions of the marble over his tomb and continues to grow there until sunset of the next day. This substance grows in such quantity that it reaches a palm's breadth in height above the stone, which is eight palms long and five wide. It is said to have the power of curing several serious diseases, which Muntaner records in detail.

Four days after Rocafort and Muntaner reached Ephesus, Roger also arrived with all his army. Everybody was happy to see Rocafort, old friend and comrade of the Sicilian wars. The help he brought them, away in enemy lands, was very important and augmented the Aragonese forces considerably. Roger gave Rocafort the office of Seneschal that had been vacant since Corbarán's death, and in order that the newcomer should succeed his lost favorite in everything, he also gave him as wife the daughter who had been promised to Corbarán. By this new relationship, Roger assured Rocafort's rank and responsibility, suitable for his new plans. He gave the new Seneschal a hundred horses with equipment for the people he brought with him, and paid them four months' wages.

Pachymeres records that Roger and the Catalans resorted to atrocities to extort money in Ephesus, cutting off limbs, torturing, and beheading the unfortunate Greeks. In Mytilene a wealthy, prominent man named Macrami was beheaded because he did not promptly supply five hundred coins that they demanded of him. Such is the military license and customary audacity of badly disciplined warriors.

Roger sent all the money, horses, and weapons that he could collect in taxes from local cities to the city of Magnesia with a good escort. He determined to spend the winter in this town, which was the strongest in the provinces. The rest of the people left Ephesus and joined Fernando de Aonés and the fleet at Anaia. The soldiers stationed there gave Roger and Rocafort a rousing welcome, coming out to meet them with gaiety and rejoicing, sure that there were now plenty of them to throw out the Turks and recover Asia.

Roger was pleased and gratified with this inspiring welcome. He paid wages to all the soldiers of the fleet and sent some people for the safety of Tire, since it had been left unfortified and defenseless. Diego de Orós, Aragonese nobleman and fine soldier, was sent with thirty horsemen and a hundred foot soldiers, which seemed sufficient to guard the city and countryside, trusting more to the reputation of their arms than to the number of their men. Fame often wins what force cannot.

REFERENCES

1. The medieval name for Ephesus was Altobosco, probably quite deformed from a classical version. The historical maps of the period of the Byzantine Empire refer to the city as Alterlocus. Some geographical dictionaries call it Ayasaluk, which is reported as a corruption of Hagios Theologus. This is the title it was given by John the Evangelist, bishop of Ephesus, the saint of whose legends Moncada speaks. Ancient Ephesus was the chief of the twelve Ionian cities on the western coast of Asia Minor. The temple of Artemis stood on the plains outside the city walls until it was burned down by Herostratus on the night Alexander the Great was born in 356 B.C. All the Ionian cities joined forces to rebuild the structure, which was considered one of the wonders of the world. After the establishment of the Christian church at Ephesus, John the Evangelist and Paul of Tarsus visited it and addressed epistles to the congregation there.

THE COMPANY CURBS THE DARING OF SARKAN THE TURK,
AND CARRIES ITS BANNERS TO THE BOUNDARIES OF
ANATOLIA AND THE KINGDOM OF ARMENIA

OUR CAPTAINS HELD COUNCIL concerning the road
they should follow, and all agreed to return to the Eastern provinces. They crossed the mountains and went into Pamphylia, where
they believed that most of the Turkish forces were, and hoped to
be able to force them into battle. This was always their intention,
because the army was so small they could not make war on a large
scale or occupy cities and regions where they would have to leave
a garrison. Such tactics would divide and destroy their strength, so
that it always seemed best to them to search out the Turks to
fight them.

But while they were discussing plans for their departure, Sarkan
the Turk, even though he knew that the Catalan army was in
the city, dared to raid the outlying plains and put to blood and fire
everything that came in his way. He soon paid for his daring and
madness; the Catalans were so offended by the insolence of the
barbarian that they rushed down on him in wild haste, without
keeping order or waiting for their captains. The Turk tried to retreat then, but could not without serious damage, because he was
attacked on all sides and had to fight his way out. The Catalans
chased them till nightfall, and then returned to the city full of
enthusiasm, leaving a thousand enemy horsemen and two thousand foot-soldiers dead on the field. The feat was scarcely believable for those who stayed in the city — because the Catalans had
gone out so late and in so disorderly a fashion.

Roger and the other captains, realizing how dangerous the delay
would be if the soldiers learned the perils of the expedition and
the intended route, decided that the camp should leave within six

days before the enthusiasm of their victory passed. They left Anaia, crossing the province of Caria and all the wide provinces that lie between Armenia and the Aegean Sea, with no enemy opposing them.

The camp moved forward very slowly, depending on the accommodations of the countryside, comforting the Christian towns and encouraging them to defend themselves. The Catalans were received with universal admiration by all the Christians, who were happy to have arms of their faith so near. Those living at that time had never seen Christian soldiers, although they had always hoped and often prayed for them. But the weakness of the Greeks did not permit them to come to those distant provinces until the Catalans and Aragonese appeared among them.

Seventeenth Chapter

THE CATALANS AND ARAGONESE FIGHT THE TURKS WITH
ALL THEIR POWER IN THE FOOTHILLS OF MOUNT TAURUS
AND WIN A REMARKABLE VICTORY[1]

SHORTLY BEFORE THEY ARRIVED in the foothills of Mount Taurus, which divides the provinces of Cilicia and Lesser Armenia, the Catalans halted and inspected entrances and dangerous mountain passes, expecting as always, as indeed was the case, that the enemy was watching for them. Our horsemen, sent out to scout the field, observed the enemy army camped along the valleys of the mountain foothills. The signal for attack was sounded in both armies; the Turks, realizing that they had been discovered and that their strategy was useless, decided to go out on the plain to attack their opponents, who seemed somewhat travel-fatigued, before they could rest or improve their position.

There were two thousand soldiers and ten thousand horsemen in the Turkish camp, most of them survivors of past defeats. The riders were lined up on the left and the infantry on the right of the Christian camp. Roger and his horsemen opposed those of the enemy who attacked his front and flank. Rocafort headed the infantry and Marulli, his own men. The Almugavars gave their customary signal used for the hardest encounters, sticking their sword points and lance picks into the ground and crying, "Iron, awake!" And what they did that day was remarkable, for even before going out to conquer, they congratulated each other and were animated with the confidence of a good outcome.

The battle began with everyone in an equal position; loud and varied shouts filled the air, and the fighting was savage because the lives and liberty of both sides depended on the victory of that day. If ours had been defeated their deaths were certain, because they knew so little of the terrain and had so far to retreat, or what might be considered worse, captivity in the power of those offended barbarians. The Turks suffered the same danger, since the natives of the Christian provinces would probably finish them off, satisfying their own just revenge, if their oppressors came back routed and defeated.

In the first encounter, the infinite number of barbarians made the attack costly; the victory looked doubtful. But they caught new spirit and vigor when their leaders cried the name of Aragon a second time. From then on it seemed that this cry filled the enemy with terror and our own men with a strength never seen before. And now they came to blows with scimitars and swords on both sides, with our men showing such advantage over their defensive weapons that the battle began to lean their way. The Catalans executed on the defeated all their fury and severity customary in wars against infidels. The Turks on the other hand were all desperation, facing death with such determination and stamina that there were no indications toward surrender, only a resolve to die like men of courage, since they lacked any hope for pity from their conquerors. As long as their weapons made wounds they did what they could; when they weakened, their eyes and expressions showed that only the body was beaten, not the spirit.

The Catalans were not content with chasing them from the field; they followed the Turks as energetically as they had fought them. Finally, night and the fatigue of killing brought them to end the pursuit, but even the next morning found them still with weapons in their hands. The sun came out, revealing the extent of their victory, and a vast silence hung over the blood-soaked earth, piled here and there with the bodies of men and animals. Muntaner claims that they reached six thousand horsemen and twelve thousand foot-soldiers, and remarks that the day bore witness to so many courageous feats of arms that better had scarcely ever been seen. But with this observation he makes reference to no particular men, to the misfortune of our times, since such valor deserves perpetual memory.

The Company was so elated with this victory that its men forgot their fears of all major difficulties and began to clamor for crossing the mountains and invading Armenia. They wanted to go to the farthest boundaries of the Roman Empire, and recover in a short time what the Emperors had taken centuries to lose. But their captains calmed this daring determination, and proceeded with the prudence worthy of the difficulty of such an undertaking.

REFERENCES

1. On the manuscript of Barcelona, a marginal note, corresponding to the passage now labeled as the seventeenth chapter, says: ". . . here it should be enlarged." (Samuel Gili Gaya, Clásicos Castellanos edition of this work, p. 119.)

Eighteenth Chapter

THE CATALANS RETURN TO THE COASTAL PROVINCES WITH
THE COMING OF WINTER, AND THE PEOPLE OF MAGNESIA
REBEL. ROGER ATTACKS THEM, BUT, SUMMONED BY
ANDRONICUS TO COME TO THE MOUTH OF THE
STRAIT WITH ALL THE ARMY, RECALLS HIS TROOPS

T HE CATALANS STAYED at the scene of the battle for eight days, and were too few to carry off all the booty. They continued on their way to a place that Muntaner called the Iron Gate,[1] boundary between Anatolia and Armenia. Roger stopped there for three days, uncertain of which road to take. But at last, seeing that autumn was near and not being sure of the loyalty of the provinces where he was, decided with his captains' approval to go back to Anaia for the winter. He planned to stay there until it was the season to go out on the field again, since the enemy had already been routed four times that year and as many provinces restored. Nicephorus says that they did not press forward because they lacked spies and civilian guides in the land, without whom advancement was a dangerous business. Roger was too astute as a leader to make such a foolhardy venture.

They made short daily marches, so that their retreat would not appear to be from fear, traveling from one position that they knew to another. Greek historians charge our people with cruelty and insolence along the way, declaring that they did more damage in the cities of Asia than the Turkish enemies of the Christian faith had ever done. Although there was undoubtedly some destruction, I do not believe that it was so great as claimed. One reason for my contention is that our people were in Asia for only a short time, most of which they spent chasing and defeating Turks, from whom they took such infinite quantities of possessions that they often left them behind because they did not consider them of sufficient value or because they were not able to carry them off. What the Greeks claim is probably true, but it does not lessen the glory of the Catalan victories. What army ever recorded has been a model of moderation and temperance — particularly when its wages were in arrears? There is no doubt that a badly disciplined ally army is as dangerous in a province as enemy troops; consequently, the Greeks allot the major part of their histories to complaints about the damages, with more exaggeration than is worthy of a historian.

The army was approaching Magnesia, where Roger had stored most of his possessions and treasure, when they received word from the natives that their chief, Ataliote, had rebelled and had destroyed the Catalan garrison they had left. He made off with their treasure, which he gathered into the city. The incident had happened this way.

Magnesia was a large, strong city, for both of which reasons it was hard to invade when the citizens were united. Roger had entered the town and announced, in an ill-advised manner, that when he returned he would expect horses and money for the support of his men. The Magnesians, influenced by the hatred that their Alanic comrades bore for the Catalans, and moved by greed for possession of the treasure collected by Roger, decided to take arms and rebel. They consulted Ataliote with their plan; since he approved, they prepared to carry it out. Having always lived in a free city, they feared subjection. The citizens were many and armed, their ranks augmented by the Alans; the storage houses were full of wheat, weapons, money, and military supplies. Finally, they took oath among themselves and put most of the Catalans stationed in the city to the sword, depositing the survivors in secure prisons. After this, they were all committed to rebelling; for nothing can secure revolt more than such a deed, since an atrocity ends all hope of pardon. Apparently the event did not seem so to Pachymeres, who instead of considering it blameworthy, approved and praised their action: a stand that indicates clearly that his work must be regarded as an apologia rather than a true history.

When Roger heard of the Magnesian rebellion, he wanted to punish them at once, so that he took some of his Alans, part of the Romanics, and all of the Catalans, and went to besiege the city, intending to repay them for the ugly treachery. He organized the machines and weapons for battle with remarkable energy and a few days later made a general attack. But the citizens barricaded in the town beat them back scornfully, abusing and insulting the Catalan leader. Roger wanted to destroy the aqueducts into the town, but the defenders received warning of the plot in time to prevent it.

The Catalans continued their siege until they received a dispatch from Andronicus, who ordered them to leave Magnesia and join his son, Michael, who was helping Roger's brother-in-law, the Prince of the Bulgars. He said that one of the Bulgarian ruler's uncles had risen in rebellion with part of his estate, and the hard-

pressed prince was about to lose the struggle if he did not get help
soon. I am sure that this uprising was invented by Andronicus for
the apparent purpose of drawing Roger from Asia. He must have
been afraid that the new Archduke with so many victories to his
credit would use his strength to seize the land and deny obedience
to the Emperor. And, thus, to press Roger more with the obligation, he added his brother-in-law's plight to the story. The captain
who serves a small prince or tyrant lives always subject to these
dangers; suspicion and misgivings have first place in the councils
of such rulers. Happy is a man who serves a great, proud monarch,
whose majesty can take no offense in the advancement of his
vassals.

It is very difficult for me to get a clear picture of the next movements of the Company, for Nicephorus does not speak of them,
but rather he suggests a different cause for our people's failure to
press forward with their victories. He writes that the Catalans were
mortally afraid of Andronicus, for which reason their good fortune
was halted and they failed to restore all the cities and provinces of
the ancient Roman Empire. These are the very words of Nicephorus: "Roger took council with his men and decided to answer
the Emperor, and, in the meanwhile, to try to take Magnesia; but
the resistance from within was so strong that he was forced to
retire with both loss of fame and people. Then he attempted to
bargain with the citizens for the return of his money, but with no
success. Because of this rebuff, and the departure of the Alans from
his ranks, he prepared to raise the siege, announcing that the Emperor had ordered it." But his people retained a hidden resentment
against leaving the provinces without punishing the Magnesians
for their action and abandoning what they had won to the fury
and cruelty of the barbarians, who would occupy them again as
soon as they saw them defenseless. Among the ordinary soldiers
some there were who were secretly agitating spirits for new movements, by saying: "What point is there in our winning so many
victories if the prizes are taken from our hands? Is this why we
left our land and the comfort of our own country, to be paid for

our mortal danger, so often endured, with a small wage? After we take a province, are we to be ordered out of it and rewarded for so many services with a new and dangerous war?" The captains and noblemen hid their feelings and appeared to accept the new decision, but were nevertheless disappointed with the departure and convinced that it sprang more from the suspicious of Andronicus than from the situation in Bulgaria.

The Catalans reached the city of Anaia, where they took the road through all the coastal provinces toward the mouth of the strait. The fleet sailed always at the same speed as those who marched overland. In this way they all arrived at the cape that faces Gallipoli across the channel, called the Mouth of Aner by Muntaner. From there they sent word to the Emperor that they were ready to embark according to his orders. Andronicus was quite gratified by their prompt obedience, and sent them letters praising their punctuality in fulfilling his orders. He also informed them that the disturbances in Bulgaria had been settled with the mere knowledge that the Catalan army was on the way. This is according to Muntaner, but Pachymeres seems to be nearer the truth when he says that the second dispatch reported the control of affairs due to intervention by the Emperor's son, Michael Palaeologus, with his offended Greeks and the soldiers of other nations in his service. Michael had written to his father in apprehension of the Catalan strength and numbers and asked him not to send Roger's men to join him because he feared civil wars. He argued that he could not stand the insolence of their manners nor the habits of living that the army had been allowed in Asia, and added that George of the Alans still felt the death of his son so keenly that seeing Roger and his men would be the cause of an open break.

With this it seemed to Andronicus that it would be advisable to look for some means to alleviate the situation. He sent word, accordingly, to his sister, Irene, and his niece, María, to go at once to Gallipoli in order to urge Roger to leave most of his men in Asia and join Michael with only a thousand picked soldiers. Roger consulted his captains about the suggestion, but it was agreed that the division of the army would be a dangerous move, especially since they began to suspect great treachery in the offing. Roger told his mother-in-law that he did not have the heart to split his men, taking a thousand to Greece and leaving the rest in Asia. Irene took to her brother the Catalan's answer. This marked the end of the war in Asia in less than two years, a short time for the achievement of enough distinguished deeds to make a century illustrious.

REFERENCES

1. Moncada is vague about the location of this farthest outpost captured by the Catalans, which is the modern town of Kula, about twenty miles northeast of Alaşehir or Philadelphia through rugged mountains. Pachymeres (II, 426, ff) describes their route past Germe, Khliara, and Aulax in the Aegean provinces of Anatolia. Prof. W. M. Ramsay (*The Historical Geography of Asia Minor*, Amsterdam, 1962, p. 211) says: "The castle Phourni, which he [Roger] captured on the same excursion, is probably Magidion, near Saittai. But the Byzantine name for Koula was Opsikion, as we may argue from the fact that it was included in one bishopric with Maionia, three hours to the west of Koula."

Nineteenth Chapter

ROGER QUARTERS THE COMPANY ON THE THRACIAN
PENINSULA AND LEAVES FOR CONSTANTINOPLE

FOLLOWING ANDRONICUS'S ORDERS, the army embarked in the ships and galleys of their fleet to cross the strait and make land on the Thracian peninsula, where they established headquarters for their weapons and lodging at Gallipoli.[1] In those days the city, located at the mouth of the channel and facing north, was the largest in the province. The isthmus or peninsula of Thrace extends seventy miles with a width of six miles, narrowing in some places to three, On the east it is bathed by the strait that the ancients called the Hellespont, dividing Europe from Asia. On the west and south it is girdled by the Aegean Sea, and on the north by the Sea of Propontis, now called Marmara.

In the past this neck of land was inhabited by the Chrysei, and in the section connected to the mainland were the city of Lysimachia, made famous by its founder, Lysimachus,[2] and Sestus, known for the story of the two unhappy lovers.[3] But by the time the Catalans and Aragonese got to the province, only the ruins remained, among them the castle of Examille in ancient Lysimachia. There were now many country towns and small communities, and it was among these that our people spent the winter, using Gallipoli, a medium-sized city, as the center of main concentration and the garrison for common defense. They adopted the same arrangements for billeting that they had used the year before on the cape of Artace, apparently to the satisfaction and peace of all.

Roger went to Constantinople with four galleys and the most select men of his infantry to report to Andronicus the details of the restoration of several provinces and to receive the privileges and honors merited by such victories. They arrived in the city, where they were universally admired and accompanied to the palace by all the citizens. There Andronicus received Roger with demonstrations of honor and affection such as he had never used before. The Catalan leader gave him a full account of the provinces he had freed, and asked for money to make a general payment to his men. The Emperor answered with great courtesy, assuring him that such valor did not deserve a delay in wages so well earned, and promised to distribute the money immediately.

But although the answer was, on the surface, what Roger desired, the Emperor was secretly annoyed by the request. It seemed to him that after taking such abundant plunder and rich spoils in his campaigns, Roger's demand for petty wages was plainly insatiable avarice that all the wealth in the Greek empire would have a hard time feeding. But that which a soldier takes in victory serves more as a luxury than for necessity, and he spends it liberally on gambling, comrades, and feasting. Wages he deems due to him for his blood and labor, and necessary to meet the requirements of his existence. If they are denied or delayed, he resents it greatly, particularly when his ruler is spending the money lavishly on a vain display of his own majesty, ignoring the obligation on which is founded and depends the true grandeur of kings.

REFERENCES

1. In October of 1304.

2. Lysimachia, a major Thracian town on the Gulf of Melas, was founded by one of Alexander the Great's generals, Lysimachus, who fell heir to Thrace and named himself king in 360 B.C. He moved the inhabitants of the neighboring town of Cardia to his city and began a long, tumultuous reign, during which he conquered Antigonus at Ipsus, invaded Getae and was taken prisoner by King Dromichaetes, expelled Demetrius from Macedonia, and became king there himself. When he was quite old, his wife Arsinoe persuaded him to kill his own son, Agathocles. His subjects were alienated by the bloody deed, and Lysimachus died in a battle on the plain of Corus.

3. The lovers were the beautiful girl, Hero, who lived at Sestus, and the manly Leander of Abydos on the opposite side of the Hellespont at its narrowest reach. According to legend, Hero was sacrificing turtle's blood to Venus in the temple of the Thracian town when she met Leander, who had come across the strait for the festival. When they fell in love, Leander began to swim the channel at nights to visit her, guided by a torch that she burned in her tower window. But one night the man's strength failed in the rough sea of a storm; his body was washed onto the Sestus shore, where Hero found it and threw herself into the sea in grief.

Twentieth Chapter

BERENGUER DE ENTENZA ARRIVES IN CONSTANTINOPLE WITH
REINFORCEMENTS, WHERE HE IS MADE A GRAND DUKE,
AND ROGER IS OFFERED THE TITLE OF CAESAR

ROGER STAYED IN THE CITY for several days, waiting for the Emperor's official order and dealing with the administrators of his possessions, who maliciously hid the money and put all sorts of obstacles and difficulties in the way of his collecting it. Such arts are always practiced by those who manage the affairs of rulers, but in this case the Emperor cooperated.

About this time, Berenguer de Entenza, a man known for his noble blood and valor, arrived at Gallipoli at the urgent request of the Emperor.[1] Although Berenguer had already offered to come and serve, Andronicus sent a special ambassador to him the second time with many advantageous propositions. Berenguer left Messina, wooed by this second call, and came to Greece with some galleys and five armed ships, manned by a thousand Almugavars and three hundred horsemen, all distinguished men. They stopped in Gallipoli ten days, where they were joyfully welcomed by their countrymen. Berenguer sent out two riders to inform Roger of his coming and waited on the peninsula for his orders.

Roger was quite pleased to have Berenguer de Entenza in his Company. There had long been a close friendship between the two and strong mutual interests to preserve it. Roger wrote his countryman to come to Constantinople, where the Emperor wished to honor him personally, and this invitation was confirmed by two letters from Andronicus, sealed in gold and enclosed in Roger's message. Thus, Berenguer went to the capital, where he entered the imperial palace, accompanied not only by Roger and all the Catalans, but also by many prominent Greeks who publicly professed friendship. The Emperor gave all appearance of receiving him happily, but he was hiding mounting fears and suspicions that were promoted by the Catalan increase, not only in reputation but in reinforcements as well. Although he had procured Berenguer's services by his own particular insistence, this had been done before the Catalans achieved the series of victories over the Turks. Since then his misgivings had grown with his estimation of this powerful Company in his realm. Pachymeres says that he hesitated to receive into his employ all of the new troops, explaining that there were more companies than he had asked for.

Displaying one of the traits for which he was famous, Roger de Flor felt the gratitude he owed his friend and recognized in public his obligations to Berenguer de Entenza, who had come to his rescue and changed his fortunes when he arrived in Sicily poor and friendless. Roger asked the Emperor's permission to renounce his own rank of Grand Duke and bestow it upon the newcomer,

giving as his reason for the change the Catalan's courage and nobility, equal to that of kings, and declaring that the first position
in his army belonged to a knight of such pure blood. In a similar
expression of friendship, Berenguer begged the Emperor to bestow
the title of Caesar that had been offered to himself on Roger, a
man of such great services whose marriage to the Emperor's granddaughter had already admitted him to the royal household. He declared that he would feel sufficiently recognized if Roger were so
honored. Such a competition in deference is rare, not only in these
days, but also in ancient times when moderation and sobriety were
apparently more valued. Roger was powerful with riches, credited
with victories, and honored by his royal relationship. Berenguer
was illustrious both through ancestry and bearing. Both men
would have had reason to seek the supreme position. But the same
qualities in them that should have inspired rivalry caused these
men to behave with the dignity and temperance for which they
were noted, being concerned more for another's advantage than
for their own.

The day after Berenguer arrived, the entire nobility, foreign as
well as native, turned out at court to watch Roger de Flor transfer
his rank to the new Catalan with Andronicus's permission. Roger
took off his helmet, the insignia of his rank of Archduke, and,
with the seal, emblem, and banner of the office, offered it to Berenguer. But his countryman rejected the honor, and doubtless
would never have accepted it at all if the Emperor had not expressly ordered him to do so. Roger's courtesy caused intense admiration among the Greeks, and Andronicus bestowed upon him
the signal honor of the title of Caesar, one of the greatest of the
Empire, which prescribed mutual obligations between the two. But
Andronicus's countrymen were not pleased that their ruler had
placed on a foreigner the ancient title that had been long unused
in that Empire because it caused distrust of the princes.

In ancient times when the Roman Empire flourished, to name a
man Caesar was to name him successor to the Empire, as among
Western emperors is the case of the king of the Romans, the Dau-
phin in France, and in our Spain, the Prince. Since the decline of

Roman power with the division of the Empire, Greek emperors had bestowed the title of Caesar without the accompanying right of succession. But the office retained its prestige, although a mere shadow of what it had been. Later the title of Sebastocrator took its place, when Alexius Comnenus received second highest rank to Isaac in the Empire. This office also lost its prestige when the same Alexius, having no sons, married his eldest daughter to Alexius Palaeologus, to whom he gave the title of Despot. This title carried with it the implication of lord and undoubtedly Palaeologus would have become the next Emperor if he had not died before his father-in-law did. Consequently, the rank of Caesar had reached third place in the Empire, being preceded by Despot, the first high-ranking title, and then that of Sebastocrator.

Curopalates says[2] that these three ranks fall into no order of precedence, but that among them the Caesar is called "lord," a presumptuous title that was applied only to God Himself in ancient times, even by the emperors themselves, for we read that Augustus, Tiberius, and some others did not permit themselves to be called lords. The Greeks referred to the Caesar as His Majesty; crowned him with a helmet of gold and fine cloth almost like that of the Emperor; dressed him in a scarlet cape and sky-blue shoes and stockings; seated him in a chair like the Emperor's except for the eagles; placed him next to the Emperor at public gatherings and appearances; and lodged him within the palace. All these events conform to Muntaner's history and the memoirs that Berenguer left us. But there is some variation in the eleventh chapter of the twelfth book of George Pachymeres's report. What he says cannot be reconciled with the above stories, but in order to present a clear record to the reader, I will include all so that he may judge for himself what seems nearest the truth.

Since the Emperor was determined to receive Berenguer de Entenza among his forces, he sent to Gallipoli for him several times, when he heard that he was camped there. In his letters sealed with gold, he assured the Catalan that he wanted him to stay with him, and swore he would treat him in good faith and friendly spirit, allowing him to leave the service without hindrance whenever he

wished. When Berenguer received the dispatches with the faith
and word of the Emperor, he sailed for Constantinople with two
ships, but when he arrived he sent word to the Emperor of his
landing, instead of leaving the ships himself.

Then Andronicus sent for him, ordering horses and coaches to
transport him through the city in due dignity and authority. But
Berenguer did not feel disposed either to leave his ships or to obey,
and instead asked the Emperor to send him as hostage his son, the
Despot, John. This obvious distrust of his word and oath did not
sit very well with the Emperor or with anyone else, and he left
the Catalan to cool his heels for several days on his ships. Finally,
on Christmas Day, Andronicus sent for him again, bidding him be
of good cheer, since he had assured Berenguer with his pledged
word. The Catalan was still hesitant for a long time, but at last
made up his mind, and went to see the Emperor, who received
him magnificently. But rather than stay in the court, the Catalan
went home every night to his ships, where the ruler always made
a point of extending his hospitality.

On Christmas Day the Emperor administered to his new officer
the oath of fidelity, giving him at the same time the rank of Archduke of the Senate and the golden staff, Andronicus's own new
invention. The Catalan was clothed in the manner and guise of a
Senator. Shortly afterwards he left his ships and went to lodge at
Cosmidio, where his Catalans were, some of whom had also been
honored with great titles and privileges. After that Berenguer began to wield tremendous influence among the confidants and in
the councils of Andronicus.

When he took the oath of fidelity, Berenguer dissimulated his
treacherous designs, and appeared to be all truth and simplicity.
He swore to be a friend to the friends of the Emperor and an
enemy to his enemies — with the exception of Fadrique — to
whom, he declared, he had previously sworn friendship. The wiser
among the onlookers scented some deep secret beneath the surface
of the proceedings. Others approved Berenguer's attitude, pointing
out that since he had been loyal to Fadrique, so he would be to
the Emperor. By this method, he gained good will and approba-

tion and followed Plato's observation that honest appearances are the best manner of winning a good reputation and to enable one to deceive.

REFERENCES

1. The Entenza family was related to the Moncadas. Matrimonial agreements are preserved in the archives of the Dukes of Medinaceli, dated 1285. Guillén de Entenza, first son of Berenguer de Entenza and his wife, Saurina, is proposed on one side for marriage to Berenguela de Moncada, daughter of Guillén Ramón de Moncada and his wife, Elisenda, of the other party.

2. The work cited here is *De officiis magnae ecclesiae et aulae constantinopolitanae,* published in Paris in 1648 and in Venice in 1729, and written by the fifteenth-century Byzantine compiler, Georgius Codini Curopalatae (Gili Gaya, p. 138). Curopalates is a title rather than a surname, as Moncada seems to accept. There were eighteen ranks of Byzantine titles, of which the three highest honors, *Caesar, nobilissimus,* and *curopalates,* were rarely bestowed and only on members of the Imperial family. Others included Despot, Grand Domestic, and Eparch, or city official.

Twenty-First Chapter

THE GENOESE PERSUADE THE EMPEROR TO WAGE WAR AGAINST THE CATALANS, WHICH MICHAEL PALAEOLOGUS UNDERTAKES, AND THE SOLDIERS RIOT AT GALLIPOLI

THE GENOESE OF PERA, who had just finished fortifying their city with trenches and battlements, were the first to raise suspicion against our forces and cast doubt upon their loyalty. They reported to Emperor Andronicus that they had news from the west of the preparation of a large, powerful fleet, apparently for a spring attack on the provinces of the Empire. They were sure of this, having arrived at the conclusion by accurate deduction, and also that the Catalans formerly in his service and those recently arrived with Berenguer de Entenza were united for the Emperor's damage rather than his defense. The Catalans were in secret correspondence with Sicily, whence the bastard brother of

Don Fadrique, the king of the island, was on his way, it was understood, with twelve ships to join their fleet. They were undoubtedly waiting for these reinforcements to declare their position and put their plans into execution.

With these lies the Genoese attempted to ruin the Catalans, establishing themselves at the same time as faithful vassals deeply concerned for the common good of the Empire. According to Pachymeres, they advised Andronicus to attack the Catalans in open war immediately, offering the fifty ships they had ready, to be combined with as many more as the Emperor had armed or could give them money to fit out. They promised to put his ships to sea, even if he were obliged to pay them in long installments. They were moved to all this generosity only by dislike of seeing the mistreatment of the Greeks and the destruction of the country they now considered their homeland by the people who had come to defend it. The Emperor, however, did not give much credit to the Genoese stories, regarding them as groundless complaints invented by their malicious and envious imaginations ever since the Catalans had set foot in Greece. The Catalans' good faith and oaths reassured him. Consequently, he replied to the Genoese that he appreciated their concern for the troubles of the Greeks, but ordered them to be quiet, for he would decide what should be done, and when he decided, he would do it.

At the same time, the honor and deference that Andronicus accorded to Berenguer irritated the soul of Michael Palaeologus, to the misfortune of the Catalans. Aided by the persuasion of the Greeks, he began to plan for our downfall, using all the means he found most effective and violating the law human and divine. The Greeks were so envious and arrogant that they plotted treachery and perfidy with incredible fury, although they managed to keep their scheming secret. With glib tongues and eloquent hands they begged Michael, who was now strongly inclined against our people, to observe the increasing prestige of Catalan arms and their occupation of the supreme positions in the Empire, to its disgrace and loss of honor. The Greeks had always believed our Catalans to be like the Alans and Turk-fathered Greeks, with no expectations beyond their meager, miserable wages. But when they saw

the offices of Caesar, Grand Duke, Seneschal, and Admiral conferred on their rivals, and realized that they also aspired to the remaining titles, they felt insulted that the honor and power of the
Empire had been placed in foreigners' hands.

While these discussions and currents of feeling were moving
among the Greeks, the soldiers in the garrisons, claiming that
their wages were in arrears, were mistreating the Greek natives in
the towns where they were stationed. Such a reaction is an unavoidable evil of war, which only the military severity of the most distinguished officers has been able to stop. Michael Palaeologus,
who had an attentive ear out for any slander against our nation,
used these disruptions to argue with his father that unless he stopped the Catalan insolence, it would bring on the eventual loss of
the Empire and dynasty: for these intruders were not content with
the excessive wages they received nor the rich plunder they had
taken in Asia; they were oppressing friendly towns to satisfy their
greed. The Empire was not free from servitude even though the
Turks had been conquered, because the Catalans, into whose hands
the common liberty had come, were more cruel and insufferable
masters. It would be in vain that his grandfather, Michael Palaeologus, had recovered the Empire from the Latins, if it was to be
surrendered to them voluntarily the second time.[1] This event was
about to happen if the Catalan insolence was not stopped and they
remained in domination. Even if their plots failed, the Catalans
must be overcome by whatever means possible. And the obligation incurred when their provinces were freed from the Turks was
now obliterated by Catalan arrogance and ingratitude. Their victories could be considered damages rather than services because,
instead of establishing a secure peace in the Empire, their arms
were making new war against friendly peoples, inflicting intoler-
able tributes and bad treatment.

Andronicus was pressed by the persuasion of his son and his
counsellors, who continually complained and cried out against the
misery and dishonor of the Greeks. The effect of their conversa-
tions was apparent in his reply to Róger and Berenguer, when they
asked for money for the war. He told them that he did not intend
to pay until they had moved into Asia and begun the war. Such

language had never been used before by Andronicus, who until then had always gone to greater lengths to reward them with more privileges and money than they asked for. When his answer came back to the men at Gallipoli, it caused such a riot in the camp that the captains were forced to attack some of the Imperial strongholds and take over their forces and garrisons. The two leaders, Roger and Berenguer, expressed great concern because Andronicus delayed so long in giving them satisfaction. It appeared to them that the Greeks were seeking aggrandisement at the cost of the Catalans' risks and sacrifices, but they did not wish to displease the Emperor, from whom they hoped for their greatest support. They refrained hence from pressing him as they should have for the wages so well earned. At last their suspicions mounted to such an extent that they decided to send ambassadors to him to ask for their pay, promising to continue their loyal service and even to punish the excesses of any of their men who dared to insult or abuse friendly peoples.

This delegation was, according to Pachymeres, particularly courteous because of the Catalans' fear of the army that Michael Palaeologus had gathered to check their boldness and bravery. Andronicus received the ambassadors, but the great payment they asked for seemed to him impossible to satisfy. But to avoid an open break and declared war, he sent them back to Berenguer de Entenza with part of the requested money, hoping to quiet them this way. They were satisfied with what he gave them and went back to Gallipoli. When they arrived, they found that Roger had come with his wife, mother-in-law, and brother-in-law, who had wanted to accompany him. He had taken them, I suspect, in order to have Irene, his wife's mother and the Emperor's sister, on hand to hold as hostage, in case Constantinople should pursue any action against him as a rebel in the event that the riot in camp reached larger proportions.

REFERENCES

1. Michael VIII Palaeologus (reign, 1261-1282) recovered Constantinople on July 25, 1261, when his general, Alexius Strategopulus, happened to find the city un-

guarded. It had been under the rule of Latin crusaders since it fell to them in April of 1204, after which Count Baldwin of Flanders was elected from their ranks as the first Frankish Emperor of Byzantium.

Twenty-Second Chapter

THE SOLDIERS ARE PAID SHORT WAGES BY ANDRONICUS'S ORDER, CAUSING NEW RIOTS

FORCED BY NECESSITY, Andronicus, with Greek fraud and guile, ordered the delivery of the silver coins that had been given to the ambassadors for payment, though they were greatly diminished to about a third of their original total, and requested that the soldiers accept them as full settlement. The captains, unaware of his treachery, were easily persuaded, took the money, and left for Gallipoli, where their men were demanding wages almost mutinously. The muster was called; the money divided amid grumbling and complaints. But finally, simply because they had been paid they were calmed, though they realized that the wages were short. There was a different reaction soon afterward when the Genoese, who had arranged with the Emperor for a certain amount of money to send their fleet against the Catalans, were paid in the same coin. They sent it back immediately and dispersed their fleet.

After accepting the currency as their wages, the Aragonese and Catalans tried to satisfy their local Greek creditors fully, but the natives refused to take the money at the value at which it was offered to them. Since the necessity for food and lodging did not permit delay, the Greeks were forced to take what was given them. The natives were angered by this, and the Catalans had to look for their food with weapons, so that many towns of that region were deserted. Infinite complaints of the disorders and outrages of the soldiers poured into the capital, so that Andronicus was inclined to follow his son's suggestion for a violent and effective remedy for the damages. He might have undertaken to stop them if the several officers of our army had maintained total authority over their inferiors or if they had been united. Whenever a ruler uses devices so unworthy of his obligations as it was to pay the Catalans in devalued coins, without issuing an edict to all the subjects of his Empire to accept the money at the same value, he is creating the occasion for a break between the people and the military forces. It seems certain that this outcome was planned by the two Emperors, Andronicus and Michael, to the end that the Catalans would maltreat the Greeks, who would then take arms to revenge the offenses. If the Catalans lost, as appeared likely, the rulers would be free of their obligation. The plot succeeded as far as inducing our men to invade villages and large towns when they needed money. When they met resistance, they extorted tribute with customary military license, abusing by hand and tongue whoever opposed them.

Since the Greek author, Nicephorus, belongs to the offended people, his account deals at length with the excesses of the army. George Pachymeres's history does even more so; he gives free rein to his passions, reviling the Catalans maliciously. But Muntaner denies that the Catalans were cruel or implacable to the Greeks. He recalls how the foreigners had helped many of them who had fled from Turkish servitude in the Asian provinces and collected in Constantinople, where they were dying of hunger and poverty in the slums. The native Greeks were unmoved by pity for the misfortunes of their friends and comrades, but the Catalans had been liberal and helped generously many who suffered in this common trouble. He who reads this relation can judge readily what credit should be given to these historians, if he looks first into their qualifications. The Greeks, Nicephorus and Pachymeres, are frequently careless with the truth and preoccupied with the offenses of our people even when they do not relate to the case in hand. Muntaner, the Spaniard, was eye witness of all these events; the simplicity of his style and of the times in which he wrote seems to assure the truth of his accounts.

The Emperor, Andronicus, began to fear that Roger would

openly take up arms against him in response to the urging of the Catalans, who were offended by the deceit in the coins of their wages. He summoned Prince Marulli, general of the Romanics[1] who had fought beside Roger in the Orient, to send him on a mission to invite Roger to Constantinople, where the Catalan was to be reassured of the Emperor's good will and reminded of his many honors and distinctions. In addition, the emissary was ordered to require his sister, Irene, to come with Roger, since he believed that she had the influence to persuade her son-in-law in important matters. Marulli reached Gallipoli with the messages. Roger answered him plainly that he could not consider leaving Gallipoli to confer[2] in Constantinople because of his men's suspicions. Irene also excused herself on grounds of ill health that did not allow her to travel.

With this reply Marulli returned to Constantinople and frankly explained to the Emperor that if he did not pay the army in full, there would be no contracts. In spite of all this plain talk, Andronicus tried again through his sister to persuade Roger to depart for the East with some help that would be sent to him. Philadelphia was in greater distress than it had been the year before; they were suffering so much there that even the dead were not spared of their need. Roger did indeed wish to obey the Emperor, but his men were angrier than ever; if he had displayed a willingness to give in to Andronicus on this point, it would have been at the risk of his authority and his life.

Meanwhile, Berenguer de Entenza was feeling the suspicion and fear of the Greeks, who regarded him as a Catalan, and at the same time the lessening of faith in him among the Catalans because he held such a high position in the Imperial government. They felt that he could not be fulfilling his charge unless he approved the wrong that the Emperor had done to them. At last, in matters that involved Andronicus and the Catalans, he could no longer remain neutral nor act as intermediary in their differences without great risk of destroying them all. He resolved, therefore, to return to his original obligation and to sacrifice his personal interests in preference for the estimation and honor of his nation, which were on the point of being lost. He asked permission of Andronicus to return to Gallipoli, and, in spite of the Emperor's efforts to detain him with pleas and offers, embarked immediately in the two galleys he had at the port of Blachernae. Passing by the Emperor's gate, he departed, according to Pachymeres, with a troubled countenance, revealing the internal conflict that was tormenting him. From his galley he sent back to the Emperor thirty gold and silver vessels that he had given him. The same author adds that he tossed his insignia of the rank of Archduke into the sea to show that from then on he was renouncing his friendship to the Empire. The Greeks condemned this action as infamous and vile, but it was the most praiseworthy deed of this great knight in the Orient, for neither his honors nor his distinctions had changed his outlook toward justice: a worthy example to those who plot to promote themselves through damage to the public welfare or to the reputation of their homeland, and who often forget what they owe to their blood and background, leaving those neglected for more petty interests. Such men are often left with no reward but infamy in their ruin.

While Berenguer was preparing to leave, the Emperor sent to call him back several times, unable to believe that Berenguer would actually abandon him. Certain men of Malvasia offered to the Emperor to attack the Catalan's two galleys and take vengeance for the small value he placed on their friendship, as well as to recover one of the ships in which they had part interest. But the Emperor did not allow them to carry out their plan, because he believed that he could subdue Berenguer. That night the Catalan set sail for Gallipoli, where he found the town reeking with a thousand suspicions and misgivings.

REFERENCES

1. Moncada's word is *romeos,* which he uses as a synonym for the Greeks of the Byzantine state. They called themselves Romaioi ῥωμαῖοι as the inheritors of the Roman Empire in the East. All the contemporary historians refer to the European lands under Byzantine domination as Romania. (Gili Gaya, p. 85.)

2. The manuscript word is *asistir,* which suggests to serve in some charge or responsibility.

Twenty-Third Chapter

ANDRONICUS GIVES THE PROVINCES OF ASIA IN FIEF
TO THE CATALAN AND ARAGONESE LEADERS

THE EMPEROR SOUGHT to divide the Catalans among themselves, in order to be able to punish them more safely later. Through Canavurius, personal advisor to Irene, the mother-in-law, he attempted again to persuade Roger of his concern for the honor and advancement of the Catalans, which would have been great indeed, had he kept his word. Making frequent trips between Constantinople and Gallipoli, Canavurius handled the negotiations, reporting what the Emperor offered. But the insolence of the soldiers, the jealousy of the Greeks, and the pressing arguments of his son began to change Andronicus's interest in and devotion to our affairs into mortal hatred. Hence, the Emperor and his son planned to give apparently honorable satisfaction to all the Catalan demands, while secretly scheming for their downfall. Although the historians do not trace this development, it can be easily inferred from what took place afterward.

Andronicus was harassed by the fear of Catalan arms and their reinforcements that rumor claimed were on the way from Sicily. Through the agency of Canavurius, he explained that the exchequer and the Imperial treasury were depleted by the large payments and that the taxes from the Empire were insufficient to meet even ordinary expenses and obligations. As the ruler he was obliged to formulate a plan for the remedy which he hoped that his allies and obligated captains would help him to execute for their mutual benefit. Finally, after long and weighty discussions, the Emperor and Roger agreed upon the following arrangement: that Andronicus would give the provinces of Asia to the Catalan and Aragonese nobility and knights in fief, on the condition that they would be available on call to him or his successors to help at their own expense in time of need. After the contract took effect, the Emperor would no longer be obligated to pay wages to the soldiers beyond thirty thousand escudos and a hundred and twenty thousand Roman measures[1] of wheat as donation every year. He would, however, continue their wages up to the day of the agreement. With this bargain, our affairs appeared to be advantageously settled. The Catalans found themselves masters of all the provinces of Asia, partly because the Emperor had given the area to them in payment for their services and partly because they had won these lands with their arms, freeing them from Turkish servitude. Either of these titles was enough to give them the right of lordship over everything.

This development was one of the most remarkable of the entire expedition, sufficient to make the whole history of the Catalan and Aragonese nations illustrious. For, when the Romans won Asia by conquering Mithridates,[2] they achieved one of their major glories; but, what the strength of such famous captains and armies had accomplished with many years of fighting, our people had done in less than two. If deceit and treachery had not cut short their fortune, they would probably still be absolute lords of Asia; and perhaps if they had been able to stay there, they would have stopped the Turks in the beginning, preventing the great expansion of the immense boundaries of their Empire that the infidels possess today.

These agreements were sworn before the image of the Virgin, according to an ancient custom of the Empire. Pachymeres and Muntaner agree upon this transfer of possession, with the exception that the Greek differs on one circumstance. He records that Andronicus held aside a few of the cities that he did not wish to include in the grant.

REFERENCES

1. The modius was a grain measure equal to about a peck. During the Middle Ages, when it was known to the Franks as a *muid*, it became a measure of dry or liquid capacity of varying size, commonly rendered as a bushel.

2. Mithridates the Great, powerful king of Pontus from 120-63 B.C., was a man of great energy and ability, said to have known twenty-five languages. After conquering all of his neighbors, he attacked the Roman Empire and took over its provinces

in Asia. Continuing wars with the Empire lasted the rest of his reign, until Pompey overpowered him in B.C. 66. He had savagely murdered his mother, sister, and concubines, taking poison himself in small doses until he was immune. Eventually his son Pharnaces led the whole army in rebellion against him, and Mithridates killed himself to avoid falling into the hands of the Romans.

Twenty-Fourth Chapter

THE SOLDIERS REBEL MORE FURIOUSLY THAN
BEFORE THROUGH MISTRUST OF ROGER

EMPEROR ANDRONICUS, preparing to fulfill his oath, sent Theodore Chuno to Roger with the signed contracts sealed in gold, the thirty thousand escudos, the insignia for the rank of Caesar, and the word that the wheat was now collected for delivery according to Roger's order. Theodore was traveling toward Ripi, and, as a prudent and sensible man, stopped near the city when he learned that matters with the Catalans at Gallipoli were getting worse. He decided not to go on until he knew more certainly the state of affairs, especially since he feared that Roger might be annoyed by a brother of his in Cancillo, who had often gone out on armed raids against him. Consequently, it seemed like sheer providence when Canavurius happened along on his way to the Emperor's sister. Theodore charged him with announcing to Roger that he was coming with the supplies, and asked him to bring back news of events there. When they met again, Canavurius would describe to him the situation concerning the new mutiny. The cautious Greek was not disposed to venture his person and the money he carried without more security than he had.

Theodore traveled very slowly in order to give Canavurius ample time to make his trip and return with information before the former ran into any danger. Near Brachialo he received news that filled him with more apprehension: that Roger was not planning to accept the insignia of Caesar. He was afraid that this new honor from the Emperor would antagonize his men even more, who were already showing signs of losing confidence in him be-

cause he was collecting riches and honor while they were being
defrauded of their wages. Theodore was fearful for his charge and
decided to seek security in the fortress of Ripi, where he stayed
several days. Since the rebellion was still going on, he feared that
if the Catalans learned of his presence in Ripi with thirty thousand
escudos they would soon attack him and make off with the
money. Thus, in the dark of the night he left stealthily with all
the rent-collection tribute he had with him, and went back to
Constantinople. There he explained to the Emperor that he had
been stopped on his journey and forced to return to the capital
without carrying out his order.

Roger judged that for the sake of his reputation and security he
should satisfy the low suspicions that his men were expressing concerning his good faith. He sent for the main leaders of his army to
come to Gallipoli, being careful to leave their stations in strong
hands. When they were all together, he told them that the hard-
ships and dangers that he had suffered for the welfare of the Catalan and Aragonese nation did not deserve to be repaid with
doubts of his loyalty. He pointed out that he had proved his intentions in the Sicilian War: serving the King and always governing the Catalan people. Despite the general suspicion that prevailed in those times, no one dared to offend him. During the
Asian wars he had fulfilled his obligation wherever duty called.
He assured them that, although the Emperor had bestowed many
honors upon him, they were not equal to his services, and that he
was not a man to be so impressed by recognition that he would
forget his original loyalty.

Then the Catalan chief explained to his men that the Emperor
wished to name him Caesar, but that he did not want to accept an
honor that he could not live up to with total commitment. He declared that he had left Constantinople and the Emperor, who attempted to detain and promote him, solely to help his men and
try to lift their spirits. He had resolved to share their fortunes,
even if the Emperor should send his army to attack them. Roger
would try to fulfill the oath he had made, but if he were put to
the test, he would, of course, firmly take up arms in the common
defense against the Greeks. With his speech, Roger reestablished

his credit among his men, whose suspicions were allayed, and who gratefully recognized him commander as always, blaming their doubts on the evil misgivings of a few.

Shortly afterward it happened, to the great chagrin of our forces, that the Turks attacked the Island of Chios,[1] which was under the charge of Roger and his men. They took almost all of it, except for a few of the garrison that was stationed there, who were able to escape from the fortress in forty boats that they had been able to collect. But even these were pitifully lost and sunk in a raging storm off the Island of Scyros. With this defeat, both sides were angered: the Greeks were annoyed because it seemed that the Catalans were so absorbed in extracting petty tribute that they could not be bothered with guarding against the infidels. On the other hand, the defenders blamed the loss on Andronicus because he had delayed so long in fulfilling his promises. They insisted that if they had received their wages on time, they could have met their obligations and defended their charge. Because they had no money, they were forced to go after it with much disturbance in all the towns and communities of Thrace.

REFERENCES

1. Chios, located opposite the peninsula of Clazomenae on the Ionian coast, was an important prize of the Byzantine Empire. One of the largest and most productive islands in the Aegean archipelago, it was known for its wine, marble, and the mastic trees, or *Pistacia lenticus,* from which gum resin is drawn through incisions for use as an astringent and an ingredient of varnish.

Twenty-Fifth Chapter

ARRANGEMENTS FOR ADVANCING TO THE ORIENT ARE
COMPLETED AND ROGER RECEIVES THE MONEY
WITH THE INSIGNIA OF CAESAR

WHEN ROGER'S public statement of his loyalty to his men reached the ears of the Emperors, Andronicus and Michael, they were gravely offended. They wanted to send the army that they had mustered at Adrianople to attack the Catalans, but Roger's brother-in-law, Asen, who had recently been dignified with the title of Panipersebastor,[1] persuaded Andronicus against this. The Emperor ordered his son not to execute the plans, and placed his confidence in getting at Roger through his nephew. Asen wrote to Roger, describing the Emperor's righteous indignation and suggesting that the best way to return to his good graces would be to leave for Asia with the army and start the war.

Roger wrote back to María's brother, including a reply to the Emperor in the same message, in which he pleaded the necessity that had forced him to satisfy the army, because they would undoubtedly have killed him if they felt confirmed in their suspicions of his treachery. He assured the Emperor that he would always be loyal and grateful for the many honors and privileges that he had received from his hand, and that if he had offended his ruler with his tongue, it had been done to prevent the Catalans from offending him in deed. They would have taken another captain as their chief who would allow them to follow their impulses freely. He requested the Emperor to send him some support, necessary to prevent their raids upon the countryside.

Since Asen wanted to further the cause of Roger, his brother-in-law, he persuaded the Emperor to send him what Theodore Chuno had been taking to him a little earlier, so that the Catalans would then go on into Asia. Andronicus complied by forwarding the insignia of Caesar, with which Roger was invested and acclaimed on the day of the resurrection of Lazarus.[2] With the rank he also sent thirty-three thousand escudos and a hundred thousand measures of wheat, and firmly ordered Roger to dismiss all but a thousand of his men. The Catalan chief made apparent demonstrations of his obedience, but secretly took counsel for any eventuality. He sent some of his men to Berenguer de Entenza, who was now a declared rebel and enemy of the Empire; the rest he sent to Cyzicus and Mytilene where there was already a Catalan garrison. In addition to the wheat the Emperor had given him, he collected another large quantity that the Catalans had taken in tributes.

REFERENCES

1. The position of *panipersebastor,* or *totus augustus* in Latin, was a title of honor for members of the Imperial family. Alexius I Comnenus had early used it to distinguish his relative, Michael Taronita. (Rosell, p. 24.) As nephew of Andronicus II, Andronicus Asen undertook a campaign against the French in the Peloponnesus, expanding Byzantine power there. The Emperor also granted to his control the important seaport of Monemvasia on this southern peninsula.

2. Roger was the last person in the Empire to receive the title of Caesar. Before him it had been borne by Alexius Strategopulus, the general under Michael VIII Palaeologus who had retaken Constantinople from the Latins in 1261, and by John and Constantine Palaeologus, the uncles of Andronicus II. (William Miller, *The Latins in the Levant,* pp. 214-15.)

Twenty-Sixth Chapter

ROGER LEAVES TO SEE MICHAEL PALAEOLOGUS AGAINST THE
WARNING OF HIS WIFE MARIA AND HIS CAPTAINS

DURING THIS TIME that the Catalans were so full of hopes and fears, Andronicus and Michael were scheming for the methods they could use to effect rigorous exemplary punishment on them for their daring. Although this circumstance is not specifically stated by the Greek historians, the facts are borne out by events and their treachery revealed. Roger's evil luck opened the way for them to accomplish this with maximum safety for themselves and noteworthy misfortune to the Catalans.

When the time came for the departure from Greece to continue the war, Roger resolved to go to Michael Palaeologus to report to him his father's plans for the campaign, and, according to Nicephorus, to ask for money. But Roger's wife, María, and her mother and brothers were strongly against the trip; they were members of the Emperor's household and familiar with the sort of treachery generated there. María, to whom the matter was most important, warned her husband in secret not to go nor to allow himself to fall into Michael's hands. She urged him not to provide the occasion for one who was so eagerly seeking it, begging him to consider her helplessness if she were left an orphan or that of his men left without government. She warned that he should neither trust the Greek's words nor his intentions, for reasons born not merely of her concern, but from positive indications by which she realized that Michael Palaeologus was plotting her husband's ruin. All these arguments, accompanied by tears and pleading, María gave to Roger, as a Greek and a member intimate with the household of the ruler. Although they had been suspicious of her and refrained from revealing their designs, in spite of all their caution much had come to her notice. As an intelligent woman concerned for her husband's life, she had been able to note and ferret out many of their plots against him.

Roger paid little attention to his wife's counsel, and the less concern she saw in him, the more her worries mounted. She tried to find some means to persuade him, the most effective of which was to call together the principal captains of the army to tell them of her suspicions and ask them to urge Roger to desist from his plan to visit Michael at Adrianople. At last they gathered at her instance; María's suspicions did not seem vain to them. Approaching their commander, they asked him to cancel or postpone his departure until they were more sure of Michael's attitude. He answered them resolutely that no fears they could present would stop him from complying with an obligation so compelling as his conference with Michael, to whom he owed the same respect as to his father, the Emperor. He told them that the Emperors would have ample reason for a quarrel with him if he left for Asia without giving them a full report of his plans and decisions. He pointed out that such a break would be very ill-advised for the safety of all of them, adding that María's misgivings were born of her love and fear of losing him, and since they had no other foundation, they were not logical evidence to detain him.

Summoned by his fatal destiny, Roger did not heed, or if he did heed, did not fear, his danger. It often happens that the more warning a man has, the less he is able to escape death and a disastrous end. And although God warns us with clear and manifest signs,[1] our mad confidence blinds our reason to the perils fated to bring about ruin and punishment. As in this case of Roger, neither good sense nor experience with and knowledge of Greek nature, nor the warning of his wife and pleading of his men could stop him from his voluntary surrender to death.

With his determination to depart, his wife, María, and the members of their household chose not to remain at Gallipoli, because they were sure of the destruction of the Catalans. Since they felt no obligation to stay there during his absence, they did not wish to venture their safety. Roger consequently ordered Fernando Aonés to take María to Constantinople with four galleys, three hundred horsemen, and a thousand foot soldiers. He left Berenguer de Entenza in his place and traveled to Adrianople, a major city of Thrace, also called Orestiade, a court of emperors and kings, as it was at the time by the Emperor, Michael. Zurita did not realize that the city was called by both names, and referred to Adrianople and Orestiade as different places. Nicephorus uses the more ancient name of Orestiade, while Muntaner calls it Adrianople, which was the current name in use by the Greeks, preserved today with little change.

Michael learned on the twenty-second of April from the brother-in-law, Asen,[2] that the Caesar, Roger, was on his way. Michael showed strange excitement when he heard of this arrival; he sent one of the knights from his house to meet Roger a day before he was expected and to ask if he were coming of his own free will or because Andronicus had ordered it. The Caesar answered humbly that he came only to show his obedience and respect for his obligations, and in order to consult the Emperor on his approaching journey into the Orient. Michael was calmed by this answer and expressed his pleasure at Roger's coming. He sent out men to receive his visitor with all suitable courtesy. Roger arrived on the Wednesday of St. Thomas in the second week of Easter, and on the same night went in to see the Emperor, who met him with obvious demonstrations of affection.

REFERENCES

1. The passage in the original text of Barcelona reads as follows: "And, although God warns us with manifest signs (that are like trumpets of His justice), it seems that in addition to warning us, he also puts a candle before our eyes, and ceases the discourse, so that we do not see the dangers that are so evident, in which our end and punishment is determined." In the margin of the page, an annotator, to whom the proposition must have seemed heretical, has written: "Beware of the Inquisition." Moncada or his editors apparently accepted the advice, since the published version appears as above. (Gili Gaya, pp. 163-4.)

2. Andronicus Asen, who ruled from 1316-1321 in the Morea, was María's older brother. The Asenids were no longer in power in Bulgaria in 1305, where Theodore Svetoslav had come to the throne.

Twenty-Seventh Chapter

THE ALANS CRUELLY KILL ROGER AS HE DINES WITH MICHAEL,
THE EMPRESS MARIA, AND ALL OF THEIR COMPANY

SINCE THEY WERE received so cordially by Michael, Roger and his men decided that María's suspicions were unfounded and forgot any apprehensions they had for the danger so close at hand, even separating and wandering through the city unarmed as though they were among friends and allies. Also in the town at that time were the Alans with their chief, George, whose son had been killed by the Catalans in Asia. Turkish Greeks were there, too, some under the leadership of the Bulgar, Basila, and others obeying Meleco. The Romanics were led by the Grand Primiserio,[1] Casiano, and by the Duke and great ruler of the companies known as the Triarch.[2] All of these people were suspicious of the presence of Roger, who had come, they supposed, on the pretext of demonstrating his obedience to Michael, but for the actual purpose of observing his forces and laying his plans.

The Alanic chief, George, worked hardest to move opinion against Roger and the Catalans, determined to achieve his venge-

ance by any means that he could. He finally accomplished this
— either by his own motive alone or with the permission and under order of Emperor Michael — the day before Roger's scheduled
departure. The Catalan was dining with Michael and his Empress,
María, enjoying the honor that the rulers did him, when the room
was suddenly invaded by George the Alan and Meleco the Turkish
Greek with many of their men and Gregorio. George fell upon
Roger, wounded him several times, and, with the help of his men,
cut off the foreign chief's head. The mangled body fell among the
dishes of the ruler's table, which was in itself presumed to be the
securest pledge of friendship, and not a place where the life would
be taken of a friendly captain of so many distinguished services, a
guest, and a kinsman, being honored by the hospitality of the Emperor, and in the presence of his wife and himself.[3]

No set of circumstances could be collected, it seems to me, for
greater infamy of this affair, a deed certainly unworthy of a man
who bore the name and obligations of a sovereign. The more illustrious such bonds are, the more aloof they remain from appearing
ungrateful or cruel, but in fact the truth is that rulers are rarely
known for their sense of obligation, and when demands are made
upon them, they abhor those to whom they are obliged. This enmity, however, never reaches the point that, despite any fear for
their reputations, they openly destroy their benefactors. The fact is
that, as a rule, a trifling displeasure is more likely to move a prince
to punish than great and distinguished services to pardon or over-
look offences of little or no account. But what evil is there that an
unjust ruler will not undertake when he is convinced that it is
necessary for his welfare? The judgment and punishment of God,
to which alone they are subjugated, seem so far away that they lose
sight of them altogether, forgetting the fragile means by which
they also can be punished, since the hand of one determined man
is capable of destroying both lives and kingdoms.

Such was the disastrous end that came to Roger de Flor at the
age of thirty-seven, a man of great valor and greater fortune. He
was lucky with his enemies and unlucky with friends; the former

made him a famous, illustrious captain and the latter took his life. He was of rugged appearance, with a heart ardent and most diligent for executing what he had determnied to do. He was magnificent and liberal, traits that made him a general of our people; his gifts had won friends who placed him in this post, among the highest, with the exception of king or emperor, for those times. When he died, his wife, María, was pregnant; soon afterward she bore a son who was living at the time Muntaner began his history.

According to Nicephorus, Roger was killed near the palace of the Emperor, but he does not state by whom or whose order it was done. In most of the particulars concerning the death, Pachymeres agrees with Muntaner, but says that the Caesar was attacked by George's Alans as he emerged from the imperial chamber where he had been dining with the Emperors. When Roger realized that he was being ambushed, he retreated to where the august Empress sat and fell dead near her of a sword thrust in his back. When the news of Roger's death and the tumult of the Alans' attacks on the unsuspecting Catalans reached Michael, he was in another room of the palace. He almost fainted of the shock and managed only to ask if the Empress were safe and uninjured. Later he learned the full details of the murder and summoned George to appear before him to explain his motive for killing Roger. The vengeful Alan replied that he did it so that the Empire would have one enemy less. With this description, Pachymeres excuses Michael of the evil deed, but discloses that whether or not he was the express author of the death, he did at least consent to it and allow it to go unpunished, which establishes his participation in the crime.

The Alans were not satisfied merely with the death of Roger; at the same time they attacked all the Catalans and Aragonese in his company. They dismembered them in atrocious slaughter. Pachymeres reports that Michael ordered his uncle, Theodore, to stop the Alans and their fellow barbarians, who, thirsty for Catalan blood, were leaving Adrianople to cut the throats of any of our nation they might happen to meet, where many of them were quartered in the surrounding villages. He says that Michael did this because he feared that his men would not emerge victorious and that their fighting spirit would soon be lost.

But with this development, it seems clear to me that Michael's intention was without doubt to finish off all the foreigners at once. All the assembled horsemen were attacking Catalans and Aragonese both in the city and outside, although many of the wounded and abused seized weapons and did equal damage to the enemy before they died. Only three knights managed to escape the pitiful tragedy, contrary to Nicephorus's report that most of them were able to get away. One was called Ramón Alquer, the son of Gilabert Alquer, native of Castellón de Ampurias, and the other two were Guillem and Berenguer de Roudor from Llobregat. The few who did not die immediately were placed in irons and afterward cruelly burned, as will be told later, according to Pachymeres's account. The three knights defended themselves courageously by taking refuge in a church, where they were forced to retire to a tower. They held it by fighting so desperately from above that no one was able either to kill or capture them. When Michael's cruelty had been carried out, he began to look around for means to bolster his reputation for clemency and compassion. He ordered that no one molest the three remaining Catalans and gave them a safeconduct to return to Gallipoli.

Nicephorus differs somewhat on this part of the story from Muntaner. The Greek says that Roger came to Adrianople with only two hundred horsemen and that he came to see Michael, not only for the purpose of giving him the details of what he was planning on the subject of war, as Muntaner states, but also to ask for money. And if he were refused the financial aid, he was prepared to take it by force. So Nicephorus writes, with, as far as I can understand, little argument against the fact already stated that the Emperor was in Adrianople with the powerful army. It does not seem probable that a captain as prudent as Roger, whom even the Greeks call "wise" whenever the occasion offers, would make such a blunder as to arrive with three hundred horsemen to threaten an emperor surrounded by a strong army within a great city.

REFERENCES

1. The "Grand Primiserio" was the *primicerius* or *mayordomo mayor*, whose office was usually as chief steward for the royal household.

2. *Etriarca* appears to be a proper name in Moncada. Probably he refers to the *hetriarca*, or chief of the personal guard of the Emperor. Dr. Sharp suggests that "Etriarch" may be a form of *triarch*, (Τριάρχος) or "triumvir."

3. Roger de Flor was killed in April of 1305 in Michael IX's palace at Adrianople, two years after he had entered the service of the Byzantine Emperors.

BOOK THREE

THE SOLDIERS BEAR ARMS OPENLY AGAINST THE GREEKS,
AND CATALANS ARE SLAIN IN VARIOUS PARTS
OF THE EMPIRE

HE SOLDIERS with Berenguer de Entenza and Rocafort decided on a last attempt to induce Andronicus to pay their wages. They sent three ambassadors to the Emperor with the resolute message that if he did not pay them at least part of what he owed them within a fortnight, they would have to withdraw from his service and use their weapons to obtain what they could not with reason and justice. The Emperor received the three envoys, Rodrigo Pérez de Santa Cruz, Arnaldo de Montcortés, and Ferrer de Torellas, in the presence of most of his counsellors and ministers. He spoke to them curtly, assuring them that the Greek Empire was not so weak and impoverished that it could not assemble a powerful army to punish their daring and rebellion. He told them that whatever services they had done him in the Oriental wars were now erased by the excesses, outrages, and lack of respect they had shown for the crown. Andronicus cautioned them that he would do what he considered reasonable and warned them against rushing into any desperate action that would only result badly for them, or violently demanding anything that he was capable of denying just as violently. He pointed out that the loyalty of which they were so proud would have no value if they attempted to force indulgences from their ruler. Then, without waiting to hear their answer or giving them more satisfaction for their requests, the Emperor ordered them to discuss the matter among themselves, come to a decision, and speak to him.

A few days later the news of Roger's death at Adrianople and the savage reaction of our men at Gallipoli arrived in Constantinople. As a result, the Greek people rose up in vengeance against the Catalans, according to Pachymeres; but Muntaner says that the Catalans and Aragonese were being slain at the same time in all the cities of the Empire by order of Andronicus and Michael. It is possible that Muntaner lost his objectivity on this point in blaming the Emperors entirely; but I am sure that they made no attempt to stop their angry people from carrying out this evil.

In Constantinople the people rose up to attack the Catalan quarters, raging through the city, cutting throats, and killing as though they were on a wild-animal hunt. After beheading many of them, the mob arrived at the house of Raúl Paqueo, a relative of Andronicus and the father-in-law of the Catalan Admiral, Fernando Aonés. There they demanded that all the Catalans inside be delivered to them, and when this was not done as quickly as they wanted, they set fire to the house. It burned completely with all inside; among them, I am sure, perished the three ambassadors and the Admiral. The Patriarch of Constantinople appeared in an effort to check the rioting mob, but his presence had little effect and he was forced to retire in danger. The only obstacles that prevented the complete destruction of the Catalans at that time were their well-defended stronghold at Gallipoli and the soldiers stationed in outlying villages with their arms at hand, who received more warning than others in other areas.

Michael, who feared a Catalan attack at Gallipoli when they heard of Roger's death, sent the Grand Primiserio with the main body of the army to take the town. His order was carried out by dispatching some captains ahead on fleet horses to attack before the garrison was warned. They seized many Catalans scattered among their lodgings, unsuspecting and asleep in bed, who thought that it was needless to take care for being on their guard since they were among friends. The horsemen rode through the country settlements putting to the rigor of the sword all the Aragonese and Catalans they ran across. Many were alerted in time to escape by the screams and groans of their tortured comrades; others got away because of the greed of their conquerors, who left off killing in order to rob. In Gallipoli, although at considerable distance, the noise and confused cries of our people taking arms could be heard. Some soldiers wanted to go out to reconnoitre the countryside and assure themselves of the mischief that they feared, but Berenguer de Entenza and the other captains checked this impulse of their men, who at all costs sought to sally forth. Since the army's discipline was not as it should have been at this point, Berenguer did not dare to send out troops to patrol the roads and seek information. He reproved them, because he feared that the rest of the men would follow them, leaving Gallipoli defenseless, much to the jeopardy of the common welfare.

There was much excited discussion among our men about the cause of the disorder in the villages and open country. Some suggested that the Greeks were fed up with their oppression by the military forces and had conspired to fight for their freedom. Others believed that the Turks had crossed the narrow stretch of sea and were no doubt attacking our garrisons. But in all the variety of conjectures, no one guessed the inhuman truth of the situation. With the aid of nightfall and the general confusion, a few of our countrymen were able to escape to Gallipoli, but they could report only that they had been attacked in their lodgings by armed soldiers.

Twenty-Ninth Chapter

BERENGUER AND HIS MEN INSIDE GALLIPOLI, HEARING OF ROGER'S DEATH, SLAY ALL THE INHABITANTS OF THE CITY, AND ARE BESIEGED THERE BY THE ENEMY

IN THE MIDST of the wholesale riot, word came of Roger's death and the general massacre of the Catalans and Aragonese in Adrianople, as well as in the region of Gallipoli, under the orders of Michael. So great was the outrage and fury of the Catalans, according to Nicephorus, with whom Pachymeres agrees, although Muntaner is silent on this score, that they killed all the natives of Gallipoli without consideration for sex or age. Pachymeres emphasizes more the inhumanity of the episode, telling how even the children were impaled, a ferocious and abominable evil, if it is true, which is doubtful since the chronicler is Greek and an enemy. But if such reaction could ever be justified, it was in this case, since animated by wrath, they dealt with the Greeks they had before them in retribution for the greater cruelty carried out against them, premeditated and without cause.

From this point on the war raged on both sides in all fury, wrath, and cruelty, more like a struggle between wild beasts than men. But Greek atrocities undeniably outdid the Catalan excesses, since the latter had never violated the law of nations nor failed to respect the terms of truces with their enemies. It is true, however, that in other matters our men were undisciplined and did not observe the rules of a just war. But this was because the Greeks made no attempt to observe them, providing justification on their part for the actions of the Catalans and Aragonese, who were compelled to wage war in the same way.

The Catalan captains met in grief and confusion to consider their possibilities. They were in such a lamentable state that even their enemies could have pitied their misery. They had lost all they had earned with which they had hoped to win quiet and rest; their punishment was particularly humiliating in the eyes of the world because it came from the people for whom they had won such victories. A large part of their supporters was dead and their own deaths faced them.

They found themselves at that moment without supplies or fortifications, faced by an enemy of about thirty thousand soldiers and fourteen thousand horsemen including men of the three nations of Turkish Greeks, Alans, and Greeks. They were besieged almost to their very walls and threatened with a pitiful end because Emperor Michael was collecting forces all through Thrace and Macedonia, pressing into service in addition those who customarily fought for the wages of the Empire. In order more vigorously to pursue his project, he had left Adrianople for Pamphylia and had sent the Grand Duke Triarch to Basila and the Grand Bausi,[1] Umberto Palor, to Brachialo near Gallipoli to add their pressure to the siege.

Our people decided first to fortify the outskirts of the town, so that the enemy could not occupy it without great cost in time and lives, under cover of the houses, reaching our fosses and ramparts; although the effort required a great deal of labor because there were so few Spaniards left and the area of the suburbs was so broad. This done, they resolved to send envoys to Emperor Andronicus to withdraw from his service in the name of all our nation and to challenge him — one hundred Catalan fighters against a hundred of his men, or ten against ten, according to the usage of the times. They wished to take satisfaction in such a battle for their insult of the shameful deaths of Roger and his men, so treacherously accomplished by his son, Michael, and the rest of the Greeks.

A knight who Muntaner calls Siscar, a chieftain named Pedro López, two Almugavars, and some seamen were sent to represent all the branches of the Catalan forces. They left before the news reached Gallipoli of the deaths of the first three envoys that Berenguer de Entenza had sent. While the Catalans were awaiting the final response from Andronicus by means of this delegation, the enemy forces, now grown powerful, tightened the siege of the city, and our men, with their customary valor, were hindering and delaying their progress with raids and small skirmishes.

REFERENCES

1. The rank of "bausi" does not appear in lexicons nor Byzantine histories. The entire paragraph is not in the manuscript of Barcelona of 1623. Rosell believes this word to be a transcription error.

Thirtieth Chapter

THE COMPANY TAKES COUNSEL AND DECIDES TO FOLLOW THE
PLAN OF BERENGUER DE ENTENZA, NOT BECAUSE IT IS THE
BEST STRATAGEM, BUT HE IS THE MOST POWERFUL

T HERE WERE AMONG the captains at Gallipoli diverse opinions about the manner of waging the war, so that the principal chiefs assembled in council to reach a decision. Among them

Berenguer de Entenza spoke up: "Friends and comrades, if the courage and strength of men well-born as ourselves were ever desperately needed, I believe that they are in what we suffer today. Our misfortunes are the greatest and most cruel that the human race can inflict upon other mortals, because we are being persecuted, tortured, and killed by people who should be aiding and defending us. To what purpose do all our victories, our shed blood, the provinces we acquired, serve us, if, when the time comes for us to receive just recompense for so much effort, we are paid instead with such barbaric cruelty that we can scarcely believe our eyes?

"I consider our comrades who died without feeling our dishonor as luckier than we are; we are left to perish with such bitter awareness alive within us. Without taking vengeance for this offense, we cannot return to our homeland, where we would be unworthy of the name and fame that we have cherished for so many years, where neither kindred nor friends would receive us, nor would the fatherland recognize us as its sons, unless we undertake to revenge our companions who died through treachery and erase our outrage with enemy blood. The little strength that is left to us, inspired by humiliation, will be able to oppose the greater power because we have right so clearly on our side. Your invincible spirit takes on courage in difficulty; the greater the danger, the more strength you will have. Asia was freed from Turkish subjection by our weapons; our reputation likewise will be preserved by them. If Greece is astonished by our victories, she will soon feel the rigor of our swords that she was not wise enough to keep in her defense. Everyone seems to have given us up for lost, or at least believes that we will sail back to Sicily in the ships and galleys still left to us. But their peril will soon undeceive them; our spirit is not daunted and our insult does not permit us to leave before taking our revenge.

"The defense of Gallipoli is now our main goal; since it is at the entrance of the strait, we can effectively control shipping and commerce on these seas as long as no fleets superior to ours sail these waters. Thus, we will have to look for money and supplies to defend the town. Whatever help we get will have to come from far away and will probably be too late if it comes at all, since our kings are busy with problems closer home. We are completely surrounded by enemy nations and rulers; the only support we can hope for will be what we can win from our enemies with our own ships and galleys. Consequently, we must do two important things: look for the sustenance that we need now, and divert the enemy from the siege that is pressing us so hard. Since we must fight, as we are now resolved, it is best to do so where the enemy is not so superior, and where we can achieve victory more easily, so that the credit and reputation of our arms may be restored to their rightful place and esteem. The coasts of these nearby provinces are completely unsuspecting, since they deem that we lack even enough men to defend ourselves in Gallipoli and will not be leaving the ramparts as long as the siege lasts. This negligence offers us a sure opportunity for doing much damage with our ships and galleys against the islands and coasts of the Empire. And since this plan is my idea, I will also undertake to carry it out."

At Berenguer de Entenza's last words, Rocafort rose with a stormy voice and countenance, indicating a soul full of wrath and resentment, and said: "It is only just that the grief and rage I suffer for the deaths of Roger and our captains and friends should trouble my voice and countenance, since my soul as well burns for a just and honorable revenge. We must make a decision today, more on the basis of our severe insult than on reason: for in such cases, speed and less consideration tend to be fruitful, while deliberation brings difficulties. If we were to return to our homeland now, our name would be disgraced and affronted, unless vengeance had been so marked and fierce that it equalled the treachery and deceit of the Greeks. I agree with Berenguer de Entenza on this point, but I must oppose him on his manner of carrying out the war. It seems to me a terrible mistake to divide our forces when united they are so few and so unequal to the power of the enemy that besieges us. I am sure that Berenguer could rob, destroy, and burn the neighboring coasts as he offers, but in the meantime, while he is raiding the seas, who can assure that the few remaining at Gallipoli will not be lost? And then, Berenguer, where could you put in your fleet with your spoils of victory? No port or secure haven is left open to us this side of Sicily. I feel certain that we will lose Gallipoli; an enemy victory is guaranteed if you take away our soldiers to man your fleet.

"All renowned captains give most of their attention to the support of a position besieged by the enemy, devoting not only the best and soundest of their forces, but all they have. And Berenguer wishes to leave the fortress? Who can assure the soldiers that he will ever return? Their common fears and misgivings will not be quieted, even though Berenguer's blood and accomplishments are secure enough pledges for those well-born as he was. The demand for our vengeance does not permit such caution nor doubts, nor does it behoove us to delay the war now because it is small and shall become less. We might as well act upon our wrath and venture our lives in the critical danger ahead. Therefore, it is my opinion that we should get out into the field and give battle to those who face us. And, although the vast enemy army makes death more likely than victory, the just cause that motivates our weapons and the same courage that conquered the Turks, conquerors of the Greeks, will also defeat the latter. We can trust this same strength to break through their copious squadrons, and overthrow the eagles as we overthrew the crescents.[1] And if we should meet our end in this battle, it will be worthy of our glory that the last day of life found us with swords in hand, occupied with the ruin and destruction of such a perfidious people."

This last opinion prevailed in the votes of those at the council, because it was the quickest action, although more gallant and dangerous. But the power of Berenguer de Entenza was greater than that of Rocafort and did not permit the execution of what was approved by the majority. And Ramón Muntaner reports that the pleas and arguments of many of his comrades did not succeed in changing Berenguer's mind.

At this point the Catalans received word that the Prince, Don Sancho of Aragón,[2] had arrived on Mytilene, an island of the archipelago nearest to Gallipoli, with ten galleys from the King of Sicily. Berenguer de Entenza and the other captains sent word asking him to come to the fortress to receive their homage and their oath of fidelity to the Sicilian ruler. They emphasized their perilous position and the discredit that would come to the name of Aragón if he did not succor them, subjects who had made him great and illustrious. Don Sancho demonstrated his desire for their welfare with his swift action. He left Mytilene and reached Gallipoli with his ten galleys, where he was received with universal acclaim. The Spaniards believed that he would help them take full satisfaction for their insults. They shared with him the few supplies and funds that they had, and, without precise obligation to obey him, they all recognized him as chief.

REFERENCES

1. The eagle was the Greek symbol, while the crescent, or new moon, was borne on the standards of the Turkish Moslems.

2. Sancho was the second son of King Jaime I of Majorca. His older brother, Jaime, had removed himself from the succession by becoming a Franciscan friar. Sancho soon afterward (1311) became Sancho I of Majorca. When he died in 1324 without children, he was followed by his nephew, Jaime, the son of his younger brother, Prince Fernando.

Thirty-First Chapter

ON THEIR RETURN FROM CONSTANTINOPLE, THE ENVOYS OF
OUR ARMY ARE IMPRISONED AND CRUELLY MURDERED IN
THE CITY OF RHODESTOS BY ORDER OF THE EMPEROR

T HE ENVOYS of our nation, sent for the purpose of breaking the agreements that they had with the Emperor, and, this done, to challenge him, reached Constantinople after a thoroughly dangerous journey. They presented themselves to the Knight Commander of Venice, the mayor of the Genoese community, the Consuls of the people of Ancona and Pisa,[1] and all the magistrates and chiefs of the nations in commerce and correspondence with the Imperial provinces. To these representatives they made their declaration: that they understood that Emperor Andronicus and his son, Michael, had given the order to destroy all the Catalans and Aragonese to be found in Adrianople and the other towns of the Empire — all these people who had been living under their protection and favor, merchants as well as soldiers. They declared that the Catalans and Aragonese remaining at Gallipoli were resolved to die to gain vengeance for the deaths of their countrymen, but they regarded the honor of their own word so highly that they would not declare open war until it was publicly announced, in the name of their whole nation, that they were withdrawing from the agreements and alliances they had made with the Emperor. From that time on, these previous manifestoes would be considered invalid and without force. Instead, the Spaniards challenged the Greek as a traitor, offering to defend this charge in the field with one hundred men to a hundred or ten to ten, and trusted to God that their swords would be the instruments of his justice to punish such foul play.

The crime had been more than a violation of the public faith by killing foreigners who traded peacefully and unsuspectingly in their lands; besides that, they had dealt brutal, disgraceful death to the very people who had brought them freedom by defending their provinces, fighting their enemies, and enlarging the Empire. Soldiers' insolence was insufficient cause for such inhuman retaliation. The guilty soldiers had been punished for their crimes without any consideration for the services they had rendered to moderate the severity. They could have given the foreigners ships and supplies to return to their homeland, and it would have been ample punishment to send them without reward. But instead they had been destroyed with utter cruelty, without discrimination for sex or age, or separation of the innocent from the guilty, the good from bad.

Receiving the manifesto, the Knight Commander of Venice and the other representatives reported the notice from this delegation to the Emperor. They tried to bring about some concord, but were not able to achieve it because spirits were so generally offended and whatever word or faith given was so seriously mistrusted.

Thus, it was deemed that under such conditions an open war was better for both sides than an insecure peace; when there is no faith, the name of peace is a pretext and opportunity for even greater treachery.

The Emperor answered the challenge with the insistence that the action against the Catalans and Aragonese had not been done by his order; accordingly, he made no move to make amends to them, though the fact was that shortly before he had ordered the death of Fernando Aonés, the Admiral, and of all the Catalans and Aragonese who had come with him to Constantinople with the four galleys bearing the Caesar's wife, María, to her mother and brothers. Muntaner emphasizes the deed even more, for he says that the killings were executed on that very day.

The envoys asked Andronicus for security for their return trip to Gallipoli, which he conceded in the person of a commissary who accompanied them as far as Rhodestos, a town about thirty miles from Constantinople. There, by the order of the officer, they were imprisoned with about twenty-six servants and sailors in the public slaughter house. There, they were, while yet alive, drawn and quartered.

Such an evil seems to me to justify any cruelties that were done to avenge it, since none of them could be more savage than this violation of the universal law of nations, defended by human and divine commandments, as inviolable customs of both civilized and barbaric nations.

This unfortunate outcome was the reward of an ill-advised captain. Confidence is praiseworthy when there is some security in the faith and word of the enemy ruler, but when it is doubtful, such a venture is a sad mistake. When our king, Emperor Charles V, went to Paris and placed himself in the hands of his greatest rival, he was praised for his confidence in the good faith of Francis. But if the queen, Eleanor, had not been informing Charles, her brother, of all that was being said, such confidence could have been strictly judged as rashness, and his faith in his rival's integrity could have been called self-deception. This clearly shows that our praise or criticism is based on results, not on reason. Berenguer

de Entenza made a serious mistake in sending envoys to a ruler of
such doubtful honesty — to a man who had taken the lives of
Roger and his men with such treacherous cruelty. For a man who
so treacherously and cruelly had taken the lives of Roger and his
troops should hardly have been expected to keep his word in other
matters, nor to have deemed as legitimate envoys those who came
to him from men whom he considered traitors. Moreover, since
they had dealt with such cruelty with the inhabitants of Gallipoli,
they could well be expected to commit another even greater atrocity whenever the occasion presented itself to them.

REFERENCES

1. Ancona and Pisa are two ancient Italian cities, the first, on a promontory into the
Adriatic Sea for which it was named "the elbow," and the second, one of the twelve
cities of the Etruscan federation, located at the junction of the Arno and Serchio
Rivers.

Thirty-Second Chapter

BERENGUER SENDS ENVOYS TO SICILY, SAILS WITH HIS
FLEET, WINS THE CITY OF RECREA, AND CONQUERS
ON LAND CALO JOHN, THE SON OF ANDRONICUS

AS SOON AS THE NEWS of their envoys' deaths had
reached Gallipoli, words cannot exaggerate the angered souls and
hearts burning for revenge for the inhuman treatment that had
been accorded to men who should have been protected and defended. Meanwhile, more reinforcements were surrounding Gallipoli every day, pressing those inside more by preventing the move-
ment of supplies from the land than by force of arms. Berenguer
de Entenza and all the captains, still resolved not to leave Greece
without taking vengeance, considered where they could turn for
help. They decided to name the King, Don Fadrique, the master

of their forces and to oblige him to come to their defense by swearing fidelity to him. Such was their principal motive, although they used arguments of more careful consideration and purpose to persuade him.

A knight of Don Fadrique's household, called Garcilópez de Lobera, received the oath of fidelity in the King's name. With this soldier, who followed the banners of Berenguer, two more were elected to serve as envoys. They were Ramón Marquet, Barcelona citizen and son, I presume, of the Ramón Marquet who was an illustrious sea captain under the great King Pedro, and Ramón de Copons, who were to serve as witnesses to the oath taken before Garcilópez and to describe at length the state in which they found themselves. They were to beg Fadrique, if he remembered their former services, to show them favor; to assure him that his erstwhile vassals were interested not only in his help, but also in his own advancement and glory; and to point out that they had opened the way for him to occupy an empire in the East, if he would assist them to relieve their determination for vengeance in their desperate situation.

The three envoys sailed from Sicily, leaving their comrades with some hope for help from Don Fadrique. For hope, however faint, always encourages and gives heart to those in dire need.

The Prince, Don Sancho, at the departure of the messengers, offered not only to follow and accompany Berenguer in the campaign he was planning, but also to assist with his ten galleys until they received word of the reaction and decision of the King. Entenza accepted the offer in the name of all and thanked the Prince for such an honorable resolve, worthy of a son of the House of Aragón. After this, Berenguer made rapid preparations for the departure and put to sea with his men. But when the time came to sail, Don Sancho suddenly changed his mind, going back on his word given such a short time before, much to the detriment of his own honorable reputation. The matter surprised everyone, because the time had been so brief since he had announced his resolution that it was impossible that any new situation could have developed that would demand his attention. If there was any event of such importance as to oblige the prince to break so to his discredit this pledge based on a rightful cause, it is not to be found in the written histories left to us by the ancients. But when Berenguer asked him to fulfill his word, his reply was that he was acting in his brother's interest. It can be surmised that the Prince realized that there was peace between Andronicus and Fadrique, so that he should have an express order before he manned his galleys against a friendly ruler. This possibility seems to me a plausible excuse for the Prince's refusal to act on his offer. But he had pledged his word, and when he saw the abuse of his brother's best vassals and subjects, he displayed disgraceful ingratitude in not standing by to help them, especially since Andronicus had broken the peace first by destroying the Catalans and Aragonese who were to be found in his Empire.

With the indignation that could be expected of him, Berenguer reported in an account that he sent to the King, Don Jaime II of Aragon, that, as he departed on his expedition, the Prince, despite pleadings and arguments, had gone on his own account, and not as his father's son. The Catalans did not lose heart upon Don Sancho's departure, nor did their abandonment by the greater forces cause them to change their plans. Berenguer de Entenza embarked with five galleys, two vessels propelled by oars, and sixteen ships with eight hundred foot soldiers and fifty knights. Leaving Gallipoli, he headed back toward the isle of Marmara, called Propontide by the ancients. He reached it, landed his men, sacked most of the towns, and killed the natives regardless of age or sex, destroying and burning anything whatever that could be of some use or comfort; since this was his first enterprise after so many insults, he was motivated more by vengeance than by greed.

Continuing with the same speed and vigor, Berenguer next turned to the coasts of Thrace, with more successes. He captured some ships and took Recrea, a great, rich city, which he entered by force with little loss among his own men. He dealt with the conquered with his customary rigor; took to his ships and galleys the best and richest booty; and set fire to the buildings, since he wished even silent, inanimate objects to serve as witnesses and memorials to his revenge.

Andronicus received word of the loss of Recrea at a time when he judged the few remaining Catalans to be fleeing back to Sicily. In order to stop the damage that Berenguer was doing all along the coast called Natura by the Greeks, he commanded his son, the Despot, Calo John,[1] to take four hundred knights and the infantry that he could gather in order to attack Berenguer and prevent him from landing his men. Near Puente Regia, Berenguer heard that Calo John was coming and obtained information on the number and type of his forces. In number his men were obviously inferior, but in their quality he seemed to have the advantage over his enemy. Therefore, he decided to land his men and to face Calo John. Since the Greek had also been advised by his scouts that Berenguer and his men were already on land, he made haste for fear they would retreat. No one could believe that the Catalans, rich and laden with spoils, would be willing to risk battle unless they were forced to. The two sides rushed together with equal ferocity; in a short time it became clear that victories depend upon valor rather than multitudes, for the few Spaniards stood the conquerors over the many routed and slain Greeks. Calo John escaped with his life and returned to Constantinople crushed by defeat. Andronicus forced his townspeople to arm themselves because all the fighting men were away at Gallipoli, and he was afraid that Berenguer might attack the city.

This rout of the Greeks took place on the last day of May in 1304.[2] These victories had been so sudden and in such diverse places and so timely that the Greeks believed the Catalan forces had increased and that Berenguer was not the only marauder doing them so much damage, but instead, one of many.

REFERENCES

1. The Despot, John Palaeologus, was the oldest son of Andronicus II and Irene of Montferrat. His chief accomplishment was his marriage to Irene, the daughter of

Nicephorus Chumnus. John's father-in-law, a pupil of Gregory of Cyprus and a member of the distinguished circle of Byzantine scholars, was one of the most influential personalities of the state. He wrote theological and philosophical works, opposing neoplatonic ideas as an Aristotelian.

2. 1305 in modern reckoning.

Thirty-Third Chapter

THE CAPTURE OF BERENGUER DE ENTENZA,

AN UNFORTUNATE LOSS FOR OUR MEN

OUR FORCES HAD such a fortunate beginning against the Greeks, under the leadership of Berenguer de Entenza, that it seemed they would go on with luck and good weather from one victory to another. Our men planned to attack ships anchored in ports and along the shores of Constantinople and to burn their arsenals, an undertaking that sounds more difficult than it was. They sailed for the beach between Pactia and the Cape of Gano to execute their plan, with good weather. At dawn, however, they discovered sails between their fleet and Gallipoli; when they realized that they were cut off from return to their home base, they took council on what should be done and agreed to disembark.

Once on land, they beached their ships with the prows as close together as they could manage, sterns seaward, because on the galleys whose prows were not equipped with artillery, the sterns provided the best defense with their height. They took arms and watched, in disciplined order, for the intentions of the eighteen galleys that were now bearing down on them. These eighteen galleys were Genoese, accustomed to ply these seas, for their courage or greed took them far from their native land, like the Catalans themselves in those days. Recognizing each other first on one side and then the other, the Genoese were the first to greet them, at which the Catalans dropped their weapons, and as friends and allies they conversed and spoke with one another.

From what the Genoese had heard of Berenguer's recent activities, they knew that it would be much to their advantage, as well as to the pleasure of Emperor Andronicus and the Greeks, if they could manage to capture Berenguer and his galleys. As they decided that it would be more desirable to break their pledged word than to let such an important and rich prize get out of their hands, they sent the Spanish leader an invitation, offering him the word of their Governing Council that he would receive no insult or injury. They sent a message that he should honor their admiral's ship, where they would discuss matters important to all of them. With this guarantee, Berenguer took no warning from the past nor from the dangers in which his trust placed him, and went aboard the flagship. There he was received and honored by Eduardo da Oria and many other knights. They ate and drank together with much comradery and merrymaking, so much so that Berenguer spent the night on board after continuing late in discussion on the maintenance of his forces.

In the morning when Berenguer was about to return to his own galley, Eduardo da Oria disarmed him and took him prisoner. At the same time, the men who had come with him were made captives, and the eighteen galleys fell upon the Catalan ships, which were unsuspecting and unguarded. Four of them were taken at a loss of two hundred Genoese, but the galley commanded by Berenguer de Villamarín, which had a little time to defend itself, put up such a fight that, although eighteen prows were attacking it, no one could board the ship until all the defenders were dead. They fought with such obstinacy that not a single man survived. Three hundred Genoese died in combat over this one galley, and many more were wounded.

Pachymeres says that the night that the Catalans joined the Genoese, the latter secretly sent one of their galleys to Pera[1] with the word that they had come upon the Catalans, who said they were the object of Andronicus's wrath and desire for punishment. The Catalans were trying to persuade them to join forces with them for an attack on Constantinople. When the galley arrived at Pera and gave the Genoese message to the Emperor, he ordered them to attack, offering them all kinds of rewards. The next day, therefore, they executed the plan that has been related.

Thus came to a regrettable end Berenguer's expedition, so well executed and worthy of success, though ill-starred. But how difficult it is for human plans to foresee such events! The determination of this voyage was discussed among the captains, who considered all the dangers that could overtake the group — yet however many and various perils were proposed, this accident was neither anticipated nor imagined. So is proved that the judgment of men, though founded on reason, cannot foresee the judgment of God. Blame for this event could be placed on the Prince, Don Sancho, who came nearest to being the cause of this loss. If he had gone with Berenguer as he should have done, the Catalan victories would have been greater, the Genoese would not have dared to attack, and the forces at Gallipoli would have been augmented. The war thereby would have continued with greater gain in profit and reputation.

Berenguer and some knights of his company were conducted in degrading chains to Pera, and then, because the Genoese were afraid that Andronicus might take the Catalan prisoners from them in order personally to avenge himself for the harm they had done him, they removed Berenguer to the city of Trebizond, located on the Black Sea where the Genoese had a trading post. They kept him there until the galleys returned. This maneuver was wisely planned, because as soon as they had taken the Catalan ships they came to Pera, but were not willing to turn over any prisoners nor sell to the Greeks any of the goods they had captured, even though the Emperor received them with affection and honor.

After this favorable event, the Emperor tried to get the Genoese themselves to undertake driving the Catalans out of Gallipoli, and they agreed to do so, provided he would give them six thousand escudos. Andronicus agreed to pay this amount and sent it to them. But the Genoese were wary people, alert to profit; they weighed the money, found it lacking, and sent it back. Andronicus replied that he would satisfy the deficiency, but they refused. Once they realized more of what they would be undertaking, the payment did not seem adequate.

The Emperor learned that they had taken Berenguer prisoner; he tried with threats and pleas to get them to deliver him, finally promising twenty-five thousand escudos for his person. But the Genoese denied him everything, fearing, I suspect, that the King of Aragón would not be happy to hear that a vassal of his so great and notorious as Berenguer had died a humiliating death at the hands of Emperor Andronicus. In the meantime, the Greek ruler was employing any effective means that he could, offering certain skippers of these galleys eight thousand escudos and sixteen suits of brocade clothing if they could manage some scheme to deliver him. But the attempt was discovered, and, in order to get away before Andronicus resorted to violence, they sailed, leaving an annoyed Emperor on shore.

The Genoese were met at the entrance of the strait by Ramón Muntaner in a frigate, representing the Catalans who remained at Gallipoli. He asked Eduardo da Oria to turn over to him the person of Berenguer, offering him almost five thousand escudos, which was all he had been able to collect for the ransom. But the Genoese would not accept it, either because, as I suspect, they thought the amount too small, or because they were afraid of angering Andronicus further by freeing his antagonist in a place held by the Emperor's worst enemies, whence they could still destroy his provinces and raze his cities for a second time. Despairing of the rescue of his captain, Muntaner left with him part of the money that he had brought and assured Berenguer in the name of the army that he would send ambassadors to the Kings of Aragón and Sicily to ask them for satisfaction for an insult so grievous as the imprisonment of the vassal of a friendly king while he was under oath of security.

REFERENCES

1. *Peraea* is a general Greek term for the country on the far side of a sea or river. Here it is the Genoese settlement across the strait from Constantinople, which is still called Pera today.

Thirty-Fourth Chapter

THE FEW REMAINING CATALANS IN GALLIPOLI
SCUTTLE ALL THE SHIPS OF THEIR FLEET

WITH BERENGUER DE ENTENZA imprisoned and
the best knights and soldiers who followed him dead, his Seneschal, Rocafort, was left at Gallipoli with only twelve hundred
infantryman, two hundred horsemen, and four knights who were
able soldiers: the Catalans, Guillén Siscar and Juan Pérez de Caldés, and the Aragonese, Fernando Gori and Jimeno de Albaro,
with Ramón Muntaner, the captain of Gallipoli. This was the
small number of men who were defending the town, but when
they heard that Berenguer and his fleet had been lost and realized
that the help they had been expecting through his efforts was no
longer forthcoming, they did not lose heart, even though they were
aware of their certain danger. With the advent of adversity came
greater courage: they left a rare example for posterity of what
should be done in cases when honor, which has been preserved for
long years without a note of infamy, runs the risk of having its
purity stained by an ill-advised decision.

The Catalans took counsel, at which there were differing opinions. To some of them the abandonment of Gallipoli seemed im-
perative and the discussion of its defense foolish. They were in
favor of sailing back in their ships to the Island of Mytilene,[1] because they could easily take and defend it. From there they could
raid the seas with more security for themselves and more damage
for their enemies, which was the most that their depleted forces
could accomplish. But this suggestion was so badly received by
the majority that they shouted against it with speech full of
threats, declaring that they would defend Gallipoli and hold as an
infamous traitor anyone who refused to do so. They were so de-

termined that they prevented all possibility of altering their decision by scuttling the ships, which ended all hope of retreating by sea and left only the avenue of escape that they could cut through enemy squadrons with their swords.

With this act they were following the example of Agathocles[2] in Africa and providing it for Hernán Cortés in the New World,[3] both of which instances are revered in the memory of man as the most illustrious that human valor could undertake. Agathocles, King of Sicily, sailed with a fleet to Africa against the Carthaginians. There he landed his people and sank his ships, forcing the Sicilians to win or die. But he had more reason and assurance for victory, for he took with him thirty thousand men, and Carthage was the only nation against which he was making war. The Catalans found themselves isolated and few, far from their country, and at war with all the nations of the Orient.

The determination of Cortés surpasses the greatest praise: for who could sink his ships and choose an almost certain death for an impossible victory in unknown provinces, separated from his country by immense distance, except a man God has chosen with admirable providence to spread his true faith over the major part of the world? I do not wish to judge between his deed or that of the Catalans as the better done, because I believe that they were both so great that it would be doing unjust insult to the one to look for something less illustrious in the other, in order to deem him inferior. They were all Spaniards who undertook these deeds: let them share the glory!

REFERENCES

1. Mytilene was the largest city on the island of Lesbos, located in the eastern Aegean Sea off the Lydian coast. It had been colonized by the Aeolians and became an important naval power, which then founded colonies on the Mysian and Thracian coasts. Here the Aeolian school of lyric poetry began, and the writers Terpander, Sappho, and Theophrastus were born.

2. Agathocles (361-289 B.C.), the Sicilian ruler who grew up as a potter in Syracuse, was taken into the home of a rich nobleman who had noticed his strength and personal beauty. When his benefactor died, the youth married the latter's widow and became one of the wealthiest men of the city. After collecting an army and declaring himself king, he defeated the Carthaginians under Annon and raided Italian settle-

ments. In his old age he suffered the murder of his son, Agathocles the Younger, at the hands of his own son, Archagathus, in an attempt to inherit the throne. The king himself died from a horrible poison that was concealed in the quill he used to clean his teeth. According to legend, he fell into a cataleptic sleep. Later historians believed that he was probably burned alive in this condition on his funeral pile without being able to give a sign that he was not dead.

3. The Spaniard, Hernán Cortés, followed to Mexico Francisco Hernández de Córdoba, who had landed on Yucatán in 1517. Cortés left Cuba with an expedition of eleven ships, about five hundred men, and some horses and cannon, to undertake the conquest of New Spain. He reached the little island of San Juan de Ulúa in the harbor of Veracruz, which he named, on April 27, 1519. After unloading his equipment, he ordered his men to burn their ships, so that they might have no alternative but success on their mission. Cortés then moved into Mexico, making allies of the Totonacs at Zempoala and encountering no real opposition until they reached Tlaxcalan territory. There the inhabitants found themselves no match for the invaders' armor, weapons, and cavalry, and swore allegiance in their defeat. Cortés — swordsman, rider, explorer, statesman, historian, orator, and one of the most determined men in history — moved on to the Aztec capital ruled by King Moctezuma II and became master of the vast land within two years.

Thirty-Fifth Chapter

THE COMPANY LEAVES GALLIPOLI TO FIGHT THE GREEKS
AND WINS A REMARKABLE VICTORY OVER THEM

AFTER SINKING THEIR SHIPS, the men of the Company, satisfied at having prevented the possibility of damaging their reputation with a retreat, reorganized their government. They gave Rocafort twelve counsellors by whose advice he was to govern. These men were elected by a majority vote of the army to have authority in the council equal to that of Rocafort. He was to carry out the decisions made by the group as a whole.

The Company designed for its dispatches and official messages a seal with the image of Saint George and with these words written around the edge: "Seal of the host of Franks who rule in Thrace and Macedonia." Wisely enough, in my judgment, they used the name "Franks" instead of "Catalans," because it was a more general and less hated one, indicating that the army was composed of almost all the anti-Greek nations of Europe and that it was a common cause for everyone to help them.[1] For I deem it grandeur of spirit for our men not to confine themselves to the name of their fatherland alone, as the name of Franks does not exclude the Spaniards of other provinces, the Italians, nor the French. On the contrary, this name was thereby made known throughout the whole sphere of the earth, the common fatherland of all living men.

The enemy was closing in on the walls of Gallipoli and pressing on the besieged. As there were several skirmishes in which the Catalans lost some men, although they managed to do worse damage to the Greeks, they decided to go out with all their troops and fight, risking their lives and liberty in a single battle. Such is the necessary decision for men who cannot continue war for very long.

Of the defenders at Gallipoli, there were barely fifteen hundred soldiers and knights available to sally forth for the fight. Nicephorus, however, puts the figure at three thousand, but he was writing according to the account of the Greeks, who could well have been deceived by fear to the point of doubling the number of their enemies. Before going out to fight, the men of the company hoisted their standard with the image of Saint Peter over the highest tower in Gallipoli, knelt in earnest demonstration of their faith, prayed briefly to the saint, and then invoked the Virgin. Shortly after they had repeated the "Salve Regina" in confused but devoted voices, the sky, which had been clear all day, suddenly clouded over, and a gentle rain fell on them until they finished their prayers. Then just as suddenly the cloud disappeared. They were amazed by such a great miracle, feeling profound piety in their hearts that lifted their spirits and accepting their victory as certain, since heaven had just favored them with such a clear sign.

The Catalans slept that night fearing that it might be their last. The next morning, Saturday, the twenty-first of June, the Company left the walls and battlements of their city. Meanwhile, the enemy, leaving part of the army to guard the camp at Brachialo, two miles from Gallipoli, were advancing to attack with eight thousand horsemen and even more foot-soldiers. The Company ranged its cavalry along the left flank of the infantry, leaving the right side to the protection of the rough terrain. An old knight from Catalonia, Guillén Pérez de Caldés, carried the emblem of the King of Aragon, and Fernán Gori bore the banner of Don Fadrique, King of Sicily. Although both rulers had forgotten them, the Catalans never failed to honor their kings. Jimeno de Albaro received the standard of Saint George, and Rocafort commended his own emblem to Guillén de Tous.

The sentinels posted on the towers of Gallipoli, who had a better view of the enemy, gave the signal for attack when they saw the enemy strengthening his positions in the hills. Both sides closed in bravely, clashing with such fury at the first encounter that Muntaner claims that the people left at Gallipoli felt the ground of the whole area shake as though in an earthquake. Although they had them greatly outnumbered, the Greeks could not win a victory against soldiers so fierce and experienced. They prepared to go back to their camp in order to rally. When the guard they had left behind saw their men routed, they went out to stop the enemies who were pursuing their victory with incredible fury and savagery. At first the fresh reinforcements held the conquerors somewhat because they were the Greeks' best men. But the Company shouted the name of Saint George,[2] charged in with undiminished courage, and beat down the Greeks a second time, even taking the camp.

Umberto Palor, Basila, and the Grand Triarch turned tail and were chased twenty-four miles as far as Monocastano. The Catalans slit the throats of those they overtook without resistance, because in their haste the Greeks had left their weapons with which they might have defended themselves against the few tired and scattered men who followed them. But Greek cowardice was so great that one author reports that they did not dare to turn back to look for fear of wounds in the face, even though at this risk alone they might have found opportunity to save themselves. This must be the ultimate misery of a man when he fears injury more than infamy. Most of the routed Greeks died from drowning, because they had no hope of a fair battle, pursued by the Catalans of whom they rather expected insult and death. Consequently, they threw themselves into small boats and galleys along the shores, crowding them with so many people that they sank under the weight or split at the seams. The Catalans themselves assisted in the loss, leaping into the water, seizing the gunwales of the boats, and attacking the occupants with knives, until they were forced to go overboard or die.

At nightfall the Company left off its chase and was back in Gallipoli around midnight, for they were more interested this time in taking the lives and shedding blood of those who had so wickedly done the same for their friends and comrades.

The next morning they went out to collect the booty that was so immense that eight days passed before they got it back to Gallipoli: great quantities of silk and gold clothing, more valuable in those days than now because it was less common; shining weapons, precious stones; three thousand pack horses; and supplies so abundant that there was no fear of a lack of food in Gallipoli for many days. Twenty thousand enemy foot-soldiers and six thousand horsemen had died, but the Company lost only one knight and two soldiers. I would hesitate to record such an impossible ratio, had not creditable authors told of like events. Paul Osorius,[3] an ancient Christian writer, describes the destruction of thirty thousand Carthaginians together with their general, Annon, by Agathocles and two thousand followers, who lost only two men.

REFERENCES

1. Muntaner frequently uses the term *francos* for the members of the Catalan Company. In this choice he follows the usage of the Byzantine historians who describe the domination of the Franks of western Europe over the Latin Empire centered at Constantinople. Bronze dies and seals have been found inscribed with variants of the motto Moncada reports: *Felix Francorum exercitus in Romania* ("Fortunate Army of the Franks in Romania"); *Universitas felicis Francorum exercitus in partibus imperii Romaniae existensis; Societas felicis Francorum in Athenarum ducatu morantium.* Also in Catalan: *Host dels Franchs qui regnen en Romania.* (Setton, p. 18.) Saint George is often depicted on the seals slaying the dragon.

2. The Catalan war cry of *"Sant Jordi!"* and *"Aragó!"* were indispensable attributes of their battles, as were the Frankish cries of *"Saint Denis!"* and *"Montjoie!"* to French-speaking armies.

3. Paul Orosius (390?-418+) was a Spanish priest who, as author of the *Histo-riarum adversus paganos, libri VII,* is regarded as the first Christian historian. As a young cleric in Hippo, North Africa, in 414, he was commissioned by the bishop, Augustine, to write a book to prove that greater calamities had occurred in pagan than in Christian times. He drew on earlier writers for the first part of the book, but the period of 377-417 is a contemporary account. The work, which became a historical supplement to Augustine's *City of God,* carried great prestige for several centuries. Over two hundred manuscript copies have been found in medieval libraries.

Thirty-Sixth Chapter

MICHAEL PALAEOLOGUS PREPARES TO MARCH AGAINST
GALLIPOLI; THE CATALANS TRAVEL OUT THREE DAYS
TO MEET HIM, FIGHT THE BATTLE BETWEEN THE
TOWNS OF APROS AND CIPSELA, AND WOUND
AND DEFEAT MICHAEL

THE GOOD FORTUNE of Catalan arms began to put the Emperor, Andronicus, and his son, Michael, on guard; until then they had been unable to believe that so few men could compel them to employ all the forces of the Empire for their defeat. But after the affair at Gallipoli, the Emperors resolved to collect their men and march against the enemy before any help could reach them from Catalonia or Sicily. A Greek spy warned our men of these plans and preparations for war. Muntaner had sent him after information with deep misgivings about the probability of his return, since others of the same nation had been dispatched to diverse areas and had not come back. Catalans could not serve on these missions because they were always recognized, even though they sought to disguise their nationality with Greek clothing and language.

With this warning they all decided to go out in search of the enemy in his own interior, a resolution as gallant as any they had made. I do not think that such boldness and nobility is recorded in other histories, for which reason I sometimes fear that my honesty and credibility may be doubted. But I assure you that Nicephorus Gregoras and Pachymeres, Greek — and, hence, hostile — authors, agree with Muntaner, the Catalan, on what seems most incredible, so that what we have written can be accepted as the truth. Muntaner claims that the main reason for the Catalan move to follow this course was their affection for the riches that they had accumulated and their fear that losing them might be detrimental to their fame.

They decided to follow more prudent and less honorable counsel, leaving their property, women, and families at Gallipoli with a garrison of a hundred Almugavars. They marched for Adrianople, which had become the garrison of the army that was being assembled against them, firmly determined to engage Michael even though he was backed by the full power of his Empire. The Catalans traveled for three days through Thrace, destroying and laying waste to the countryside as they went. One night they reached a place to pitch their camp on the slope of a mountain that was not particularly rugged. The sentinels that they stationed on the heights reported that they had seen great fires burning on the other side. Scouts were sent forth to reconnoitre, returning a little later with two Greek prisoners, from whom they learned the occasion of the fires: Michael was camped with six thousand cavalry and many more infantrymen between the two small villages, Apros and Cipsela, to await the rest of his army.

Some of the Catalans wanted to cross the highlands between them that same night to attack the unsuspecting enemies. It appears to me that this counsel was not approved, for what reason I do not know. Since they were placed in a position where fighting was inevitable, it would have been easier to venture themselves in the darkness and confusion of the night than to await the morning when the scarcity of their number would be more quickly recognized. Instead, they all confessed and received the sacrament of the Eucharist, made one squadron of the infantry that was flanked by the cavalry divided equally into two troops, and left another squadron in the rearguard to help where they might be needed.

They began to march toward the enemy; as the sun came up

they found themselves on the other side of the mountain. They looked down upon the enemy, discovered to be more powerful than the scout had told them, since the major part of the army that had been lacking had arrived just two hours before. By this time the Greeks were aware of their approach, and, since they estimated that between infantry and horsemen there were no more than three thousand Catalans, they judged that the enemy had come to surrender their arms and beg Michael's clemency. They were so sure of this that they made no effort either to take up weapons or to leave their quarters. But Michael knew from his own sad experience the valor of his enemies. Armed and mounted, he mustered his squadrons as follows: the infantry was divided into five squadrons under the command of Theodore, Michael's uncle who was general of all the militia that had come from the Orient. On the left wing he put the troops of Alanic and Turkish Greek horsemen under the charge of Basila; on the right wing were posted the most select horsemen from Thrace and Macedonia, together with the Wallachians and mercenaries under orders of the Grand Triarch. Michael and his bodyguards remained with these nobles responsible for his defense in the rearguard. He was also accompanied by his brother, the Despot, and by Senancarip Angelus, who did not wish to have men of war in his charge that day because he found himself occupied with the protection of the Emperor and the responsibility for the security of his person.

Michael reviewed his squadrons and encouraged them for battle. They began to close in. The Catalans, divided into four squadrons and fortified with great spirit and resolution, first clashed with the Alans and Turkish Greeks when their cavalry drove against the first squadron of invincible Almugavars, who broke their fury. Pachymeres says that they retreated pellmell, though Nicephorus states that the Massagetes and Turkish Greeks had fled when the trumpets sounded for the attack because the Alans had resolved to serve the Emperor no longer and the Turkish Greeks had reached an understanding with the Catalans. However it may have been, before or after the command to charge, they abandoned the infantry, exposing its left flank where all the horsemen supporting it had been, and leaving it, as Nicephorus says, like a ship without mast or sails in the deepest fury of a tempest.

Part of our cavalry, which had been joined by the Almugavars and mariners, had dismounted and were attacking on foot on their side. The occasion for these troops leaving their horses was simply that they found themselves useless in close combat and could not have fought still mounted. The remaining squadrons of the infantry, now free of most of the flanking enemy cavalry that could threaten them, closed in on the front lines of the attackers so vigorously that they cut to pieces the first ranks, where the most shining, valiant soldiers were. All the rest of the infantry was put to flight. Only the cavalrymen from Thrace and Macedonia, stoutest and most famous of those provinces, maintained their position for a long time. They fought our horsemen, defending one of their squadrons that remained undefeated until the Almugavars opened their flank and attacked the front. The enemy cavalry then suffered great loss, left the post, and fled back to Cipsela.

Michael, as a good ruler and valiant soldier, seeing his squadrons broken and his cavalry, in which he had placed his greatest hope for victory, partly destroyed and partly in flight, headed his horse back toward the enemy. Suddenly his bridle broke and the horse ran away toward the foe. Stopped by some of his bodyguard, he mounted another animal, rushing on at his peril to encourage some and help others with great energy, without paying attention to the evil omen of the broken bridle. Threatening some and begging others, he called on his captains and officers in the field by name to turn their heads and to resist so that the day would not be lost with so much disgrace to the reputation of the Roman Empire. But both soldiers and captains, who had lost to fear their concern for their fame, had rushed on to commit the ugly deed of abandoning the person of their Prince, his pleas and complaints without effect upon them. For, the greater the infamy of a deed, the more difficult is the repentance. Then Michael tried to do by example what he had failed to do with words. He realized that it was a cowardly act not to risk his life for his men; turning to the few who stood by him, he told them:

"The time has now come, comrades and friends, when death is better than life, and life more cruel than death itself. Die with glory rather than live with infamy!" He lifted his face to the sky, asking for help, and hurled his horse into the midst of the Catalan ranks. About a hundred of his most faithful men followed him and for some time put the victory in doubt. So much can be accomplished on such occasions when the ruler ventures his own person!

He killed two men and wounded many. A Catalan mariner named Berenguer, who appeared for the expedition that day on a good horse and in shining arms, the spoils of the past victory, went among the enemies so bravely that Michael, for both reasons, took him for some distinguished captain of our nation. With the desire to show his valor he attacked the man, slashing his left arm with his sword. The mariner turned on Michael so quickly that he shattered the Emperor's shield with his war club and wounded him in the face before he could move his horse. At the same moment his horse was killed and he was almost overcome, but some of his bodyguard rescued him valiantly. One of the soldiers offered Michael his horse on which to save himself, giving his own life to free his prince.

Having lost most of his men and finding himself out of danger through his courage and good fortune, Michael came out of the battle more as a result of the strength of his men than of his own will. Several times he tried to come back into the fighting to regain his lost reputation, but he was always stopped, so that his fortitude finally broke down into tears. He retreated into the castle at Apros, and the victory was declared for the Catalans. The conquerors made no attempt to pursue their victims, because they knew that the Greeks still had armies, as yet uncommitted, to fight again. Pachymeres says they were afraid of ambush, adding that this fear was the particular providence of God that prevented them from pressing a victory that could have been much greater and protected Michael from falling into their hands. They contented themselves with remaining masters of the field and waiting for the morning to confirm their suspicions. They kept their weapons at hand all night long. When morning came, they realized that their victory had been complete.

That same day they fell upon Apros and took it easily, since it was defended only by its inhabitants. There they stayed eight days to heal their wounds and rest from the labor and fatigue of the battle. They learned from the spies' reports that the men whom Michael had been awaiting had joined him before the battle, and that all were now conquered. Muntaner's calculations were that the enemy lost ten thousand horsemen and fifteen thousand foot-soldiers in comparison to our twenty-seven infantrymen and nine knights.

Michael, who had retreated into Apros, did not consider himself safe there and that same night after the battle escaped to Pamphylia and from there to Didymocheion, where his father was. According to the account of Nicephorus, the son was gravely reprimanded for placing his person so daringly at risk. What should be praised in a soldier or captain was reprehensible in an Emperor — words born of a father's affection rather than valid counsel. I do not know when a ruler bears the obligation of venturing what Michael risked if it is not when he sees his squadrons destroyed, his reputation endangered, his people dead, and his land lost. What great ruler, celebrated in the memory of the world, has not wagered his life in a situation of similar significance and grandeur?

With this victory, most of the province of Thrace was left open to the pillage of the Catalans. The strong, populous cities did not suffer in this common tempest because there were too few Catalans to risk losses in sieges. They did take a few cities where the enemy's carelessness invited them in without much being ventured. Most of the inhabitants of the Greek villages and settlements throughout the province were so terrified when they heard of the rout of their army that they abandoned their houses, possessions, and the wheat that was now ready to harvest and wandered through neighboring kingdoms, spreading the fear of Catalan vengeance. Pachymeres says that refugees were pouring into the cities in hordes; Constantinople seemed like the sphere of Empedocles.[1]

But this victory was the occasion for the horrible end in Adrianople of the Catalan prisoners who had been held there since the murder of Roger de Flor, sixty men in all. When the captives heard of the victory of Apros, they were motivated to attempt their liberty. Held in the tower of a strong prison, they broke their chains and rushed the door, but it would not give way. They climbed to the top of the tower to reconnoitre some way to their freedom, but none was possible. Since they despaired of any pity from the Greeks, they fought valiantly from above with the arms that they had been able to get. The citizens of Adrianople besieged the tower and attacked it with full force of arms, but such was the courage of those who were defending themselves that they could do them no damage. Finally, after many of the townspeople had been wounded, they gave up trying to make the prisoners surrender and resolved to set fire to the whole building and tower. They started flames in several places so that the edifice was soon burning furiously. But the prisoners kept up the struggle, hurling stones and darts until they were half burned alive. At length they said farewell to each other, embraced, signed themselves with the cross, so says Pachymeres, and leaped into the fire. Among them two courageous brothers of noble spirit and lineage embraced with great sorrow for the circumstances and threw themselves from the tower. They had escaped from the fire, which had pardoned them with more mercy than did the iron of the perfidious Greeks, who cut out them to pieces. Among these sixty men only one had shown signs of surrendering; the others had thrown him from the tower.

The rest of the Catalans destroyed and laid waste to most of the province until they returned to Gallipoli. They enjoyed great increase of reputation, property, and numbers with the Italians, Frenchmen, and Spaniards who joined their ranks to escape the cruelty and fury of the Greeks.

REFERENCES

1. Rosell (p. xxi) explains the comparison: "This simile is used effectively by Pachymeres, not to describe the battle at Apros, but rather in Book 6, Chapter 25, of the *History of Andronicus*. We believe it needs some interpretation. The sentence

is completely metaphorical, and alludes to a certain sect of philosophers of Corinth, called Anemocetas, who were supposed to have dominion over the winds. They kept them enclosed and dormant in a kind of wine skin or sphere, reduced to rigorous oppression, as in the Cave of Eolus or the wine skins of Ulysses. Empedocles belonged to that sect, and it is to his wine skin or sphere that the simile refers. Because certainly the Greek forces, crowded with the other subjects into Constantinople, seemed to those from the districts to be compressed into so small a space. One who desires more complete clarification of the expression, 'sphere of Empedocles,' may consult the *Glossary* of Pedro Posin to the *History of Pachymeres* by Michael Palaeologus in the Rome edition of 1666, page 417." Empedocles, Sicilian philosopher born about 444 B.C., was so famous for his wisdom, eloquence, and skill at curing diseases with the aid of a translucent sphere that he was considered a magician. When he disappeared suddenly, the people believed he was a god. But after Mount Aetna discharged one of his sandals in a volcanic flow, they realized that he had thrown himself into the flames.

Thirty-Seventh Chapter

THE STATE OF AFFAIRS WITH ANDRONICUS AND THE GREEKS

THE IMPARTIALITY of divine justice has demonstrated itself in all times and ages, but in some it has been more manifest in the scourges of pestilence, famine, and war. This last disaster was taken to be the punishment of Andronicus and the Greeks, who had withdrawn from obedience to the Roman Church, the universal mother of those who serve in God's ranks on earth. They had fallen into a thousand errors; for these and the other sins that followed, God had permitted the Catalans to become His ministers of justice. Added to the evils of war were the malice and family quarrels that are always of disastrous import among rulers. Thereby counsels are confused, forces are weakened, and it is a short path to the country's ruin.

Andronicus's wife, Irene, judged it to be unworthy of her position and noble blood, that her three sons, John, Theodore, and Demetrius, should have no part in their father's Empire because he had by another mother sons who had been named first in the succession: Michael, who was already named Emperor, and Constantine, the Despot. She attempted through all possible means to persuade her husband, Andronicus, to share some of the provinces of his Empire with her sons, but he did not cede to her demands. Then she tried another measure, more compromising and dangerous to the Empire than the first: that he should declare them successors and companions to their brother, Michael. He refused this also. At last Irene, an ambitious woman who knew her husband's great love for her, decided that separation would double his constancy and that the desire for her return would be more effective than her pleas had been. She went to Thessalonica against her husband's strong opposition, although he outwardly pretended not to be displeased in order not to publish such secret, intimate dissension.

But absence has never been a means of increasing affection; instead, it almost always happens that even the greatest love is weakened thereby. The love and affection of Andronicus little by little grew cold; when she despaired and saw the door closing upon her pretentions, she changed her entreaties to threats. She opened relations with foreign rulers and made agreements with the enemies of Andronicus. She sent for her son-in-law, Crales, ruler of the Bulgars, who was married to her daughter, Simonis.[1] To him she gave all her jewels and so much money that Nicephorus has it that with it a hundred galleys could have been maintained for the defense of the seas and coasts of the Empire. With such division, what power would not be destroyed, what kingdom would not be overthrown, particularly when faced with an army of hostile men whose desire for vengeance continually drove it to victory or death?

REFERENCES

1. Irene (Yolande) of Montferrat went to Thessalonica, which had been part of her inheritance, after the quarrel with her husband over the division of rule among her sons. She made contact with the Serbian king, Milutin, to try to arrange for one of her sons to succeed to his throne. But the boy himself was not interested, finding the Bulgars too primitive. Milutin had also been flatly rejected in his suit for Eudocia, Andronicus's widowed sister. But Milutin did become the son-in-law of the Emperor when he was given their five-year-old daughter, Simonis, as wife, even though he had a Bulgarian wife at the time — his third wife. See Ostrogorsky, pp. 424-444. Since Irene was of Latin origin, she wished to introduce the Latin custom of equal inheritance among all her children.

Thirty-Eighth Chapter

THE CATALANS GO RAIDING AND TAKE THE CITIES
OF RHODESTOS AND PACTIA

AFTER THEIR VICTORY, the Catalans retired to Gallipoli, remaining the absolute masters of the countryside. Andronicus and Michael felt so threatened by our arms that the first did
not dare to leave Constantinople nor the second, Adrianople.
Complaints about the many injuries that the Catalans had done in
the provinces came pouring in. But Andronicus shrugged his
shoulders, blamed his sins for the punishment that God was sending him, and confessed that he was powerless to resist. The conquerors had even entered Maronea, Rhodope, and Brizia,[1] a hundred and seventy miles from Gallipoli, on many raids. The provinces suffered universally from fear and wonder, for there was no
place free from the invader's fury, no matter how distant or isolated. The cities, although protected from attack by the strength
of their walls, felt the scourge in their meadows and gardens,
where the most valued land was burned and wrecked and many
prisoners were taken and held for heavy, continuing ransom.
Sometimes these forays were made by four or six soldiers instead
of whole companies.

One night Pedro de Maclara, an Almugavar who served in the
cavalry, was gambling with his comrades and lost everything in
the game. He resolved to replace his losings and at the same time
revenge himself in a profitable way at the cost of the enemy. He
and his two sons mounted and rode off into enemy territory until
they reached the farming country outside of Constantinople.
There, to their good fortune, two Genoese merchants, father and
son, fell into their hands. They took them prisoners and rode all
the twenty-five leagues back to Gallipoli without being molested

by anyone along the road. The Catalans demanded fifteen hundred escudos, with which the Almugavar paid his debts and won acclaim as a brave and clever soldier.

The boldness of the Catalans reached such a degree that Muntaner reports many other such exploits equally fortunate and remarkable. Rome was once the capital of the world, reigning in such grandeur and glory that swollen with conceit she believed herself to be eternal; but all her victories and triumphs have disappeared. The hordes of Goths and Vandals swept down to prove how brief was her glory and how false her attribution of grandeur. The same fate was now happening to Constantinople, capital of the Eastern Empire, where power and piety together were promoted and deserved by the great Constantine.[2] His strength was preserved in his successors until God's wrath brought their punishment and delivered them up for pillage to foreign nations. During this age these people who had given laws to so many kingdoms and nations were now almost forced to accept them from a handful of Catalans and Aragonese.

In the hearts of the Catalans there burned the desire to take vengeance for the disgraceful death of their ambassadors upon the citizens of Rhodestos, by whom the envoys had been savagely killed and torn to pieces. Therefore, they set out on the campaign, taking even the children, who also felt the powerful passion of revenge in spite of the weakness of their age. The city was situated on the seashore, sixty miles by road overland from Gallipoli. In order to reach it, the Catalans had to pass through enemy territory that separated them from their stronghold. Realizing this, the residents of Rhodestos were careless of their safety because they did not imagine that the Catalans would venture where they had no retreat through the countryside. But these difficulties would have been a serious obstacle had our men not been spurred on to overcome them by their sense of outrage.

At dawn they scaled the walls and entered the city without meeting resistance. Then they set about killing with such ferocity that as a result of this first deed and others that ensued, the curse that remains even today was established: "May you suffer the vengeance of the Catalans!"[3] So well preserved is the memory of that havoc that it is still the most terrible curse of malice and hatred among the Greeks. Muntaner emphasizes the disorder of our soldiers, whose captains and knights could not stop or hinder the cruelty of the conquerors against the vanquished. Forgetting their fear of God and respect for their captains, and even their own nature, they dismembered the bodies of many innocent children who were incapable of guilt in the matter because of their ages. They even sought to put to death all the animals, so that no living thing would be left in that place.

From there they marched to Pactia, a neighboring city, which they won as easily and treated as harshly as they had Rhodestos. The captains decided to garrison these posts, since the numbers of the Company had increased enough to allow a division of their forces. Now they were approaching Constantinople, whose overthrow and ruin were the goals of our dangers and fatigues. They left only Muntaner in Gallipoli with some sailors, a hundred Almugavars, and thirty cavalry.

REFERENCES

1. The Thracian districts were named for the great mountains there. Rhodope, one of the highest ranges in the province, was considered sacred to Dionysius by the ancient inhabitants.

2. Constantine I the Great, Emperor of the Roman Empire from 306-337, who rebuilt the Greek colony of Byzantium on the Bosphorus as the new Eastern capital that took his name and was the political, economic, and military center of the Byzantine state for a thousand years.

3. In Thrace the curse, (Ἡ ἐκδίκησις τῶν Καταλάνων εὕροι σε) , or "May the vengeance of the Catalans catch you!," can still be heard. In other places around the Mediterranean where Catalan is still spoken, or the Catalans remembered, such as the Alghero district of Sardinia, along the Adriatic coasts, and in the Kolonja region of Albania, the word Katallán-i retains an evil, threatening connotation. In his work, La expedición y dominación de los catalanes en Oriente juzgados por los griegos, Rubió i Lluch discusses the popular works of non-Greek literature that have been inspired by the theme of the curse. They include El señor del Olimpo, Juan el Catalán (The Lord of Olympus, Juan de Catalán) by Marino Koutoubali (1873) and Spyridon P. Lampro's El último conde de Salona (The Last Count of Salona) of 1870. Epaminondas Samatiades discusses the references to the Catalán domination that appear in the popular Greek tradition in his work, (Οἱ Καταλάνοι ἐν τῇ Ἀνατώλῃ) (The Catalans in Anatolia), Athens, 1869. Gili Gaya, p. 223.)

BOOK FOUR

FERNAN JIMENEZ ARRIVES IN GALLIPOLI, BEGINS INLAND
RAIDING, AND DESTROYS TWO THOUSAND ENEMY
INFANTRYMEN AND EIGHT HUNDRED
CAVALRY ON HIS RETREAT

ONE OF THE MOST EMINENT Aragonese captains who came to Greece with Roger de Flor was Fernán Jiménez de Arenós. As we have told before, Fernán had left the Catalan Company after a quarrel. With the few men who followed him, he went to the court of the Duke of Athens[1] and stayed there for some time, serving in the many and varied wars that the Duke waged against his neighbors. In all of these tribulations that are unavoidable for small states with powerful rulers for neighbors, Fernán distinguished himself by honorable service. But when he heard that his countrymen were in danger, he was moved to leave his own growing security to risk his person for their aid. Receiving the Duke's permission, he left for Gallipoli in a galley with eighty veteran soldiers. There he was welcomed with real gratitude and furnished with the horses and arms that his men needed. Three hundred foot soldiers and sixty cavalrymen among his friends who wanted to join them traveled with him to the interior.

Fernán went to see the captains stationed at Rhodestos and Pactia, telling them of his plans to march with his men to Constantinople. Then he began the campaign, crossing the river that the ancients called the Batinia and sacking and burning many towns within sight of the capital. Andronicus watched their progress from the walls of his city by the smoke of the burning houses. Believing that all of the Company ranged outside, he would not allow his men to sally forth, but distributed them on guard on the walls of Constantinople, expecting that the Catalans' swords would be used for his own ultimate ruin that day. Andronicus's misgivings were well founded and advised, because his people, full of dread and accustomed to idleness, did not attempt to take up arms in their own defense. The Alanic and Turkish Greek mercenary soldiers, who were bound neither by nature or benefits to the service of their ruler, feared and avoided the danger, increasing the suspicion that they had made a treaty with the Catalan captains.

Andronicus was filled with these fears and uncertainty when he learned that Fernán Jiménez de Arenós with only three hundred men was the cause of so much damage and that Rocafort remained with the bulk of the army at Rhodope. He picked eight hundred horsemen and two thousand infantrymen and ordered them to go out to charge Fernán Jiménez as he was retreating with his rich spoils. They went off with spirit and determination, crossed the river during the night, occupied an advantageous position through which the Catalans had to pass, and waited in ambush.

But the scouts of Fernán Jiménez discovered them; and since the Catalans had no other route of retreat, the captain, having called a halt, said to his men: "Now, my friends, the enemy has closed the way to us, so that we can get through it only with our courage. Nothing less than our lives are at stake here, placed in ultimate danger. These opponents before us are the same people that you have overcome so many times when there was even greater inequality of numbers; their multitudes have served only to make our conquests grander. Our victory here is as sure as it has been on other occasions, since it appears that they do mean to stay and fight. Their advantageous position gives them confidence, but they have forgotten that our swords penetrate the most impregnable defenses. Let these cowards know that everywhere they shall be overtaken by the rigor of our just vengeance!"

So saying, he ordered his Almugavar infantry to close in behind him and himself led the charge upon the troops of enemy cavalry with his few horsemen. Both sides fought savagely. The three hundred Almugavars attacked the two thousand Greek foot soldiers and destroyed most of them so promptly that they could then turn to the aid of Fernán and his horsemen. Their help was so effective that the route was left free of enemies, with a loss of six hundred cavalry either dead or captured. Laden with victory and spoils, they pressed on and reached Pactia, where Rocafort had just arrived from raiding Rhodope.

REFERENCES

1. Guy II de la Roche, the last Burgundian duke of Athens, who died on October 5, 1308, and was succeeded by his nearest relative, a cousin, the fifth Gautier de Brienne. This Duke Gautier became the last French ruler of the duchy.

Fortieth Chapter

FERNAN JIMENEZ TAKES THE TOWN AND CASTLE OF MODICUS

IT BECAME APPARENT to Fernán Jiménez that, in order to assure his position, he must take some town where he could occupy quarters apart from those of Rocafort, since his character precluded their ability to live together. Fernán's nobility of blood and bearing was attracting to his ranks many of those who followed Rocafort; but since they feared the latter's resentment as the more powerful leader, they did not dare to leave him openly without having the security of some city.

The nearest enemy town was Modicus, located along the strait south of Gallipoli. He decided to try taking it by surprise, and, when they failed to do so, they laid siege to the town and dug trenches. Those who were experienced in military strategy condemned Fernán's resolution to take a town that had seven hundred men under arms within when he had only two hundred soldiers and eighty horse. But the Aragonese believed that the poltroonery of the townspeople in comparison to the constancy of his own men would make the impossible easy. When a nation lacks courage and energy it will necessarily give way to the enemy that undertakes to subjugate it, because neither a numerous populace nor strong walls will serve as protection.

Seven hundred miserable Greeks cowered inside of their walls in fear of fewer than three hundred Catalans, as though they were besieged by the entire enemy army. They made no attempt either to go out against the invaders nor to undo their efforts for their ruin. Fernán Jiménez raised a catapult and spent several days using it to bombard the parts of the walls that seemed weakest. But the machine could fire only light stones, which made little impression on the strong, high walls. Next, they tried to put up ladders but all was fruitless. Muntaner sent food and supplies from Gallipoli, while our men concentrated upon securing themselves within their own fortifications, harassing the enemy until they were forced to relax their guard.

The Catalans' diligence and stubbornness finally won what they had undertaken. After seven long months of siege, the Greeks began to feel contempt for their enemies and grew careless about keeping their walls guarded. Their sentinels became fewer and less regular on the watch. Around the first of July the Greeks prepared to celebrate one of their festivals with great solemnity. Since their first delight is wine, a vice that has disgraced that nation in all ages, they drank until they forgot that the enemy was at their walls, watching for any opportunity to attack them. Some of them danced; others slept in the shade, leaving the walls without their usual garrison.

Fernán Jiménez, who by this time had begun to despair that Modicus would ever surrender or that he could overcome it, was inside his tent, wondering what he should do, when the voices and clamor of the dancers above drew him from his lodge. Little by little he approached the walls, which were discovered to be without men. Fernán ordered a hundred men to scale the walls and led the rest to attack the gate. His commands were put into action with incredible efficiency. Of the hundred men climbing the walls, about seventy got over before they were noticed and were able to occupy three towers.

When the Greeks awoke from their costly sleep, they seized their weapons, incited more by the effect of the wine than by their valor, and tried to dislodge our men from the towers. In this effort they were all absorbed, so that none defended the gate Fernán was attacking. Since there was no one to impede them, the Catalans pushed the gate to the ground and walked in openly through the breach. They approached the combatants at the towers from the rear. The townspeople retreated and fought from the slender defensive towers along the streets until they finally sought safety in flight, leaving free the town and castle with most of their possessions to Fernán. So ended the siege of Modicus because of the pertinacity of an Aragonese during the eight months that the siege lasted.

Of the Catalans who were garrisoned in the other towns, I find nothing of interest to write. They were engaged in routine raids on the interior countryside, looking for their necessary sustenance.

Forty-First Chapter

THE CATALANS DIVIDE INTO FOUR HEADQUARTERS, AND
MUNTANER DEFEATS GEORGE OF CHRISTOPLE

W HEN FERNAN JIMENEZ DE ARENOS had taken the town and castle of Modicus, he established his garrison and headquarters there. Rocafort had divided his men between Rhodestos and Pactia; Muntaner, the quartermaster, remained in charge at Gallipoli where the arms and supplies for the whole army were collected and stored. When soldiers in the other fortresses needed weapons, horses, or clothing, they sent to Gallipoli for them. Merchants of all nations, the wounded, the old men, and other useless people lived there, since it was considered the most secure garrison because of its distance from the enemy.

The Catalans were sustained by this organization of government for five years. In none of their districts was either field or vineyard cultivated; only the natural produce of the land was harvested during this time. Time has changed and improved this approach to making war; today the conqueror's main intent is not desolation and the reduction of fields into deserts, but rather their preservation for his own use. To take a province in order to destroy it and impede the cultivation of its land completely is the same as not winning it at all, particularly when its produce is necessary to the invaders if they wish to maintain themselves. But our people were not aware of this logic, nor did they moderate their cruelties. They had driven the farmers from their settlements, until they found themselves in such need — in spite of their many victories — that the lack of food forced them out of Thrace and into much danger and hardship.

Around this time, George of Christople, a rich and important gentleman of Macedonia, was traveling from Thessalonica to Constantinople with eighty horsemen for an interview with Emperor Andronicus. Hearing that Gallipoli was now sparsely guarded, it occurred to him to take advantage of this opportunity. He turned aside from his route, and, with the aid of expert scouts, was able to come close to Gallipoli without being apprehended.

They met up with a group of mule-drawn carts that were coming out of the city in search of firewood. A veteran cavalry soldier named Marco was at the head of the caravan. When George and his men suddenly attacked, Marco sent his people on foot to take refuge behind the walls of a mill while he himself rode off back toward Gallipoli. The Macedonians did not stop to force the mill, but pursued the soldier, so that they and the warning of their appearance would arrive at the same time. But Marco knew the land so well that he reached Muntaner, the captain in Gallipoli, first to give him the alarm. The Catalans all took up arms and defended the walls, while Muntaner went out with fourteen horse and some Almugavars to meet and delay the attackers. As they moved out, the men who were scattered outside the walls had time to collect within.

Muntaner and his small troop of fourteen horsemen closed in

on the eighty Macedonians and fought so valiantly that George
was forced to retreat, leaving thirty-six of his men dead or captured. Muntaner pursued them as far as the mill, where the mules
were recovered and the men rescued. Then he returned to Gallipoli, where he freed the few prisoners and divided the money they
had taken. To the men at arms he gave each twenty-eight gold
coins,[1] fourteen to the light horsemen, and seven apiece to the foot
soldiers.

REFERENCES

1. According to Zurita (Book V, Chapter CV), the coins taken by Muntaner were
Byzantine *perpres de oro*, worth ten Barcelona *sueldos*. (Gili Gaya, p. 233.) José
Salat in his *Treatise on Catalonian Coins* says that the *sou* of Barcelona minting
equalled twenty contemporary *sous*. Muntaner mentions the coin in his chronicle in
discussion of his negotiations for the ransom of Berenguer de Entenza: *"E yo entrel
veure, e volgui donar X milia perpres de oro, qui val hu X sous barceloneses, e
quelnos lexassen, e non volgren fer."* He indicates that the Byzantine coin was worth
ten Barcelona *sous*. (Rosell, p. 38.) All the gold coins minted under Andronicus
II, called *hyperpyron*, were greatly depreciated with alloys until they contained about
fourteen carats, or less than two thirds of their face value.

Forty-Second Chapter

ROCAFORT AND FERNAN JIMENEZ DE ARENOS TAKE
ESTAÑARA AND RECAPTURE THEIR FOUR GALLEYS

AT THE SAME TIME that Muntaner had such good fortune against George, Rocafort and Fernán Jiménez de Arenós
collected their forces that were divided among Pactia, Rhodestos,
and Modicus and marched through Thrace toward the Great Sea,
proceeding as always with sacking and setting fire to towns, cutting down and burning the crops, killing, and taking captives as
they went. Their thirst for vengeance never relented. They decided
to try to take Estañara, a busy trading port on the shore of the
Black Sea, where most of the ships of Thrace were built. They

crossed the forty long leagues and entered the place without finding resistance, since the natives had never feared the Catalans because their fortresses were so far away.

After they had taken the town, the Catalans attacked the ships
and galleys in the harbor. Muntaner claims that they seized a hundred and fifty vessels, all of which they mastered as easily at sea as
they had on land. They made off with rich capture, recovering
their four galleys that the Greeks had taken in Constantinople
when they killed the Catalan admiral, Fernando Aonés. The
spectacle of that day was tremendous; they changed the order of
nature itself, flooding the land by breaking the dikes that held the
water of the irrigation ditches, setting fire to the ships at sea, and
in other ways using as ministers of their vengeance the elements,
which overflowed their natural laws and limits for the ruin of their
opponents; the havoc was so great that everything seemed to return to primeval chaos. Many perished by burning in the waters,
while others drowned on land. They spared only the four galleys
from the fire, which, loaded with spoils and Catalan crews, were
sent back to Gallipoli.

They passed through the strait by Constantinople, with more
terror of their enemies, who had no one to oppose them, than peril
to themselves. Rocafort and Fernán moved on toward their fortresses little by little, while making forays into the land on all sides
in search of the necessary sustenance, which they took from the
foe. The natives abandoned their towns to their enemies and fled
into the most rugged areas of the mountains.

Andronicus realized his losses but did not consider his forces
strong enough to restore them or to go out to block the way of the
marauders. On the contrary, he despaired, delivering his provinces
to the rigor of the armed invaders, doubtful not so much of their
courage as of the loyalty of his men. Such is the situation that all
rulers suffer who make even their most faithful subjects disloyal
with their cruelty and tyranny.

In the Greek Empire rulers were established more through the
acclamation of the army than by right of succession, and they
feared the loss of their rank by the same arts that had gained it.

They lived in perpetual suspicion and fear both of their subjects who were superior to the rest in courage and wisdom, of the rich, the honored, or the respected, as well as the daring or rebellious, equally afflicted by the virtues of the ones and the vices of the others. From these anxieties were born the atrocities of that nation: putting out eyes, cutting off ears and noses, banishments, exiles, executions for suspicion of imagined or pretended crimes in order to allay the pangs of jealousy. And as often as not they were oppressed by those they had never feared. Andronicus was a ruler of singular sagacity, but in his last years his grandson, Andronicus,[1] took the Empire from him, and his wisdom was forestalled by the daring of a boy. So end all reigns and empires that place their security and undertakings on reasons of state alone.

REFERENCES

1. Andronicus II and his son, Michael IX, ruled as co-Emperors, a tradition in the Byzantine state established to insure succession and distribute the responsibility for governing the distant parts of the Empire. But Michael died at Thessalonica in 1320 of illness, aggravated by shock at the knowledge of the accidental assassination of his younger son, Manuel, in a love affair involving the older son. He left this elder son, Andronicus, as co-Emperor with the boy's grandfather. The young Emperor waged civil war against the old, taking Constantinople on May 24, 1328. He forced his grandfather to abdicate and two years later to enter a monastery, where he died as a monk in 1332.

Forty-Third Chapter

THE CATALANS AND ARAGONESE WREAK VENGEANCE
ON THE MASSAGETES, ON THE SLOPES
OF MOUNT HEMO

THE CATALANS AND ARAGONESE did not consider themselves satisfied as long as the Massagetes with their general, George, principal minister of the death of the Caesar, Roger, and the men who went with him, were retired into their own country without having received just recompense for the outrage they had committed. Our men learned that, with the permission of Andronicus, the Massagetes were returning to their land, tired from the labors and fatigues of war. They preferred servitude and subjection under the Scythians, their ancient lords, to the liberty they enjoyed among the Greeks; so great is the love of homeland that oppression within it can seem sweet, while liberty away from it is insufferable.

The Catalans decided that it was necessary to overtake them — since they had resolved to seek them out — before they had gone beyond Mount Hemo, which divides the Greek Empire from the kingdom of Bulgaria. It would have been an ill-advised resolution to follow them into Bulgaria, where retreat through the narrow passes, entrances, and exits of the mountains was difficult, and the inhabitants were warlike and friendly at that time to Andronicus.

Together at Pactia the captains resolved that this action would require most of their forces. In order to draw more men, they abandoned Pactia, Modicus, and Rhodestos, leaving only Gallipoli. There all the women were sent under the rule of Ramón Muntaner with two hundred soldiers and twenty horse. Muntaner objected that his reputation was damaged by not going along on a expedition on which everyone else was venturing. But the entreaties of the army, as well as their confidence in his person as defender of their women, children, and possessions, obliged him to remain. They offered him one third of the fifth that would fall as their share of the booty and another part to his soldiers. But many of Muntaner's men felt that this was small proportion from a victory that was certain and without danger; they sought rather to go with the army and many left during the night to join Rocafort. Ramón Muntaner gave others permission to go, since he saw that they were resolved to depart without it. He was moved to this action somewhat in his own interest, because they promised to divide with him their share of whatever booty was taken. After this he was left with one hundred thirty-four soldiers out of his two hundred, and six of the cavalry from twenty.

More than two thousand women remained, so that Muntaner

wrote: "We were Latins poorly accompanied by men, but well accompanied by women."[1] All the women who had been in the fortresses were sent well escorted to Gallipoli, after which our captains went out from Pactia in forced marches in pursuit of the Massagetes, who had hastened their own departure when they learned of the Catalans' intent. But their diligence could not have been as great as their misfortune, because their enemies caught up with them after twelve days on the road before they had passed Mount Hemo. One evening scouts from the Catalan camp discovered the Massagetes and learned from the natives of the land that there were three thousand horsemen and six thousand infantrymen, with numberless pack animals for carrying families and belongings.

Rocafort and Fernán Jiménez gained credit with their men by assuring that the Massagetes would not get away and allowing them to rest for a day within their lodges. At dawn the next day, their strength renewed after their repose, they gave battle to the enemy. The Massagetes, most valiant of all the peoples of the Levant, were more surprised by than fearful of their situation. They armed and went out to receive their attackers in defense of their women and children. George, the general and principal minister of the death of the Caesar Roger, with a thousand horsemen opened the terrible and fearful combat against our cavalry who penetrated the enemy's defensive positions made up of their carts. A bloody battle ensued when the rest of the troops of infantry closed in from both sides. Remarkable feats of arms were seen that day because those who fought were equal in courage, though not in numbers. The theater of this tragedy was a plain that stretched for two leagues toward the slopes of Mount Hemo. The horse-troops with their weapons destroyed, swords and maces broken, and horses dead, sustained themselves in the struggle with their hands and bodies. The insatiable desire for vengeance inspired some; for others it was the last necessity of their own defense. Everyone was subject to fate, because the Massagetes were all outside their defenses, fighting confused and interlocked with the Catalans.

Until noon the victory was uncertain and changing. But when the banners of George and the most valiant captains fell, the battle inclined to our side. The defeated tried to rally within their defenses, but it was not possible because the conquerors pursued them inside, dealing out death to them in the arms of their women. These also fell to the sword because, without distinction for sex or age, they came to the defense of their children and husbands, exposing their bodies to the rigor of death.

The victory became more certain for the Catalans when the Massagetes stopped fighting to put their women and children on horses for flight. If they had been concerned only with their own persons, few would have failed to reach freedom in flight. But natural love, powerful enough even among barbarians to make them scorn death, delayed them to their own ruin. They scattered over the plain, riding for the refuge of the mountains, but the horses were so tired, and they were so little helped by the women, who were terrified and laden with the children they carried at their breasts and in their arms, that they could not save themselves. Almost all perished as they were overtaken, because the men turned back in desperation to face their pursuers so that their women could escape, and were torn to pieces at the hands of the Catalans. Nicephorus and Muntaner agree that of the nine thousand men under arms only three hundred survived.

An incident as strange as it was pitiful happened during the chase. One brave Massagete youth, realizing that the battle was lost and Catalan arms were everywhere, tried to escape, more in order to rescue his beautiful young wife than in fear for his own life. With the urgency that the danger demanded, he pulled his wife from the defenses and tents, where all was now covered with blood and death, and put her on a horse — the first one that chance offered him. He mounted another and they rode off toward the mountain.

Close behind her came three of our soldiers, motivated by lust or perhaps by the beauty and gallantry of the woman. Her husband recognized their enemies and their zealous pursuit. He urged his wife's horse on by shouting and beating him with his scimitar, but the animal was already overcome with heat and fatigue. He then decided it would be the lesser evil to leave the woman than to die himself and, giving spur and rein to his horse, passed on ahead. But he was stopped by the tears and complaints that so justly flowed from his wife. He turned his horse, and coming up beside her, wrapped her in his arms and took leave of her with passionate kisses; weeping, he then drew away from her, lifted his scimitar, and cut off her head with one stroke.

What a strange confusion of events that such fierce, barbarous cruelty could combine embraces with the knife, kisses with death, all the result of a lover's passion! While tender love inspired the kisses and embraces, unbearable jealousy brought the knife and death; in order that enemies could not enjoy what he had lost, jealousy had conquered. Love and the desire to live are equally powerful in the spirit of man.

At the same moment that the girl fell dead from her horse, Guillén Bellver, one of the three who was following her, caught the rein. With incredible fury and bravery, the Massagete youth, bathed in the blood drawn by his own hand, cut off with one blow Guillén's arm and life. Then he turned on Arnau Miró and Berenguer Ventallola, giving and taking wounds until he fell dead beside the body of his wife. It seemed that he could not have fulfilled the laws of a lover if he had not sacrificed his own life to love after sacrificing hers to jealousy.

In any case the incident seems unworthy of a rational man, even though he was not a Christian. Tacitus tells us a similar story about Rhadamistus, son of King Pharasmanes of Iberia. The prince and his wife, Zenobia, were fleeing on two horses along the River Araxes, when she was overtaken with labor pains. Fearing that she would fall into the hands of his offended enemies, who would take vengeance upon him by abusing and insulting her, he wounded her five times and threw her into the river. But Zenobia's fate was different from that of the Massagete's wife. Some peasants rescued her from the water, cured her, and delivered her to Rhadamistus's enemy, King Tiridates.[2]

After the victory, the Catalans collected their spoils and captives and marched back to their fortresses with great glee and exuberance at having so satisfactorily fulfilled their revenge. The way home was tiresome and dangerous because it was so long, through enemy lands where the armed inhabitants had recently gathered into their strongholds all the fruits of their fields, so that food often had to be bought with blood and lives.

There are some differences between Nicephorus and Muntaner on the relation of this march. The Greek says that the Catalans tried to persuade the Turkish Greeks to join them, reminding them that when they all fought together under the banners of the Empire, the Massagetes always took a unfair share of the spoils because of their reputation for power. They suggested that the Turkish Greeks should take this route for satisfaction of the insults they had suffered. Muntaner says only that the Catalans merely considered this approach, which could well be believed, but the Turkish Greeks did not have to be solicited to seek their vengeance. What I am sure of is that the Turkish Greeks were the ones who had warned the Catalans of the departure of the Massagetes, and that some of them joined the Catalans on the expedition, but not the whole nation. Their captain, Meleco, was not with them, because it was not until after this victory that he left the service of Emperor Andronicus. That story will be told in its place.

REFERENCES

1. Moncada quotes Muntaner's Catalan phrase: *"Romangui mal acompanyat de homens, y ben acompanyat de fembres."*

2. This tale is to be found in Tacitus's *Annals*, 12: 51. A modern English version (by A. J. Church and W. J. Brodribb, in *The Complete Works of Tacitus*, New York: The Modern Library, Random House, 1942, p. 275) may be of interest here:

Rhadamistus had no means of escape but in the swiftness of the horses which bore him and his wife away. Pregnant as she was, she endured, somehow or other, out of fear of the enemy and love of her husband, the first part of the flight, but after a while, when she felt herself shaken by its continuous speed, she implored to be rescued by an honourable death from the shame of captivity. He at first embraced, cheered, and encouraged her, now admiring her heroism, now filled with a sickening apprehension at the idea of her being left to any man's mercy. Finally, urged by the intensity of his love and familiarity with dreadful deeds, he unsheathed his scimitar, and, having stabbed her, dragged her to the bank of the Araxes and committed her to the stream, so that her body might be swept away. Then in headlong flight he hurried to Iberia, his ancestral kingdom. Zenobia meanwhile (this was her name), as she yet breathed and showed signs of life on the calm water at the river's edge, was perceived by some shepherds, who inferred from her appearance that she was no baseborn woman, bound up her wound and applied to it their rustic remedies. As soon as they knew her name and her adventure, they conveyed her to the city of Artaxata, whence she was conducted at the public charge to Tiridates, who received her kindly and treated her as a royal person.

Forty-Fourth Chapter

THE GENOESE ATTACK GALLIPOLI AND RETREAT AFTER
THE LOSS OF THEIR GENERAL

WHILE ROCAFORT and Fernán Jiménez were achieving victory over the Massagetes, Ramón Muntaner, the captain at Gallipoli, won it from the Genoese. It was a remarkable event, one of those that show clearly how varying are the accidents of war, with victories and losses sometimes born of causes neither foreseen nor expected.

Antonio Spinola arrived at Constantinople with eighteen Genoese galleys to deliver the marquisate of Monferrat to Demetrius, the third son of Andronicus and Empress Irene.[1] He discussed with the Emperor the state of affairs with the Catalans and offered, with more temerity than prudence, to take Gallipoli and force them out of Thrace, if the ruler would give his word for the marriage of his third son, Demetrius, to the daughter of Opicin Spinola as a reward for such significant service. Andronicus accepted the agreement and pledged the marriage of his son.

This done, the arrogant Genoese sailed with two galleys to Gallipoli under security. He asked for the captain, and, taken to where he was, said with lofty, uncivil bearing: "I am Antonio Spinola, general of my Republic. I come to order you to leave these provinces without objection or delay and to return to your own country, because otherwise we will eject you by force and you will be subject to the rigor of our arms."[2]

Ramón Muntaner, realizing that he was without forces and being a discreet and sensible soldier, answered with courtesy and restraint, explaining that the departure from Gallipoli and Thrace was not a matter to be undertaken impetuously even if he were able to do as Spinola wished. He pointed out that threatening them with force was outside all reason since peace existed between their kings and his Republic, which he was obliged to keep as long as they observed it. A second and third time Antonio replied, challenging all the Catalans with a thousand abuses, and undertook to express his challenge through the public assertion of a notary.

Irritated by so much insolence, Muntaner lost his patience and answered boldly that the war declared by Spinola on behalf of his Republic was unjust and that, consequently, he protested before God and the faith that they professed in common, all the injury, shedding of blood, robbing, burning, and deaths that would result were the responsibility of the Genoese since the Catalans were forced to oppose such an unfair offense. The Republic of Genoa did not have jurisdiction to require them to leave Thrace, since that land was not subject to its sovereignty. If their right to rule was based only on their power, then they should come to attempt the banishment, at which time they would learn the difference between saying and doing. He claimed that Andronicus was a false schismatic and that the Catalan forces would be employed to bring about his ruin in spite of the Genoese.

After this answer, Antonio returned to his galleys and sailed to Constantinople, where he reported to the Emperor what had happened and offered to take Gallipoli for him at once, since it had so little defense. Eager to win the fortress from his greatest enemies, Andronicus gave Spinola seven galleys under their captain, Mandriol, a Genoese by nation, so that, joined with the seventeen, they could more easily undertake the enterprise. Antonio sailed with Demetrius and they arrived at two in the afternoon the following day with twenty-five galleys at Palomares near Gallipoli, where they began to disembark their men.

With the few horsemen that he had, Muntaner rushed out boldly to the shore to prevent the unloading. But ten of the galleys moved away from the rest and freely put what men they carried on land. When Muntaner was wounded and his horse killed, the Genoese believed that the quartermaster was gone and shouted out: "The captain is dead and Gallipoli is ours!" But a servant helped the Catalan leader, who escaped from their hands with five wounds. Returning to Gallipoli bathed in his own and the blood of others, he caused concern among the people, who feared that the wounds of their captain were fatal. But after they had been examined, they turned out to be so slight that they did not hinder either his fighting nor his governing. Two thousand women garrisoned the walls, with a Catalan merchant as corporal for each ten, and pikes, stones, and swords for weapons. They found themselves successors to their husbands, not only in responsibility, but also in courage.

The Genoese now found themselves masters of the field. They formed their ranks, marched to Gallipoli, laid up their ladders, and threw innumerable darts. They pressed the assault gallantly, especially when they saw that the walls were defended only by women. But their resistance proved that these were women only in name, while invincible men in their strength and endurance. Though they were beaten back from the walls with many deaths and wounds, the Genoese were convinced that the naturally weak sex could be overcome if obstinately combatted.

They attacked again, but retreated with even greater damage. Watching the struggle from his flagship, Antonio Spinola saw that his men were exhausted and despaired of winning success with the contingent he had on land. He therefore went to their rescue in person with four hundred horse, bringing energy to the assault. As he came up to the walls, he saw the carnage and numerous dead at close range and wished he had not undertaken the enterprise. But he encouraged his men, who assaulted valiantly. The combat began anew, and the women were inspired by the danger. Even though covered with blood and wounds, they remained at their posts, some with as many as five injuries in the face, refusing to leave the places that they regarded as honored because their husbands usually occupied them, and would not relinquish them except with their lives.

The Genoese fought stubbornly, ashamed of being beaten off

by gallant women. As soon as one man fell dead from the ladder, another was there to expose himself to the same danger. Ramón Muntaner saw the punishment that the Genoese had received, observing that they no longer had darts to shoot; their squadrons were undone; most of the men were wounded and the rest worn and fatigued by the combat and the heat of a July day. Shortly after midday he sallied forth to fight with one hundred men and six cavalry without defensive arms in order to maneuver more freely. After one of the gates of Gallipoli had been opened, he charged out with his six horsemen against the enemies, who were breathless from the exhaustion of the heat and their weapons. The hundred soldiers followed, conquering and slitting the throats of their attackers with little resistance. The beaten army fled back to its galleys, constantly pressed by their enemies, so that almost all of them perished during the chase. The ships had dropped their ladders to the land, so that one Catalan followed his prey up and finally killed him on board. Many of the Genoese galleys would have remained in Muntaner's power that day if he had had more men for reinforcement.

Demetrius, the Emperor's son, and the other captains who remained alive, raised anchor and sailed away, fearing the daring and determination of their conquerors. The four hundred horsemen had all died with their captain, Antonio, on the some spot from which he had challenged all the Catalans and declared war on behalf of his Republic: an end justly merited by a man so arrogant and unreasonable as to initiate a war. His death served as a warning to those who represent to rulers as easy and secure those enterprises that are subject to the uncertainty of war. One who kindles the flames of war and grasps a sword finds that the quite certain becomes doubtful, and that which is already in doubt, even more so.

When the Genoese captain, Antonio Rocanegra, found the passage out of the strait blocked for his galleys, with around forty soldiers he took up a defensive position on the summit of a small hill. After the few remaining Genoese had retreated to their galleys and escaped in them with so much disgrace and damage,

Muntaner heard about this band. He took a group of men to where they were and attacked them, leaving some dead and some overcome. Only Antonio Rocanegra was left standing alone with his broad sword, giving brave and extreme proof of his valor. Muntaner admired a man of so much courage, even though an enemy, and stopped the soldiers in their attempts to shoot and kill him. He asked the Genoese courteously if he would accept prison. But the reckless captain, resolved to die before surrendering his weapons, scorned Muntaner's chivalrous pleas. Whereby he provoked the ire of his conquerors, who closed in on him and cut him to pieces. The Catalans were thus left the victors and masters of the field.

The seventeen Genoese galleys did not dare to return to Constantinople, although they were in severe need of men and supplies. But, as they feared the indignation of Andronicus and the insolence of the Greeks, they sailed through the mouth of the strait and back to Italy, taking Demetrius with them. The other seven galleys commanded by Mandriol returned to Constantinople and advised Andronicus of the event.

At last the word of Gallipoli's danger reached our army that had dispersed to its own fortresses after the victory over the Massagetes. Fearing to lose their stronghold before they could come to its aid, they pressed on the way and arrived two days after the conquered Genoese had embarked. They were universally grieved that they had not come in time to punish the Genoese who had been so treacherous as to break the peace during their absence and to attack a fortress held only by women. Their anger increased upon finding their wives wounded and abused, but the joy of the victory overcame it at length and together they celebrated the pleasure and elation of both victories.

REFERENCES

1. Irene (or Yolande) of Montferrat, second wife of Andronicus II Palaeologus, was the daughter of the Marquis, Guillaume VII of Montferrat, and Beatriz of Castile. In addition to the marquisate of Montferrat as her inheritance, Irene had also received Thessalonica as her dowry.

2. Spinola's use of the familiar form of address was insulting: "Yo soy Antonio

Spínola, general de mi república: vengo a ordenaros que sin réplica y dilación dejéis libres estas provincias, y os retiréis a vuestra patria; porque de otra manera os echaremos con las armas, y estaréis sujetos a su rigor." (Rosell, p. 41.)

Forty-Fifth Chapter

THE TURKS AND TURKISH GREEKS ENTER THE
SERVICE OF THE CATALANS

SINCE THE CATALAN and Greek arms were occupied in ruining each other, the Turks were freed from the fear of both that they had had when the two were in accord and combined to prosecute their war. They went back to their course of victories and occupation of the Asian provinces, no longer concerned with any army able to oppose the current of their prosperous fortunes. According to the account of Pachymeres, by the twenty-fourth year of the reign of Andronicus, or the year 1306 of Christ, the Greeks had abandoned all of Asia — three years after the Catalans had left there. From this can be seen clearly the disaster that resulted from division and discord between the Catalans and Greeks, who lost the opportunity to subjugate that arrogant nation at the outset, when it could have been accomplished with little difficulty.

As the absolute lords of Asia, the Turks contemplated entering Europe and expanding their conquering arms into the West. For several years they were delayed in this effort by the lack of ships to get by those who were on the other side of the strait at Gallipoli. Recognizing the present occasion with the Catalans as enemies of the Greeks, they sent messengers to our men at Gallipoli to explore their attitudes and learn if they might favor a treaty that would allow them to enter Catalan service.

The Catalans indicated that they were not displeased by the idea. They sent to the messengers an armed frigate to bring their captain, Ximelix, and ten companions to conclude the treaty. On the Turkish side, he offered eight hundred horsemen and two thousand infantrymen to swear fidelity to the Catalan general. The conditions of the agreement were separate quarters where they could live with their families; half the amount of spoils paid to Catalan soldiers; and freedom to return to their homeland when they wished without any violent attempts to detain them. When their proposal was presented, the Catalans admitted the Turks to their service by common consent and assured them by oath that these conditions would be fulfilled. With this matter closed, Ximelix sailed back through the strait to prepare his people for the arrival of the fleet. Shortly afterward they embarked on the ships and galleys that they were able to gather, reaching Gallipoli with the two thousand Turkish foot soldiers, eight hundred knights, women, children, and possessions.

This deed of the Catalans has been condemned by ancient and modern writers as most unworthy: to bring into Europe the barbarian infidels, enemies of the Christian name, thereby staining the glory of that expedition with such an impious and detestable decision: for the way to Europe was thereby opened to that brave and powerful nation. This is without doubt an unjust charge against the Catalans by those writers, who are carried away by their passions or careless in their search for the truth: both grave errors for a historian. The decision would have been impious and dangerous to their own liberty for the Catalans, if the Turks whom they admitted to their favor had been superior in forces. The Easterners would then have been able to introduce their false religion freely and to threaten our faith, combining to oppress the liberty of those who had accepted them as comrades. Reinforcements and allies should not be greater than one's own, so that they may not bring about what happened to Scipio in Spain, when thirty thousand Celtiberians treacherously abandoned him. Since his forces were inferior, he could not stop them, as Livy describes in his famous account.[1]

The Turks were fewer than three thousand and inferior to the Catalans in weapons and courage, to such a degree that they could not have been expected to do other than as their masters ordered. It is also certain that the faith of the Christians was not in danger from these barbarians, since they were too much in the minority to offend the others. Back in the times of our forefathers, in the communities of the kingdom of Valencia those who served most faithfully were the Moors, whose use against other Christians was regarded as legal and necessary. In the same way the Turks served the Catalans in Greece, where the urgency for their own defense forgave whatever error they may have committed in this matter. No republic or ruler can be found that, when pressed by foreign or civil wars, has not been forced to call for the help of people of different customs and religion. Often they have given access to their kingdoms to more powerful allies in order to free themselves from the present danger, without considering that they themselves would be despoiled, whether they became conquerors or conquered. Sometimes a close danger is prevented by a greater one, but since one must perish eventually, it is better to put it off as long as possible and seek the more distant peril that may at length cease to threaten.

If the Catalans had done what Stilicho[2] and Narses[3] did, one calling in the Goths and the other the Longobardians, for the ruin of Italy and the Empire, they could not have been more reviled by the tongues and pens of historians. Some call them impious, sacrilegious; others, pirates, common pestilence of the people, men without God, law, or reason, all because they accepted the Turks into their favor. Expressed in these terms, the act does offend Christian ears; but when the matter is fully investigated and understood, there seems little reason for casual blame, and certainly much less for abuse in words so violent and full of insults and accusations. When men are a thousand leagues from their own country, with their captains and envoys killed by treachery, how much suffering should they endure? What means, however violent, would they not use to revenge their insults? If they did fall into error, these circumstances might well moderate the judgment of a writer.

There is also some disagreement about the time when the Turks came. Nicephorus says they were called by the Catalans before the battle of Apros, when Michael was known to be preparing an attack, and that only five hundred joined the army. I take this account of Nicephorus to be false, because Muntaner contradicts him on the number of men and the date they came. Since he was an eye witness, he should be credited, even though he was Catalan and prejudiced. During the course of his history, however, he reports many matters against his countrymen, freely condemning their evil deeds without reservation. It is not believable that one who tells the truth to his own detriment would lie in a matter that is so unimportant to his glory as whether the Turks came four years earlier or later.

Zurita,[4] who follows the relation of Berenguer de Entenza, also disagrees with Nicephorus. He reports that Berenguer himself called the Turks after he learned of the deaths of his envoys and that fifteen hundred cavalry arrived at Gallipoli to pledge fidelity to him. I also discount this relation, because it seems impossible that, during the fifteen days that Berenguer remained in Gallipoli after he was declared an enemy of the Empire, he could have called the Turks, who were in Asia, come to an agreement with them, or that fifteen hundred cavalry could have been mustered, embarked, and arrived to swear loyalty to him. Even though these actions had been taken in some haste, they could not have been carried out in a fortnight. Muntaner clearly reports the truth about the time when the Turks arrived: four years after the Catalan expedition was undertaken. I am sure of this because it offers no difficulty, while there are large questions about what Nicephorus and Zurita claim. Therefore, in the affair of the Turks I follow only Muntaner, as I find him more accurate because he took part in all those events.

During this same period the Turkish Greeks in the service of the Emperor were declared rebels because, in imitation of the Catalans, they demanded payment of their wages or threatened to force contributions. Since they were few in number, they could not maintain themselves in that way. They sent word to the Catalans to ask permission to join the Company. They received the invitation to come under security and to accept the same agreement as the Turks had, but with more advantages because they were Christians.

Almost a thousand fine horsemen swore the oath of fidelity under the same conditions that the Turks had and were placed under the command of Juan Pérez de Caldés. When the Alans and

Turkish Greeks left his service, Emperor Andronicus found himself without foreign militia and so lacking in soldiers that he was unable to impede any campaign, of whatever size, against the provinces of his Empire. The strength that the Emperor lost Rocafort gained, because both Turks and Turkish Greeks respected him and recognized him as their supreme chief. Finding his security increased by their obedience and devotion, the Catalan captain grew proud and hateful to many because of the arrogant and absolute power with which he governed and commanded all.

REFERENCES

1. The *Roman History* of Titus Livius (59 B.C.-17 A.D.) is a picturesque account of the growth of the Roman state, including the campaigns of the general, Publius Cornelius Scipio Africanus, and stressing the prediction that contemporary moral laxity would destroy the Empire.

2. Flavius Stilicho (359?-408), son of a Vandal captain who became one of the most distinguished generals and statesmen under Emperor Theodosius I the Great (346?-395). Stilicho succeeded him as ruler in the West under Emperor Flavius Honorius, who reigned from 395-423.

3. Narses (*c.* 478-573) was an important officer of the Emperor Justinian, whose throne he helped save from a rebellion in 532. As supreme commander in Italy, he there defeated by the year 554 the Ostrogoths and the Alamanni and remained on as Imperial governor for the following thirteen years.

4. Jerónimo Zurita explains his opinion, differing with Moncada, in Book VI, Chapter IV, of his *Annals of the Crown of Aragon,* which reports the history of the kingdom from its origin in the ninth century to 1516. (Gili Gaya, p. 256.) Secretary to King Felipe II of Spain from 1560-1580, he was the first modern Spanish historian. He investigated archives, collected original documents, and selected his material with scientific methods of analysis.

Forty-Sixth Chapter

WHAT HAPPENED TO BERENGUER DE ENTENZA FROM THE
TIME OF HIS IMPRISONMENT AND LIBERATION
TO HIS RETURN TO GALLIPOLI

T HE CATALANS WERE augmented with the new aid of the Turks and Turkish Greeks, as well as by many other Spaniards who had been disguised throughout the Empire as merchants or people of other nations. After the Company was credited with so many victories, everyone vied for its friendship: some motivated by the desire for vengeance, but most by greed, wanting to participate in the riches acquired in the war, as fame had published.

About this time Berenguer de Entenza was freed from his long, tiresome imprisonment and began wandering through the courts of the rulers of Europe, seeking support for the Catalan enterprise in vain. He reached Gallipoli with a ship and five hundred men, all estimable people. His appearance disturbed the peace and quiet of the Company, because of the rivalry that it raised between him and Rocafort for the government. But before explaining the reasons and causes for the competition on both sides, it would be well to give a full account of what happened to Berenguer from his capture to his return.

By order of the captains of the Company, Ramón Muntaner had tried to rescue Berenguer when the Genoese galleys passed through the strait of Gallipoli on their return to Trebizond, but he had been powerless to conclude it. It was regarded as certain, however, that when Berenguer was taken to Genoa he would be put at liberty and given compensation for his treatment because he was a captain and vassal of a friendly king. But it did not turn out as they expected. On the contrary, the Republic condoned such an ugly case by neither punishing their general nor granting liberty and indemnity for loss to Berenguer; whenever a transgression is not punished, it is approved.

When the news came to the Catalans of Thrace that Berenguer was being held in a prison unworthy of his person in Genoa without discussions about his liberty, they determined by common agreement that, since they were not now strong enough to free him by force, they would petition Don Jaime, the King of Aragon, to interpose his authority for them with the Republic. They named three envoys for this mission: García de Vergua, Pérez de Arbe, and Pedro Roldán, all of the Council of Twelve. These reached Catalonia and gave the King their message. They described the great insult they had suffered when their captain, Berenguer, had been imprisoned while under word and in faith, and the continuing evil of his liberty that was still denied. On behalf of the Com-

pany they threw themselves at his feet, asking him for his clemency in forgiving their past quarrels and providing a suitable,
prompt remedy in response to their petition.

They gave the king a detailed account of their victories and of
the state in which stood the affairs of the Company and the Empire, whose lordship they offered to him if he would now help
them energetically, since the provinces were then defenseless and
exposed to the rigor of the first one who would undertake to attack
them. They would regard it as one of their greatest honors to increase the power of his crown at the cost of their own labor and
blood and to make his name obeyed in the most remote and isolated regions of Europe and Asia. The King responded that in
order to please such good vassals, especially Berenguer de Entenza, one of his greatest vassals, he would place his authority and
arms at their service whenever they might be needed. But he
excused himself from helping them on the grounds that it seemed
a matter more suitable for his brother, Don Fadrique, the King of
Sicily, to undertake, since Catalonia was so far away that there
would be great difficulty in unifying and maintaining a combina-
tion of Greek provinces with Catalonia. He did, however, thank
and praise them for their good will.

With this effort ended, the three envoys went to Rome to present to the Pope[1] his opportunity of reducing the Empire of Greece
to obedience to him if he gave the Catalans of Thrace some considerable help. They urged him to grant the investiture to Don
Fadrique, so that he could undertake the enterprise in person with
a legate from the Holy See. They asked him to declare their campaign a crusade to encourage people to join them or to contribute
alms. The Pope did not receive the embassy cordially nor approve
its requests, because he was beset by his own difficulties. One of
the most important of these was his fear that the House of Aragon
might be glorified by these means.

The King, Don Jaime, in order to fulfill his promise, sent his
envoys to the Republic of Genoa to express his deep indignation
at the imprisonment of Berenguer, one of his greatest and most
distinguished vassals. He pointed out that the capture had been in

violation of the peace treaty if it was done with the knowledge of the government. He requested that Berenguer be put at liberty and given compensation for the loss he had suffered. Otherwise the King would be required to make some demonstration of his displeasure.

The Republic decided to accede to the King's orders. They responded that they regretted what their general, Eduardo da Oria, had done to Berenguer de Entenza, explaining that it had been insurrection of the base people on the galleys that caused such an excess. The captains and general had not been able to regain control until they had carried out the sailors' demands. Now they would free Berenguer and had named eleven persons to meet with delegates sent by the King to a place to be chosen by him, where they would negotiate the indemnity for damages that he had received in the loss of the galleys and in his imprisonment. With this favorable message, the King's envoys took their leave. The Republic sent another embassy to represent their side in the same way, conveying the deep apology of all of them for the offense of their general, although blameless himself, against his vassals. They assured the King that they would take Berenguer to Sicily and would restore to him what they had taken from him. They petitioned Don Jaime to order the Catalans, after that matter was settled, to separate the Turks from their Company and to depart from those provinces where the Genoese had most of their trade, now disrupted by the raids and havoc that were continually inflicted there. The King agreed to send the order if Berenguer's claims were satisfied.

When Berenguer was freed, the King sent his deputies to Montpellier, the place designated for the discussion of the recompense. The Republic sent Lord Donizelli, Meliado Salvagio, Gabriel da Sauro, Rogerio da Savigniano, Antonio de Guillelmis, Manuel Cigala, Jacomo Bachonio, Rafo da Oria, Opisino Capsario, Guidero Pignolo, and Jorge de Bonifacio, all of their Council. These were the men who conferred with the King's delegates. After many meetings and the proposal of many settlements, none of which were acceptable to the Government's party, which always found some point too doubtful for conclusion, the conference was finally disbanded without any reparations made by the Republic. It then appeared that the courteous response from the Genoese to the King was only to move him to order the Catalans not to undertake any armed measures against the Genoese, since they had amicably offered to restore the captain's loss.

In the meantime Berenguer, despairing of receiving any recompense, went to the King of France and to the Pope in a second attempt to win their help for the Catalans of Thrace, with the same propositions that the three envoys had offered. But neither the King nor the Pope wished to give it to them. He had to return to Catalonia, where he sold part of his property; collected five hundred men, all well-known veterans; and embarked in a scout ship, leaving the quiet of his home to help the friends who waited for him at Gallipoli.

REFERENCES

1. Pope Clement V (1305-1314), who pronounced anathema on Emperor Andronicus II in 1307.

Forty-Seventh Chapter

BERENGUER DE ENTENZA AND BERENGUER DE ROCAFORT
DIVIDE THE COMPANY INTO FACTIONS

W HEN BERENGUER DE ENTENZA returned to Gallipoli, he sought to resume the command he had held before he was imprisoned. But Berenguer de Rocafort explained to him that the situation had changed so that he no longer had more to command than the men he brought with him, because the rest already had a general. Each became angry, both claiming the supreme authority for himself. The friends and allies of each man spoke in strong and arrogant words, threatening to win obedience by force of arms. The Company was divided by this rivalry, with all in disorder and on the point of a great break, instigated by the gossip that went through the ranks. They were close to coming to blows, because in any great multitude there is never a lack of men who enjoy turmoil, to do injury to an enemy or win credit for themselves with a friend.

Both sides supported their pretensions with well-founded arguments. Berenguer's men said that he had been general before his imprisonment, being the first to attack successfully the provinces of the Empire. He had lost his charge through the perfidy of the Genoese, not through any default in his own responsibility. The long captivity which he had suffered because he was their general should not be the occasion for relieving him of his post, but on the contrary of honoring him with it if he had never had it. He should not be deprived by misfortune of what he had won with his valor, especially since he had sold part of his property after his release in order to bring them help. They also added what to Rocafort was most offensive: the differences between them in blood, bearing, and condition. Berenguer was a grandee, while Rocafort was a private knight. The former was courteous, liberal, and gentle; the other, rough, greedy, and insolent.[1]

On Rocafort's side his friends promoted his pretensions with arguments also worthy of great consideration. They based his right on the fact that he had governed the camp as supreme captain for six years, having taken charge of the command of our men when almost everything was lost. His industry and valor had restored their position, making the nation in his time the most powerful and respected of all the Orient. It would indeed be unjust to take the rule from him in prosperous times, when he had had it in a period so distressed that they often desired death as the least of the evils they were expecting. The fruits of labor should go to those who had suffered for them, rather than to others, even though they were noble and great. It would certainly be a notable insult if they relieved him of that post in which he had increased their name with remarkable victory and had spared the men from the sad, wretched deaths that they had regarded as certain.

While they discussed the case on one side and the other, they almost came to a break and to settling their claims by arms; so that several times there was nearly a battle within the walls of Gallipoli. They had no one who could decide the case, because the Company was divided into two parts, each with its obligations and devotions, neither being able to govern or control as was necessary for the common good. There were some well-intentioned men among them, who valued the public welfare over their particular interests and offered themselves as neutral mediators for reaching an agreement, a dangerous responsibility to accept between two declared factions. Those who are not friends are always judged to be enemies in such situations, and usually end with the hatred of both sides.

If the mediators had not succeeded in preventing the break into arms, Berenguer de Entenza's party would surely have been lost because Rocafort's side included most of the Almugavars and all of the Greeks and Turkish Greeks, who had sworn fealty on his hands and blindly obeyed him. Berenguer had far fewer men than Rocafort did, although they were the better, for the better are always in the minority. Those who were working on the agreement persuaded Rocafort to submit his claim to the twelve counsellors of the Company for their judgment of justice and the rights. They pointed out the great harm to ensue if the matter should come to a break, because, even though he should destroy all of Berenguer's party, it could not be done without great loss to his own, leaving him without the forces to resist the enemies that surrounded him on all sides. These were not the times for taking arms in the interest of personal glory, when the result could be the loss of the whole nation; more credit would be earned by ceding to Berenguer the right that he claimed than by conquering him. Ultimately, Rocafort was convinced, either in apprehension of the damages that could follow or in the belief that the twelve counsellors inclined more to him than to Berenguer, who was also easily persuaded.

The judges declared that Berenguer, Rocafort, and Fernán Jiménez should each command his own men, and that the soldiers should be free to serve under the government that best suited them, without coercion by any of the factions. It was the most appropriate solution that could have been offered in this case, because to declare one captain as the general would have subjected the other to his rival and competitor; either of them would have chosen death to that subjection. Moreover, the twelve did not have the authority to command obedience to anyone they might choose, since they were merely mediators attempting to reconcile the two sides.

After that, the camp became somewhat calmer on the surface, but tempers were secretly angry and suspicious, hoping for the chance to revenge themselves for the insult that each imagined had been done to him. Every man who does not achieve the ambition that he cherishes judges that he has been affronted. Often enterprises are rendered impossible because of the competition among those who command, when they are not governed by some ruler great and powerful enough to repress the insolence of the daring and ambitious. Even though an enterprise is begun with much moderation, malicious interpretations always follow the good or bad events. The discontented become very bold and many good men find that they are obliged to defend themselves. So many intrigues of suspicion, envy, and hatred are raised that it seems impossible to free oneself of them. For this reason, we must judge as quite remarkable that this expedition of the Catalans and Aragonese had been free from that danger for eight years.

When Godfrey led his expedition to the Holy Land, one of the most illustrious reported in the histories, it suffered from this damage in the beginning through the rivalries between Tancred and Baldwin and between Bohemond and the Count of Toulouse.[2] In some men ambition is always more powerful than piety, which was the primary motive of that undertaking.

Fernán Jiménez de Arenós was permitted by the agreement to separate himself from the rest of the Company and to command his men alone. But he chose not to part from Berenguer de Entenza, deeming that he would not lose reputation in obeying a man who was equal to him in blood and older in years. In addition, very few people followed him. Since they feared Rocafort, Berenguer and Fernán united their forces in order to command more respect and deference.

REFERENCES

1. Entenza belonged to the small, exclusive class of *ricos hombres* or great nobles with privileges that made them almost equal to their monarchs. The spoils of all conquests had to be divided between them; the king was forbidden to confer fief or honor on those outside of their ranks. They had the rights of private war and of renunciation of allegiance to their sovereigns at will, and were exempted from corporal punishment. The nobility of Aragon and Catalonia were fewer than in other Spanish provinces, such as Castile, more united, and, consequently, more formidable.

2. Godfrey of Bouillon, the Frankish baron who became the "Defender of the Holy Sepulchre," led the first crusade around the eastern end of the Mediterranean in 1096. Among his followers were Count Raymond of Toulouse; Bohemond, the son of the Norman knight, Robert Guiscard; Bohemond's nephew, Tancred; and Godfrey's brother, Baldwin. They all became embroiled in disputes with each other over the rule of the cities they conquered. Each of the knights, except Raymond, swore fealty to the Emperor of Byzantium, Alexius I Comnenus, agreeing to return to his control any territory that was wrested from non-Christians. Bohemond even offered his services to Alexius in the post of Grand Domestic to the Empire. But all except Raymond, who had refused the oath, ignored their commitment to return the cities of Asia Minor. Raymond and Bohemond fought over the rule of Antioch, which was captured on June 3, 1098. Tancred and Baldwin disputed over Tarsus on the route to Cilicia down to Jerusalem. Raymond lost out to Bohemond, who remained as king of Antioch, and led the crusade on down to its goal at Jerusalem. But there he again failed to take power, as Godfrey managed to become the ruler of the Holy Land.

Forty-Eighth Chapter

ROCAFORT BESIEGES NONA AND BERENGUER, MEGARIX;
MARTINO ZACCARIA, THE GENOESE, TAKES THE
TOWN AND CASTLE OF FRUILLA WITH
THE HELP OF THE CATALANS

ALTHOUGH ALL APPEARED to be peaceful after the agreements, neither faction felt secure and both continued to live full of distrust. Their hatred grew each day until they reached the point that all opportunity for harmony was closed. Since every man had been forced to join a side, no neutral mediators remained to investigate those matters that always occur requiring jurisdiction. Danger kept them apart, now that other reasons could not. Berenguer went to besiege Megarix, while Rocafort, in rivalry, went to besiege Nona, sixty miles from Gallipoli and thirty from Megarix. The distance still seemed short for resentful feelings, particularly for the men of Rocafort's party, who regarded Berenguer's daring to compete against them, the superiors, as an insult. The Turks, Turkish Greeks, Almugavars, and some knights followed Rocafort, while the Aragonese and all the nobles who served at sea were with Berenguer. Since Muntaner as the supply master had to remain at Gallipoli, he was not obliged to declare himself for either side. Consequently, he was the only man left with the confidence of both factions.

About this time a Genoese named Martino Zaccaria,[1] the governor of the town and castle of Fruilla, came into the service of the Catalans with a vessel of eighty oars. He arrived because he hoped that the Catalans would help him take revenge for an insult. He had been governing the castle for five years with care and fidelity, according to his report, in the name of a dead uncle, Benedetto Zaccaria.[2] Another uncle of his, who had inherited the place, then came to Fruilla and quarreled with Martino over the investigation of certain accounts. When this uncle returned to Genoa, his nephew received warning that he was sending four galleys to seize him. The Genoese felt the affront and sought to revenge himself, but could not make himself master of the castle because he did not have the forces to sustain himself alone nor enough people he trusted to overthrow the friends of his uncle. Consequently, he went to Gallipoli, hoping to receive from the Catalans what he wished.

When he did not find the generals, he explained to Muntaner the occasion that brought him. He offered to serve faithfully, so that Muntaner entered him and twelve armed knights on the books to receive their share of the profits. It was the supply master's custom to assign salary to certain knights and distinguished men for more soldiers than they actually brought, in order to give them an advantage. Martino then requested of Muntaner that the Catalans give him men, offering to put into their hands the town and castle, from which they could draw great profit. Muntaner did not concern himself with the justice and logic of the deed, but only with the obligation to help anyone who asked his aid and put himself under his protection. He gave Martino arms, horses, and other requirements to prepare his men, whose number was fifty. He gave him additional support troops, since Muntaner, a mortal enemy of the Genoese, did not wish to lose this opportunity of doing them some damage. He gave to his cousin, Juan Muntaner, and four Catalan counsellors the responsibility for the support, charging them to do nothing without consulting Martino Zaccaria.

The day after Palm Sunday the expedition departed from Gallipoli with a well-armed galley and four smaller vessels. They sailed off to the castle of Fruilla, arriving on the night before Easter. The young Zaccaria, resentful of his affront, carried out his determination. He disembarked his men in the silence of the night and set up his ladders. Thirty of Zaccaria's Genoese and fifty of the Catalans climbed the walls. When the morning dawned, the invaders were discovered and the entrance defended against them, but they fought valiantly, reaching and opening the gates from the inside so that they could give free entrance to those remaining without. More than five hundred men who were defending the castle put up a strong resistance at first, though they were not so well armed nor resolute as were their attackers. Some captives were taken, but most of them escaped in flight. After the fortress fell, the defenseless town, inhabited by Greeks, was then assaulted at once before the natives could organize any resistance or hide their property.

The spoils were rich. In addition to the gold, silver, and fine clothing taken, they found in the castle three great relics that had been pawned to the Genoese, Benedetto Zaccaria, by the Turks. According to tradition, Saint John the Evangelist, of whom we have spoken before, had left them in the sepulcher. One was a piece of wood from the Cross at the point where Christ had rested his head. Saint John had worn this fragment hanging from his neck all the time that he lived among mortals, as Muntaner reports. It was then in a gold setting with very precious stones. There was also a white priest's gown, worked by the hands of the Virgin and worn by Saint John when he said mass. There was in addition a copy of the Revelations written by the saint himself and bound in covers of magnificent art.

Since Juan Muntaner and Martino Zaccaria decided that Fruilla was too far from the Catalan fortresses to be sustained by their power, they abandoned it. The Genoese had taken satisfaction against his uncle, and all the others had taken much gold. With that decision, they returned to Gallipoli, where they repaid Ramón Muntaner and the others their shares. Of the relics Muntaner received for his good fortune the wood of the Cross, which would surely have reached these kingdoms if this great treasure had not been stolen from him on the Black Sea together with the rest of their property. Encouraged by his recent success, Martino Zaccaria resolved to undertake an expedition to win a place where he could establish himself. Muntaner gave him some men for this enterprise also, with whom he was able to take a castle on the Island of Tarsus a little later. He maintained it, not without great advantage to our nation, as we shall see presently.

REFERENCES

1. Moncada writes the name "Jaquería." Martino Zaccaria belonged to the powerful Genoese family that controlled at this period many islands of the northern Archipelago in the Aegean Sea, the Sea of Marmara, and the Black Sea, as well as the sea passage from the Mediterranean through the Dardanelles. This adventurous ruler, who became lord of the large islands of Tenedos, Lesbos, and Chios, married Jacqueline, the daughter of Rainald de la Roche of the French Burgundian house in 1327, and died in 1345.

2. Benedetto Zaccaria, who served as admiral for the French king, Philippe IV the Fair, took the island of Chios from the Byzantine Empire in 1304. His base was Phocaea on the coast of Asia Minor. The Genoese and Venetians, who controlled the southern islands, were rivals in the Aegean Sea, at war in 1294, but at "eternal peace" in 1299. Andronicus II Palaeologus supported the Genoese in this struggle, but his grandson, Andronicus III, and John Cantacuzenus took the Genoese islands in 1346. By that time the Zaccaria family was well established in mainland Greece: Bartolomeo Zaccaria ruled Boudonitza in Neopatras, and Asen Zaccaria was Grand Constable of the Morea in 1389-90. By 1416 Prince Centurione Zaccaria was powerful in Achaea.

Forty-Ninth Chapter

THE KING, DON FADRIQUE, SENDS THE INFANTE FERNANDO,
SON OF THE KING OF MAJORCA, TO COMMAND THE
COMPANY AT GALLIPOLI IN HIS NAME

AFTER THE CAPTAINS had divided the men in the siege of Nona and Megarix, the Infante, Don Fernando,[1] son of the King of Majorca, arrived at Gallipoli with four galleys. He came at the order of Don Fadrique, the King of Sicily, who had decided that it was important for the fortunes of his House to send a person posted by his own hand to command the Company of Catalans at Thrace. They had themselves called upon Fadrique and pledged the oath of fidelity. He did not take into account, perhaps, that this had happened five years earlier, when they had been compelled by necessity, but that now he might find some difficulty in being accepted.

The Infante undertook the mission as he had been charged only to serve the King, with the understanding that he would not marry in France without his cousin's consent and that he would govern those states in his name. When the Catalans' arms were proved to be superior to those of the Empire, they were held in such estimation that the Kings of the House of Aragon did not wish to relinquish their obedience, even to a prince of their own house. Don Fadrique was a ruler of singular prudence and grand master of the art of reigning. He had not wanted to risk his reputation on the Catalan Company, because he took them for lost when they came to ask for help. Neither did he choose to declare himself as an enemy of Andronicus until he saw the Emperor without forces to defend himself. But events turned out so differently from what had been expected that the King's decision, reached with so much deliberation, ultimately failed, as we shall see, to have the effect that it would have had if he had helped the Catalans earlier.

The people in Gallipoli were extremely pleased by the arrival of the Infante, particularly Muntaner, who was a great and passionate servant of the House of Aragon. Although those to be found there were few, they received Fernando as the King's lieutenant without difficulty or objection, and, as the first to receive him, were given thanks in the king's name. Messages were sent to the three principal captains, Entenza, Rocafort, and Fernán Jiménez, to inform them of the Infante's arrival and to forward to them the letters that he carried from the King, explaining that he had come to govern in Fadrique's name. Muntaner provided fifty horses and a larger number of pack animals for the service of the royal household. Then, because his dwelling was the best in Gallipoli, he moved out of it and gave it to the Infante.

Berenguer was engaged in the siege of Megarix, thirty miles from Gallipoli, when he received the news of the prince's coming by the two knights that Muntaner had dispatched to tell him together with the letter from the King. He departed immediately with a few men, being the first of the captains to arrive in Gallipoli. He welcomed the Infante and pledged fealty to him as his general and supreme ruler. After him came Fernán Jiménez de Arenós from Modicus, following Berenguer's example in everything. These two noblemen felt that their situation was improved, because, as the less powerful party, they were always fearful of Rocafort. With the arrival of the Infante, it appeared that everything would calm down and that matters, in a turmoil because of the violence of one man, would return to their proper order, with each man being esteemed according to his own merits and qualities. There was universal joy, in Berenguer's faction as well as Rocafort's, even though the latter was clearly annoyed by the untimely coming of the prince and would surely have denied his obedience then if he had not been aware of the pleasure that this new event was giving his men. Rocafort found himself in a perplexing situation: he was a man of wisdom and foresight in all his counsels, but he had been unable to foresee with his usual shrewdness this event that it had never occurred to him to fear. After consulting with his intimate friends on the matter, he decided that it was suitable to show much pleasure at the Infante's arrival, as being what all of them had desired. But he explained that the siege was so well underway that he did not dare to leave it to come offer his obedience and, therefore, he petitioned on behalf of all his men that the prince's party should come to Nona, where they awaited him with great anticipation. This was the substance of his response to the Infante, and meanwhile he persuaded his relatives and confidants to concur with his opinions and plans.

When Rocafort's message came back to Gallipoli, the Infante chose not to make a decision on the matter without the opinions of Berenguer de Entenza and Fernán Jiménez, as well as of some of the other captains who were devoted to his service and knowledgeable in the schemes and designs of Rocafort. They all agreed that delay was dangerous, so that the Infante should depart at once before the army's pleasure in his coming could cool and Rocafort should have more time to conclude or undertake new plans against the service of the King, or to exclude Fernando's person from the command.

With this resolution the Infante arranged for his departure, accompanied by most of the men of Berenguer de Entenza and Fernán Jiménez, but not by the captains themselves, as they felt it would be inappropriate for his rivals to be present in a strong position with the Infante on his first appearance, before he had the opportunity to win the good will of Rocafort and his men. Consequently, these two grandees deferred their departure until after the Infante had received Rocafort's pledge at Nona. Then they believed that a reconciliation would be possible once he had established his full authority.

REFERENCES

1. Prince Fernando was the fourth son of King Jaime I of Majorca, who had in turn been the third son of King Jaime I the Conqueror of Aragon (1208-1276). The reign of Fernando's father was a long and troubled one, interrupted for a period when he and his older brother, Pedro III of Aragon, were at enmity over the rule of the Balearic Isles, which their father had left independently to Jaime. Fernando died in 1316 on another journey to Greece.

Fiftieth Chapter

THE INFANTE IS EXCLUDED FROM THE GOVERNMENT
AT THE HANDS OF ROCAFORT

THE INFANTE LEFT GALLIPOLI as well accompanied as possible, taking with him of the well-known captains only Ramón Muntaner. After three days of traveling along the coast, he reached the camp, where he was received with universal rejoicing. Rocafort feasted him with great demonstrations of pleasure during the days that he remained to discuss his uncle's[1] orders. The prince hoped that Rocafort would have the courtesy to accept him without the necessity for his demanding it of him a second time, but since he saw that the captain was postponing his obedience to the King and was pretending to ignore the matter, Fernando told him that he wished to deliver the King's letters to the Company and to tell them orally the intention of his coming, for which he wanted the general council called together. Rocafort obeyed with a display of great pleasure and offered to summon the council the following day. For in the few days that the Infante took to arrive, Rocafort had warned his friends to send the word through the camp that it would be well to move cautiously in their determination to accept the Infante on behalf as King, and at least an immediate decision should not be made. This was done very carefully, always with the fear that when the army saw the Infante, it would choose to acclaim him as King and accept him. The idea seemed wise and prudent to everyone, since the ignorant common people rarely penetrate underlying intentions; therefore, they carried it out.

The next day the milling multitude of the general council, which included everyone who was paid wages, collected in the camp to await the Infante. He appeared in the company of his household and many captains and handed the letters to a secretary, ordering him to read them to the public. When they had been read, he explained to them briefly that the King had accepted the oath of fidelity that their envoys had sworn to him, as they had begged him to do. Even though he knew that it would not be materially profitable for his kingdoms to undertake the defense of the Catalans, he had wished to show the love that he bore for them, subordinating his interests to theirs. Therefore, he was now sending one to command them in person in his name and was promising that he would always be ready to go to their aid with major support. They answered him, in accordance with Rocafort's desires, that they would come to an agreement among themselves over what they must do, and then would respond to him. With this, the Infante left them and went to his lodging.

Rocafort remained with the army, uncertain of the decision that so many people together might take and fearful of some knights who, although they were his friends, desired that the Infante would stay to command them. He told the crowd that the subject they had to discuss could not be handled well among so many, since a multitude always engendered confusion, which was not conducive to consideration of the small details and difficulties that are involved in a matter of so much weight. Consequently, fifty persons of the greatest credit and confidence should be selected to talk about and discuss the advantages and disadvantages of the proposition before them. They would come to the decision that seemed best to them and explain it to the others so that all together they could freely condemn or approve it, a method that would obviate the problem of communication among so many.

Rocafort's opinion was accepted as sensible; when the common folk incline to believe a man, they follow him in everything without distinction between his good and bad counsels, because they are governed more by will than by reason. Then they named fifty men to discuss with Rocafort, not realizing that it is much easier to influence the few than the many. With this step he had accomplished his end, because the fifty were almost all hand picked by him, and the few he was not able to trust equally with the rest were easily persuaded; besides his own men did not lack well-founded arguments in support of Rocafort's arguments. The fifty met with Rocafort, who spoke to them as follows:

"Friends and comrades, the arrival of the Lord Infante has been one of the greatest and most fortunate events that we could desire. He has been sent by the powerful hand of that King who even until today has favored us to the great advance of our name and the confusion of our enemies. Our labors have come to an end now and our full prosperity has begun since we have such proper pledges from our kings, to whom we can safely surrender our lives and liberty. We should, however, accept this prince not as he wishes, as lieutenant for his uncle, but as our absolute ruler in his own right, without subjection or any dependence. If the choice of ruler is ours, I would hold it a great mistake to take one who is absent and occupied in governing great states, instead of him who is unoccupied and free of other obligations, who will always live among us and share our fortunes in prosperous or adverse events. If we receive Don Fadrique as king, we subject ourselves to practical servitude, because he is not able to be with us in person and must send someone else to govern in his name this victorious army and the provinces that we have subjected.

"What greater misfortune could come to us than, as a reward for our victories, to find ourselves governed by some other hand than that of our own ruler? And the King himself, Don Fadrique, will look to our defense only so long as it does not interfere with that of the Kingdom of Sicily. Then why should we accept such discrimination? The labor, danger, and losses are for us alone; but not only does the King receive more of the glory and profit than we do, he gets it safely. If we lose, we are left dead or in dire servitude, while Don Fadrique remains free and as great a ruler as before; if we win new states and provinces, they all become his. With these unequal conditions, would anyone who found himself free to choose give his obedience to a ruler under such terms? Furthermore, are you satisfied with the wages that we were given when we left Sicily? It was little more than the biscuit and sustenance that one would not deny to serfs and slaves.

"No, friends, it is not advantageous to us to accept Don Fadrique as king, since he did not remember us at the time that we asked his aid and it was so important to us to have it. But now that it suits him, it is no longer of any profit to us. This is obvious now, for he does not send us arms, men, supplies, money, or anything necessary for war, but rather a chief and general to govern us, as if we had need of that and could not go on to win many more victories without having him imposed upon us by the King.

"Let us not consent to the rewards for our services being distributed by the hand of his ministers and governors, who are always more passionate than honest, more moved by their own interest than by the common need. Since they do not intend to remain in them, they deal with the provinces as with the temporary possession of another's property, enjoying the present without any care for the future. Moreover, since the King is so distant, our complaints would reach him very late, if they were heard at all, and his help would be about as prompt as what he sends us now — six years after the time when we urgently requested it.

"In view of these matters, I am at last resolved that we should reject Don Fadrique in favor of Don Fernando. We have with us a ruler for whom we can venture our lives, and let him be a witness, since he is to be a judge, of the services that we do for him; and let him be as concerned for us as he is for himself, since our lives and preservation will share the same fate as his. Let Don Fadrique be content with Sicily, which our valor won and kept for him, and let him leave to his nephew, Don Fernando, the travail of an uncertain and dangerous war, ruined provinces, and the lone hope of conquering new kingdoms and holdings."

After this speech the few doubters that there were agreed with Rocafort's opinions. Then two of the fifty elected reported to all the camp the decision that they had taken, offering all of Rocafort's arguments. All approved the resolution as wise and determined to give the answer to the Infante then. The fifty went at once to present the message to him. As a good knight, Don Fernando answered them that he had come on behalf of his uncle, whose forces and authority he had accepted with his responsibility for that enterprise. He explained that he would be failing his obligation if he did not punctually carry out the orders of the one

who had sent him. In no case could he accept the offer that they
made him, instead of receiving him as the lieutenant for his uncle,
Don Fadrique. Rocafort spread the rumor that the prince could not
accept the offer immediately in order to palliate his conduct to the
King. He deceived most of the army with this claim. If anyone
had been able to persuade them that the Infante would in no case
stay to govern them as ruler, they surely would have accepted him
in the King's name.

A fortnight passed in this discussion, during which the Infante always believed that the offer was a matter of compliment
to him and that in the end they would obey the King. In the
meanwhile, with all of the Turks and Turkish Greeks at Rocafort's
disposition, as well as his faction of the army that followed him,
the others, who were the weaker group, did not dare to contradict
the captain. Moreover, the entire army that was under his command was determined not to accept the Infante as the King's re-
presentative. The truth was that he did not intend to exclude Don
Fadrique in favor of Don Fernando, because he would not remain
in power with either one. But, as a shrewd man, he recognized the
Infante as one of the best knights of his time, who would not be
dishonest with his uncle, the King. Therefore, he had proposed to
the army to deny the King in preference for the Infante, knowing
that he would not accept the proposal. With this deceit Rocafort
was able to get most of the army to declare for the Infante against
the King; afterwards they did not wish to choose the one they had
previously excluded. Rocafort plotted all these schemes, confident
that even though they were afterward discovered, they would not
injure him because he had the Turks, Turkish Greeks, and the
men he trusted, who were the greater part of the army, on his side.

It cannot be denied that Rocafort had some bases for his stand
in this matter, even had he been a man of more restrained character. After winning so many victories and commanding the army
for five years, he could in justice reject a superior favored by his
greatest enemies, Berenguer de Entenza and Fernán Jiménez, who
would always be preferred for their rank and closer friendship.
Even though the Infante had left them at Gallipoli in order to
allay suspicion, Rocafort's misgivings were not removed. This

very care to foresee the external appearance of things served in itself to increase his suspicion. He always believed that Berenguer
and Fernán had too much confidence in the prince, and he in
them, especially since they expressed no resentment when he did
not include them in his company. Nothing can penetrate and discover more than can jealousy and the fear of losing such a superior post as Rocafort had, particularly when they occur in a man
of such ability and experience.

REFERENCES

1. King Fadrique II of Sicily was not in fact Prince Fernando's uncle. They were
first cousins as the sons of brothers, Jaime I of Majorca and Pedro III of Aragon.
It is not likely that Moncada, a devoted subject of Aragon-Catalonia, would be in
error about this relationship. Instead, the deferential designation of Fadrique as an
uncle may reflect a difference in age that suggested another generation, or, more
likely, a matter of rank between a reigning monarch and a prince who would probably not reach the throne. Ordinarily only crowned heads called each other
"cousin." Fernando did not come to the throne of Majorca because of his early
death, but his son did. Since the oldest brother, Jaime, was a Franciscan friar, the
next one, Sancho, reigned from the time of their father's death in 1311 until his
own in 1324. He was married to Marie of Naples, but left no children. Then the
third brother, Felipe, came to power, but within a year he had entered the priest-
hood. By that time Fernando was dead. Their sister, Sancha, had become the second
wife of King Robert I the Wise of Naples. Fernando's young son, whose mother
was Isabelle de Sabran of the Villehardouin family of French crusaders in Greece,
became Jaime II the Unfortunate — last King of Majorca, losing the throne to his
Aragonese cousin in 1349.

Fifty-First Chapter

ROCAFORT TAKES NONA BEFORE THE INFANTE LEAVES THE
COMPANY; AND THE CAPTAINS AGREE TO ABANDON
THE FORTRESSES OF THRACE AND MOVE
INTO MACEDONIA

W HEN THE INFANTE, Don Fernando, came to the
Company, the besieged Greeks despaired and surrendered with
great losses at the hands of their conquerors within a few days.

Although they did not lose their lives, they were left without property. Berenguer de Entenza also took Megarix.

The Catalans were then beginning to suffer from a lack of food, because the area around Gallipoli for a distance of ten days' march was destroyed and laid waste. During the past five years of the seven that they had been in this province, they had lived on what the earth produced without cultivation, since they did not go near the trees and vines except to harvest the fruit. Eventually the latter gave out and they were forced to consider searching for a place in other provinces where they could live and maintain themselves. The move had been deferred because the enmity between Entenza and Rocafort was still so keen that they did not dare to shift their lodges or meet together for fear that the two rival factions would reach a break. To such a degree can enmities and personal interests prevent the common welfare: people prefer to perish with them rather than to yield in their mad, vain pretensions and live.

Everyone agreed to abandon Gallipoli and the other fortresses, including the rival captains, the Turks, and the Turkish Greeks. Therefore, those good men who were free of passions begged the Infante not to leave them until he established them in another province, because his authority and name could provide safety and in the meanwhile it might be possible to settle the differences between Entenza and Rocafort. The prince took this suggestion and agreed to go along. From what I can gather, he was moved by pity for Berenguer de Entenza and Fernán Jiménez de Arenós, who would be left in the hands of Rocafort, who out of respect for the Infante apparently was checking the action of his vengeful spirit. The prince sought to see whether by this delay he might reconcile their differences and leave them in peace and harmony in order that they could, united and in accord, achieve greater successes, and would, he continued to hope, eventually obey the King even though for the time being they had declined him.

The Infante met with the principal chiefs of the army and all those of the council who were determined to leave their fortresses in Thrace at once because of the food shortage, and discussed what route to follow and which city to occupy in Macedonia.

Opinions differed, but ultimately it seemed wiser to attack the city of Christople, located on the confines of Thrace and Macedonia, because the way into the two provinces would be easy and the retreat secure. The inhabitants would be powerless to prevent sea support, as at Gallipoli, where once the strait had been occupied by a few war ships they blocked any free shipping that came by sea to bring help. Ramón Muntaner was charged with bringing the thirty-six ships that there were in the fleet, including four galleys in which the women, children, and old people would be transferred by sea to the city of Christople, after all the fortresses held on those coasts by our people had been abandoned: Gallipoli, Nona, Pactia, Modicus, and Megarix.

The Infante and the captains arranged their departure in this order: Berenguer de Rocafort, with the Turks, Turkish Greeks, and most of the Almugavars, was to leave a day before Berenguer and Fernán Jiménez and would preserve this order on the journey, with Berenguer following Rocafort at a distance of one day's march. This was done to prevent the opportunities for quarrels that would occur if the two parties shared encampment, where they would inevitably come to blows over the taking of encampment positions. They decided that it would not be dangerous to divide their forces, because there was no enemy in the field strong enough to mount a sudden attack against them. Since they were separated by one day on the road, help would not be available if they needed it. But all the warriors of the cities were more concerned to defend themselves than to confront our army, an effort that they had so often undertaken with serious damage for themselves and glory for ours.

When all the other fortresses had been abandoned, the Catalans gathered at Gallipoli, from which Rocafort and his men departed on the road nearest to the sea. They were followed the next day by Berenguer de Entenza and the Infante, who always occupied the posts that Rocafort had just left. After some days of marching, they began to come into the more densely populated parts of the province where our arms had not penetrated before. The Greeks, terrified by the Catalan name, fled inland, leaving in their towns

abundant provisions. The Company moved in comfort, finding itself free of the danger and of a lack of food, a situation which the
soldiers had feared. This was one of their great enterprises, passing through unknown lands and provinces, with no security of a
central stronghold or any friendly ruler. The expedition of ten
thousand Greeks that Xenophon[1] described was one of the greatest
celebrated in antiquity, but their goal was always to reach their
homeland, using their arms only to cross foreign provinces and
nations. At the end of the Catalans' journey, however, they would
not find the repose of their homeland, but rather an attack upon
a great, strong city that they had resolved to storm before they
left Gallipoli. For them the end of one great dangerous and fa-
tiguing effort was the beginning of another even greater one.[2]

REFERENCES

1. Xenophon (434?-355? B.C.), Greek essayist, historian, and author who studied
under Socrates as an Athenian lad, marched with Cyrus's army into upper Asia.
There he was suddenly elected general upon the death of Cyrus at Cunaxa and later
retired to write the *Anabasis, Cyropaedia,* and *Hellenica.*
2. June of 1307.

Fifty-Second Chapter

BERENGUER AND THE INFANTE'S VANGUARD OVERTAKE
ROCAFORT'S REARGUARD, ALMOST CAUSING A BATTLE;
ROCAFORT KILLS BERENGUER DE ENTENZA, AND
FERNAN JIMENEZ DE ARENOS FALLS INTO
GREEK HANDS AS HE FLEES
THE SAME DANGER

ROCAFORT AND HIS ARMY reached a village at two
days' journey away from the city of Christople, located on a plain
abundant with fruit and water. The houses were empty of people,
but full of bread, wine, and other things — not only necessities,

but also pleasure and luxuries. They stayed in such comfortable lodgings longer than experienced, well-disciplined soldiers should have. Near noon time they still had not left, because the men, scattered out on the plain, enjoying the fruit to be found on the trees, had delayed there so long that they could not be collected any sooner.

Meanwhile, the vanguard from the Infante's camp, led by Berenguer de Entenza, started out from their camp earlier than usual, so that it overtook Rocafort's rearguard. They had departed before dawn in an effort to escape the sun's heat — and without realizing it, found themselves upon Rocafort's men. The rearguard was startled, turned to see Berenguer's men so close behind them, and believed that they were being attacked. Arms were taken up in great confusion; the vanguard of one group and the rearguard of the other closed together.

When Rocafort recognized his opponents, he was certain that they had come determined to carry out some evil intent, since there could be no other reason for Berenguer to change their arrangements without warning. A suspicious man never reflects on or considers explanations that would allay misgivings, only those that increase them. He did not think about his carelessness in delaying their departure until noon or why Berenguer de Entenza could have risen so early. At any rate, either through such a line of thought or by taking advantage of the opportunity of having his enemy in his hands, he ordered his men to mount and did so himself, armed from head to foot. They rode out furiously against Berenguer de Entenza's men, who were already being attacked in a cruel and bloody skirmish.

News of the disorder reached the Infante and the other captains. Berenguer de Entenza rode out ahead, unarmed except for a hunting javelin, as the person of greatest authority to stop his men and draw them back. Berenguer de Rocafort's brother, Gisbert, and his uncle, Dalmau de San Martin, saw Entenza rushing into the dangers of the skirmish, where it appeared to them that he was encouraging his men against the others. Or, what is more likely the case, they saw their chance to satisfy their ill feeling and to get rid of their kinsman's rival; Gisbert and Dalmau closed in on him. Berenguer de Entenza, the good and innocent knight, turned when he saw the two brothers bearing down on him and asked: "What is this, friends?" At the same moment, they each wounded him with a lance thrust, so that the brave and valiant knight fell dead from his horse, unable to defend himself because he had gone unarmed and heedless among his comrades.

The fight raged on more fiercely after the death of Berenguer, with the Rocaforts taking their vengeance by slaying many of his party. There could have been no greater cruelty than Rocafort's killing and tearing to pieces the conquered men, after having beaten and killed his rival, since Berenguer's people, after losing their leader, had no choice but to accept and obey the other chief. But his pride and arrogance were such that he was now making war, not against his enemies, but against his own countrymen, inhumanly calling on the Turks and Turkish Greeks to finish off all Berenguer's band to the last man.

Fernán Jiménez de Arenós was traveling unarmed with the same fecklessness as Berenguer de Entenza, and when his men were retreating before sword blows, he was informed that Berenguer had been killed and that he was being eagerly sought for the same fate. And so he left the field with the few men whom he could gather behind him and decided that he would be safer surrendering to the Greeks than to Rocafort. He went to a nearby castle, where he was received under security under the condition that he should present himself before Emperor Andronicus.

The Infante attempted to protect and defend Berenguer's men, going out armed with a few knights to oppose courageously the Turks and Turkish Greeks in Rocafort's attendance, who were subjecting everyone to the rigor of their swords. The Infante's presence was so effective that Rocafort placed himself at his side in order that the Turks should maintain their respect and then retired his men, after having killed Berenguer and so many people of his faction so treacherously. One hundred fifty horsemen and five hundred soldiers died that day, most of them from the companies of Berenguer de Entenza and Fernán Jiménez de Arenós.

After the tumult had quieted and the men separated to their own banners, Rocafort and the prince met at the center of the field where the body of Berenguer lay. The Infante dismounted from his horse, took the dead man in his arms, and wept bitterly, as Muntaner reports. While he embraced and kissed him more than ten times, the grief was so universal that even his enemies themselves cried. He turned to Rocafort and told him in bitter words that the death of Berenguer was the evil work of some traitor. The captain replied humbly that his uncle and brother had not recognized the chief until after they had wounded him. The Infante was forced to be satisfied with this explanation since he did not have the men to punish such daring. If he had not found himself with so few people, he would doubtless have made some demonstration.

He ordered that the army remain two days for the burial of Berenguer's body and the obsequy to his memory, for he wished to honor him as well as he could; and so it was done. They placed him in a hermitage of Saint Nicholas that was nearby, next to the high altar. It was a tomb hardly worthy of his person, if we consider the humility and obscurity of the place where they left him; though a celebrated and well-known one, for it was located in the heart of the enemy provinces, with an inscription and epitaph that are fame itself, preserving and spreading the memory of the illustrious heroes who lacked magnificent sepulchers in their own country, since they had perished in lands won and kept by their valor.

So died Berenguer de Entenza, noblest of blood and celebrated for his deeds, esteemed both by native and foreign kings. In his early years he served his rulers, first in Catalonia and then in Sicily, with great reputation. There he made friends and acquired property by following the road that fortune offered him to win glory and rise to an estate equal to his merits. His possessions in his homeland were vast, but not so great that the limited boundaries of the barony we today call Entenza could have contained his generous and gallant spirit. Berenguer was brave and gallant in the face of any danger, strong in fatigue, constant in decisions, and as well known for his adverse as for his successful enterprises. At the peak of his power he suffered a long and arduous imprisonment, from which he had scarcely been freed and returned to his own people, and just when fortune had begun to show itself favorable again, he died by treachery at the hands of his comrades, at the height of his hopes.

After the disturbance had been calmed, the Infante sent for Fernán Jiménez, promising him the security of his word to come to him. But Fernán answered that the prince must pardon him because he was not now at liberty to obey his orders, having offered to present himself with his company to Emperor Andronicus. The Infante excused him, and Fernán Jiménez, after collecting his men, went to Constantinople. There Andronicus received him with signs of pleasure that he was entering his service. As an effective demonstration of his good will, he gave the captain his widowed granddaughter, Theodora, as wife[1] and the rank of Grand Duke that had been held by Roger and afterward by Berenguer de Entenza. With this favor, Fernán Jiménez became the best rewarded of the captains of the Catalan expedition, the only one who maintained his position of dignity and escaped a disastrous end.

REFERENCES

1. On the Barcelona manuscript the following comment appears: ". . . such a thing is not told in the rest of the Histories; the curious reader should read them." (Gili Gaya, p. 297.)

Fifty-Third Chapter

THE INFANTE LEAVES THE COMPANY, TAKING MUNTANER
WITH HIM AFTER HE DELIVERS THE FLEET

WHILE THE INFANTE remained at the place where Berenguer had been killed, his four galleys arrived with their captains, the knight, Dalmau Serran, and Jaime Despalau of Barcelona. Relieved to have the ships so that he could separate himself from Rocafort, he ordered a meeting of the general council at which he petitioned once more for their acceptance in the name of his uncle, Don Fadrique. When they did not wish give it, he resolved to depart.

Rocafort, author of the past decision when the same proposal was made to them, was even more powerful now. Since he had no rivals who would contradict him, it was easy to bring all the camp to his opinion because his will was now stronger than that of any individual man. They answered the Infante as they had before, and with more determination. After this he realized that his mission was impossible, despaired of it, and sailed with his galleys, leaving Rocafort the absolute master and lord of the Company. He returned to the island of Thasos, six miles from the mainland where the Catalans were camped.

The Infante arrived at the island at almost the same time as Muntaner with all the fleet. After he had reported Rocafort's evil and the loss of such good knights as Berenguer de Entenza and Fernán Jiménez de Arenós, the prince commanded him on behalf of himself and the King that he should not leave his company. Muntaner obeyed gladly, being rich and fearful of Rocafort, even though he was his comrade. The friendship of an insolent man in power must always be feared, because it can be easily dissolved, leaving the stronger man free of restraints on the expression of his fury or whims.

Muntaner asked the Infante to wait for him with the fleet while he gave an account to the captains of the camp of what had been charged to him, which included most of their possessions and all their wives and children. The prince agreed to delay, after which Muntaner took the fleet to the beach where the army was encamped, one day's journey beyond where the Infante had left them. He allowed no one to disembark until he was assured that there would be no injury to the women, children, and property of the men of Berenguer de Entenza and Fernán Jiménez and that they would be left free to go where they wished. With these guarantees secured, he disembarked all those who wanted to go to the castle to which Fernán had retreated. They were given fifty carts and two hundred Turks and Turkish Greek cavalry with fifty Christians to escort them to the fortress. Those who did not wish to remain with either Rocafort or Fernán were given armed barks for Negroponte.[1]

The camp was busy with these preparations for two days. Now that he wished to leave, Muntaner called together a general council and delivered to them the seal and records of the Company. He told them that the Infante, Don Fernando, on behalf of the King and himself, had ordered the supply master to follow him, which he was bound to do, but would not until he had discharged all that had been commended to him. He said that he was grieved to leave them, although his conscience did not permit him to stay after their evil action. They had given such cruel recompense to those who had commanded and served them as their generals: Berenguer dead from their excesses and Fernán Jiménez delivered to an uncertain fate among the Greeks.

Muntaner dared to make these statements because he could depend on the Turks and Turkish Greeks, whom he had always treated with much affection and they had reciprocated, calling him "Kata," or "father" in their language. Even though Rocafort should command it, they would have undertaken nothing against him. The whole nation joined in urging him to remain, including the Turks and Turkish Greeks, who continued to urge Rocafort to detain him. But he was resolved to depart from them, especially since he had spoken with some liberty in favor of Berenguer de Entenza and Fernán Jiménez and did not wish to place himself in danger or give Rocafort the small occasion he would need to put him to death, as he had the others.

So Muntaner left the Company with a twenty-oared vessel and two armed barks, in which he carried the property of his comrades, servants, and himself. He reached the island of Thasos, where the Infante waited for him and where they stopped for several days to take on supplies and plan the navigation for their voyage. They were detained also by the good reception that they were afforded by Martino Zaccaria, that Genoese who had sacked the castle of

Fruilla with Muntaner's aid and afterward occupied the one on that island. With demonstrations of great pleasure, he delivered to them the keys of the castle, placing his life and property at their disposal. Doing a good turn is always profitable, with the recompense often coming from one least expected to give it. What is lost in many favors is occasionally repaid by one assistance so great that it is worth more than all that the others have cost. Muntaner and the Infante found security in the port and luxury in what he gave them for sustenance, all because the captain had once helped the Genoese, albeit for his own interest and profit at the time.

REFERENCES

1. The long off-shore Greek island east of the Attican peninsula was Euboea to the Greeks and Negroponte to the Latins. Negroponte was also the major city there, on the site of the ancient Greek Chalcis.

Fifty-Fourth Chapter

THE COMPANY MOVES INTO MACEDONIA

WITH MUNTANER GONE from the camp, Berenguer de Entenza dead, and Fernán Jiménez escaped, Rocafort was left absolute lord and master of all. Consequently, his desires and caprices ruled all of the council's decisions. The plan that all the captains had made before they left their fortresses was for attacking Christople and strengthening their position in it as they had done at Gallipoli, so as to be near to the two provinces of Thrace and Macedonia for their raids. At the beginning the undertaking seemed easy, because they expected to catch the Greeks by surprise without time to prepare themselves.[1] That plan surely would have come out as well as they thought it would if they had not stopped four days on the way to revenge their private insults or passions.

This delay gave the Greeks time enough, not only to defend themselves, but also to attack and defeat the invaders, had there been among them a single man of courage and foresight. Delay in the execution of war is very pernicious; whatever speed can be mustered is useful indeed. The loss of one day, one hour, or even less time, has meant for many the loss of great opportunities and occasions.

When Rocafort heard that the city was posted in defense, he resolved to cross the pass of Christople on the sea side of Mount Rhodope and not to delay in attacking the place. The following day the whole camp came through the pass, not without great fatigue on the rough road with their abundant baggage, women, children, and sick people. Although the Greeks were warned of the route that the Catalans had taken, they could not or dared not venture to impede their passage. On the other side of Mount Rhodope nearly eight thousand men of war from all the nations forming the army came down into the fields of Macedonia, an army large enough for any enterprise had their spirits been united. But Berenguer's death had made Rocafort despicable even to his own comrades, because since that time he had become too vain and offended them.

At the end of autumn the Company found itself in the middle of the province of Macedonia, surrounded by powerful enemy towns that had not yet suffered from the war. But the destruction in Thrace, the nearest province, served as warning to the inhabitants to prepare themselves within their cities, bringing in the harvests from the fields. For this reason, the Catalans were careful to choose a well-provisioned site for their winter encampment, exploring all the land and considering positions that they could occupy where they could gather enough food and supplies that might be bought with blood or money. Finally, after having done great damage throughout the province, they established a stronghold in the ruins of ancient Cassandria.[2] It was one of the better locations of the province, since it is near the sea in an area which is fertile and placid because of the many bays and fjords formed by the sea.

From there the Catalans could easily, or at least with more ease than from any other place, make their incursions inland, and keep Thessalonica, the capital of the province, in continual anxiety of losses.[3]

REFERENCES

1. The move began in the spring of 1309.
2. This was Potidaia of the ancients, a deserted city on the narrow isthmus that connects the peninsula of Cassandria to Macedonia.
3. On the route to Cassandria, the Catalans apparently raided and sacked the Christian religious communities of Mount Athos, located at the tip of the easternmost Acte peninsula below Macedonia. Their attacks are recorded in the legends of the monastery of Khilandari, even though King Jaime II the Just had expressly ordered the Company to spare the monks. (Setton, p. 5.)

Fifty-Fifth Chapter

DON FERNANDO'S IMPRISONMENT AT NEGROPONTE

WHEN THE INFANTE left the island of Thasos with Ramón Muntaner, he ordered that the best galley, the one called the *Española,* should be delivered to the quartermaster. With these four galleys, an armed vessel, and Muntaner's bark, they kept sailing along the coast of Thrace and Macedonia as far as the port of Halmyros in the Duchy of Athens. When he previously had been there, the prince had left four men to make hardtack in preparation for his return. But he found that, against their faith and the word they had given, the natives had taken the hardtack and mistreated the four men who were making it. He took satisfaction for the injury he had received by disembarking his men onto the land and sacking the town of Halmyros, where everything was put to blood and fire.

When they had sacked the city and thus made up for their past loss, they went on to the island that Muntaner calls Espol; I believe that it is the one called Skyros today.[1] They sacked all the island, but attacked the castle unsuccessfully. From that point they took the cape on the island of Euboea, where the Infante wanted to enter the city of Negroponte because he had been well received and entertained there when he had first come to Romania. Muntaner and the other experienced captains warned him, however, that it would not be prudent to risk his person and those who went with him, after they had sacked cities that belonged to the Duke of Athens, with whom the lords of Negroponte were allied.

But he did not credit their good counsels and, using his absolute power, went into the city in evident danger. There they discovered in the port ten Venetian galleys that had come in at the instance of Charles of France, to whom the Pope had given investiture for the kingdoms of Aragon when the King, Don Pedro, had occupied Sicily. The ships had brought a French knight, Thibaut de Cepoy,[2] to discuss new federations and alliances in Greece in the name of his ruler, Charles. He was particularly interested in the Catalans, whose help Charles was hoping for. He had considered coming in person to assume the rights that he claimed to the Empire, and to overthrow Emperor Andronicus.

The Infante no longer had the option of retreating or repenting because such behavior would cause great suspicion. But before he disembarked, he asked for assurance on their word that he would not be offended. First Thibaut, then the captains of the ten Venetian galleys, who were named Juan Tari and Marco Misot, and the three lords of Negroponte gave their word apparently with great pleasure. With this guarantee, the Infante believed that he was secure.

He went ashore, where they had invited him in order to reassure him more and to take from the galleys their major defense, which was the presence aboard of his person with those who always accompanied him, including Muntaner. He had scarcely put foot ashore when the ten Venetian galleys fell upon his ships and Muntaner's vessel, to which many people rushed who had heard that there were great riches on board. As they boarded the vessel, they killed almost forty men who tried to defend themselves and at the same time took as captives the Infante and as many as ten of the more important men who accompanied him. Thibaut then delivered the person of the Infante to Sir Jean de Maisy, lord of a third of Negroponte, who was ordered to take him to the Duke of Athens in the name of Charles of France. The Duke's decision would be awaited for the disposition of the person of the Infante. He was taken to the city of Athens with eight knights and four squires. There he was delivered to the Duke, who ordered him taken to the castle of Saint Omer under heavy guard, where he remained a prisoner for some days.

REFERENCES

1. Scyros or Skyros is a rocky island of the Northern Sporades group in the Aegean Sea east of Euboea. Many legends are attached to it, including accounts that Lycomedes there killed Theseus and that Odysseus found Achilles, where his mother, the nymph, Thetis, had disguised him as a woman among the daughters of King Lycomedes in an attempt to keep him from the Trojan War. The English poet, Rupert Brooke, is buried there. Muntaner, however, may have intended Scopulus or Skopelos, which means "rocky observation spot," which is nearer to Halmyros than is the island of Skyros. (Gili Gaya, p. 201.)

2. Thibaut de Cepoy was a plenipotentiary of Charles of Valois, a French prince who hoped to take advantage of the fact that the Byzantine Empire was in turmoil to gain the throne in Constantinople. Thibaut appears as Theobald, Tibaldo, Tibal, Thibaud, and Thibault de Sipoys in works by Latin writers. He soon gave up on his mission to win control of the Catalans for the service of Charles. He abandoned them in Thessaly when he realized that they were pursuing their own concerns without regard for their oath. Cf. Ostrogorsky, pp. 440-444.

Fifty-Sixth Chapter

ROCAFORT AND HIS MEN SWEAR FIDELITY TO THIBAUT DE
CEPOY IN THE NAME OF CHARLES OF FRANCE

AT THIS TIME Thibaut undertook to bring Rocafort and all the Company into the service of Charles, attempting to gain their good graces by any means that he could. He did not lack people to advise him that nothing would work better to win Rocafort's will than the surrender to him of two of the prisoners they had taken: one was Muntaner; the other, Garci Gómez Palacín, a great enemy of Rocafort. Thibaut accepted this advice and, without further inquiry, embarked Muntaner and Palacín in his galleys and set out in person for the cape of Cassandria, where Rocafort and our people were.

No sooner had he arrived in their presence than he presented to them the two prisoners, believing that they would be a means to gain Rocafort's friendship. For this very reason the friendship turned out to be so unfortunate, for it was based on the death of an innocent man. Both of the prisoners were surrendered to Rocafort, but they had different fortunes. One was taken away to be put to death, and the other was placed in liberty. They honored Muntaner with a great show of joy, but Rocafort ordered that Palacín's head be cut off, without granting him more time to live than it took for the executioner to kill him. And not one man dared to argue with Rocafort about him. It does not cause me wonder that a man as vile as Rocafort could be found among so many soldiers and captains, but it does surprise me that not one man of good will was there who would stop or object to Rocafort, warning him that such an inhuman and untimely execution would injure his own fame and darken his own deeds! Garci Gómez Palacín was a valiant Aragonese soldier and an honorable but unfortunate knight, a principal captain and defender of the party of Berenguer de Entenza and Fernán Jiménez de Arenós. By this deed, unworthy of any man who is a human being, Rocafort lost friends and reputation. To put to death a knight who was going conquered to his homeland, where he could neither offend nor hinder Rocafort's grandeur, was a manifest sign of cruelty and ferocity.

Muntaner, who had been master of supplies and ordered all the official matters of the pen, had won over the spirits of all the soldiers with his courtesy and his honesty. And so they loved him as a father, unusual though it may be for soldiers to revere a man engaged in military office work. Usually they hate and distrust such officers, who seem to them to be shirking labor and relying on tricks and red tape. They believe that the office staff members become enriched and promoted to the detriment of the fighting men, who always live in a wretched state with countless labors and dangers. Muntaner was received with general rejoicing and given one of the most honorable lodgings that they had. The Turks and Turkish Greeks first presented him with twenty horses and a thousand escudos, followed by Rocafort with a very expensive horse and other valuable objects. There was not a person of consequence in the whole army who failed to give him something. Thibaut de Cepoy and the Venetian captains who had delivered him were embarrassed to see that the man they had robbed of all he had was so honored. They feared that he might do them some injury by spoiling their plots and pretensions, but Muntaner was wise, realizing that it was not safe to remain in the Catalan camp, so that he neither favored nor impeded them.

Until then Rocafort had been doubtful about accepting what Thibaut de Cepoy was offering him on behalf of Charles of France, restrained by his respect for the House of Aragon. But when he became convinced that by refusing to accept the Infante for the King, Don Fadrique, he had made enemies of the kings of Aragon, Sicily, and Majorca, he agreed to what Thibaut desired. If the Company would receive the Frenchman as its general in the name of Charles of France, the men were promised an advantageous salary and great hopes, which represented what he would be able to give them. Accordingly, they swore fidelity to him, obliged, as well as I can judge, by the violence of Rocafort, since it seems impossible that the Catalans and Aragonese who had rejected their natural ruler would voluntarily consent to a foreign, enemy one. Nor would Rocafort have had such an intention except for his security in the Turks and Turkish Greeks and part of the Almugavars, who blindly obeyed him. What Rocafort did, however, appears not to have been an act of treason because he did not take up arms against his rulers, but merely separated himself from their service, a common and legal custom in those days, particularly when grievances had preceded.

It was not for enmity against the House of Aragon nor love for that of France that Rocafort so acted, but rather to align himself with the ruler who was then less powerful, so that he could more easily separate from him when his own affairs came to the state in which he hoped to see them. There were rumors abroad that Rocafort planned to name himself king of Thessalonica or Salonika, which were not without some foundation. He had changed the seal of the Company, replacing the image of Saint Peter with a crowned head — evidence of his high and daring thoughts. Such hubris comes to the man who has in his hand a victorious and devoted army. I believe that those ideas were more than thoughts and that he certainly would have become an absolute ruler, if his great pride and avarice had not blocked the steps of his prosperous fortunes at the time that he was offered a state in which he could have founded and glorified his house.

I am sure that if Rocafort had been alive when the Catalans occupied the states of Athens and Neopatria they would not have called the King of Sicily, but instead would have received the general for their prince and ruler. This title would have been justly placed because Rocafort had been their leader for so many years, through times of so much hardship. Under his command and government they had achieved many victories and brought to glorious ends many distinguished enterprises.

As soon as the Venetian galleys saw that Thibaut was general of the Company in the name of Charles, they returned to their homes, taking Ramón Muntaner with them. The Catalans strongly urged him to remain, but since he knew how fickle Rocafort's character was, he never considered staying, even though Thibaut himself earnestly requested it.

Fifty-Seventh Chapter

MUNTANER RETURNS TO NEGROPONTE WITH THE VENETIAN
GALLEYS AND VISITS DON FERNANDO IN ATHENS

BY ORDER OF THIBAUT, Juan Tari, admiral of the Venetian galleys, gave a ship to Muntaner for the transportation of his comrades, servants, and clothing. He himself sailed in the flagship with Tari, who served and entertained him with extreme courtesy. In addition, Thibaut gave Muntaner letters for Negroponte in which he ordered the restoration of all that had been taken from his galley when the Infante was captured, under penalty of loss of life and property for anyone who concealed goods. With this favorable dispatch, Muntaner left with the Venetian galleys for Negroponte, where they arrived in good time. There the letters from Thibaut to the Chief Justice of Venice were published. The penalties for those who did not return goods were publicly proclaimed. Jean de Maisy and Bonifacio da Verona, as rulers of the island, also made the same proclamation when they saw the letter from Thibaut, who was supreme minister from the King of France in that region. Little attention was paid to the notices, however, because they were published only to satisfy Thibaut by their proclamation. Muntaner did not collect anything of his losses, nor did he receive any other recompense for them.[1]

As a true servant and vassal of the Infante,[2] Muntaner asked Juan Tari for leave to go to the city of Athens to visit and console the prince in his prison. He explained that since he had been born subject to his House, he could not neglect to go to him in the distressing condition of his imprisonment. With much deference, Tari offered to wait four days for him at Negroponte, enough time for him to visit the Infante and return, since Athens was only twenty-four miles from the port.

Muntaner departed with five knights, going to see the Duke when he reached the city. Although he was sick, the Duke ordered that his visitor be shown in and received him very courteously. He spoke earnestly to the Catalan about his regret for the incident at Negroponte when his galley had been stolen and assured him that in whatever he needed he promised to help him. Muntaner replied that he deeply appreciated the kindness and honor that were shown to him, but that he desired only to see the prince, Don Fernando. The Duke gave him permission with much civility, ordering that while Muntaner was with the Infante any others who wished to could enter the castle and visit him.

They were then given free entrance to Saint Omer.[3] When

Muntaner saw the Infante, tears served him instead of words to express his sorrow at seeing the prince's person in the hands of foreigners. Instead of receiving some consolation from Muntaner, it was the Infante who gave it, encouraging his friend with words of great courage and steadfastness. Muntaner spent two days in his company, talking about means that must be undertaken for his liberty. At length he asked to remain himself to serve and assist Fernando in the prison, but the Infante would not consent to this because he believed that Muntaner would be more useful to him by going to Sicily to treat with the King about his liberty. He gave him letters for the King, charging him as an eye witness to report to his uncle all that had happened in Thrace and Macedonia on the matter of his acceptance in the King's name. Muntaner gave his farewell, and went back to the Duke for his permission to return. He was given some jewels that were of great value to him, because he had left to the Infante all the money he had brought with him, as well as dividing up his clothing among those who served the prince.

After Muntaner had returned to Negroponte, the galleys departed, sailing along the coasts of the Morea until they reached the island of Sapiencia. There they met with four galleys of Riambau Dasfar, of whom Muntaner had already had word. The Venetians, always suspicious, as are the people of a republic, drew away with Muntaner, asking him if Riambau Dasfar was a man who would keep faith. The Catalan replied that Riambau was a good knight who would not do damage or be an enemy to the friends of the King of Aragon, and that they could safely come together and honor him. With this, the Venetians were calmed and Muntaner passed over to Riambau Dasfar's galley. Then they all joined together, the captains inviting each other with great familiarity and security.

They arrived at Glarentza, where the Venetian galleys remained. Then Muntaner joined Riambau's fleet, in whose company he returned to Sicily. At Castronuevo he met with the King, to whom he gave a long account of what had happened, together with the Infante's letter. The King showed much concern, writing at once to the Kings of Majorca and Aragon so that they might help to free Don Fernando. In the meanwhile Charles, brother of the King of France, wrote to the Duke of Athens, requesting that he send the person of the Infante to King Robert of Naples. The Duke obeyed, and thus the prince arrived at Naples a captive. He remained for a year a house prisoner, for he went out to hunt and dined with Robert and his wife, who was the Infante's sister.[4] His father, the King of Majorca, arranged for his liberty through the King of France. Fernando then went to Collioure to meet his father.[5]

REFERENCES

1. Fifty years after Muntaner attempted to regain his property, the Serenissima, as the government of the Venetian Republic was called, in February 1356, paid to his granddaughter one tenth of the value. This was done in connection with diplomatic negotiations between Venice and the House of Aragon. (Miller, p. 217.)

2. The Catalan knight remained a devoted subject to the Prince until the latter's death nine years later, when Muntaner wrote that "he was the best knight and bravest among all the kings' sons of that day, and the most upright and the wisest in all his acts." (Miller, p. 256.)

3. This great castle was built by the Theban magnate, Nicholas II de Saint Omer, on the ruins of the ancient city of Cadmea in Thebes, largely out of the vast wealth of his first wife, Princess Marie of Antioch. Only one tower now remains of what was once "the finest baronial mansion in all Romania." (Miller, p. 165.) The castle, famous for its frescos picturing contemporary scenes, was destroyed by the Catalans between 1331 and 1335, presumably by order of the Vicar General, Nicholas Lancia, when they feared it would fall into the hands of Gautier II of Brienne, legitimate heir to the duchy of Athens through his father, who had been killed by the Catalans. It was in this edifice that the original of the famous history of Greece, the *Chronicle of the Morea,* was found. Since that manuscript is not extant and the copies we have are in popular Greek, French, Italian, and Aragonese, the author's language is uncertain.

4. When King Charles II the Lame of Naples died, his third son, Robert of Calabria (1278-1343) became King on May 5, 1309. Robert had married Yolanda, or Violante, the sister of Jaime II the Just of Aragon when he was twenty, but she died five years later. He then wedded Sancha, daughter of Jaime I of Majorca, when her brother, Fernando, was brought to the Angevin court. King Jaime I received his son in Collioure of the Aragonese province of Roussillon in the eastern Pyrenees. He was then nearing the end of his long reign in 1311.

5. Despite his disappointing experience with the Catalans, Prince Fernando returned to Glarentza in 1315 to undertake to rule as "lord of the Morea" the Peleponnesian peninsula, for or in alliance with them. He planned to press the hereditary claims of his wife, Isabelle de Sabran, to the lands in Achaea won there by her ancestors among the Frankish crusaders. Her grandfather had been Prince Guillaume de Villehardouin (1246-1278), and her cousin was now on the throne of Cyprus. But he died the next year in the battle of Manolada, fighting Burgundian swordsmen on the classic plains of Elis on July 5, 1316. (Miller, p. 202.)

Fifty-Eighth Chapter

THE IMPRISONMENT OF BERENGUER AND
GISBERT DE ROCAFORT

AFTER THEY HAD accepted Thibaut as their captain general, the Catalans swore fealty to him in the name of Charles, the brother of the King of France.[1] They maintained the base at Cassandria, supported by raids and incursions that they made inland, as far as Thessalonica, where the Empress was with all her court. This ambitious woman had collected all the treasure and riches of the Empire of the Greeks for the promotion of her sons, in grave injury to her stepson, Michael, his father's legitimate successor.

While Rocafort, suspecting no change, was concerned with his enrichment and grandeur, the end of his prosperity and the beginning of his misfortunes overtook him.[2] This usually occurs when a man feels the greatest confidence and security: thus the instability of human affairs may be clearly recognized and that no one, no matter how powerful, can be assured of himself alone, because the causes of his advancement are the same as those for his ruin. The first reason and motive that his enemies had for overthrowing him was their awareness of his deep ingratitude for what he owed to those of his own kind and blood. Besides being cruel, he was also greedy and lascivious, insufferable vices in those who command, because life, honor, and property, the greatest values of mortal man, are always in danger. His enemies had the desire to take satisfaction and vengeance for the insults they had received from Rocafort, but they hid it in fear until they had the pretext of the little deference and respect that Rocafort had for Thibaut. Secretly they began discussions about the captain's liberty, believing that they would find in Thibaut an offended man who would repay the insults that were common to all of them. They told Thibaut that he should help them escape from their hard servitude and that the insolence of Rocafort should be put down, for he had forgotten how a good governor and captain should behave according to natural laws, unscrupulously using his power for acts both illicit and beyond all reason. He treated free subjects as slaves and the property of others as his own. It was now time to punish Rocafort's evils, and to end his labor and dangers; since Thibaut was supreme chief, he should apply the suitable remedy and avenge so many wrongs.

Thibaut, alone and a foreigner, fearing that they might be spies sent by Rocafort to probe his attitude, answered with equivocations, neither charging Rocafort nor discouraging his accusers. The Frenchman was very prudent and experienced; although he had been wronged by Rocafort, he sought to find the most diplomatic way to restrain him. Since his principal motive for coming had been to win the army to his side, he did not pay attention to his own personal authority, but to what was important to the ruler whose minister he was.

His first approach was to talk to Rocafort in great secrecy and to ask him to take his pleasures in hand, pointing out to him the harm that they could cause him. But Rocafort, little accustomed to tolerating people who presumed to restrain or correct his disorders, answered Thibaut so harshly that he was obliged to use a more violent recourse. Despairing of being able to keep Rocafort in the service of his ruler unless his base actions were consented to, he decided to revenge himself upon him and to leave the Company. But he disguised this determination until a son of his came from Venice, where he had sent him some months before, with six galleys. When they arrived within a few days, Thibaut, seeing that his retreat would be safe, sent with great secrecy to ask the conspiring captains to inform him what their firm decision was in the matter of Rocafort. They replied that he should call a meeting of the Council, and at it he would learn the results of their determination. Thibaut understood, and the next day called the Council together, announcing that he had important matters to deal with in it. Rocafort arrived with his customary insolence and arrogance.

In the first discussion that was proposed, they all began to make their complaints of him. But since up to then there had not been a man who would dare to contradict or openly challenge him, he became strangely excited, trying to trample them under foot as was his wont with angry face and harsh words. Then the conspiring captains rose one by one from their seats, surrounded him, and multiplied their complaints, reminding him of the wrongs that he was doing to all. So saying and doing, they seized him and his brother, who were unable to resist because the conspirators were so many and so resolved. As soon as they had taken both brothers prisoners and had delivered them to Thibaut, they assaulted Rocafort's house and sacked everything. They stretched military license, as is usual in such cases, without being detained by the respect that they should have felt for the walls of one who had been their general for so many years, and who had defended them so often with his sword and courage.

REFERENCES

1. King Philippe IV the Fair (reign, 1285-1314) was the older brother of Charles of Valois and Louis of Evreux. They were all sons of King Philippe III, who ruled from 1270-1285.

2. Rocafort was at this time negotiating with the French Duke of Athens, Guy de la Roche, for a marriage with the Duke's half sister, Jeannette de Brienne. Guy sent two minstrels as envoys to Cassandria, where discussion went on for some time before it was dropped.

Fifty-Ninth Chapter

THIBAUT LEAVES THE ARMY, TAKING THE TWO CAPTIVE
BROTHERS TO NAPLES, WHERE THEY ARE KILLED

ROCAFORT'S IMPRISONMENT produced different effects, since his friends, as participants in his crimes, were grieved and would have made some effort toward freeing him if they had not doubted that such a grave step could have been undertaken without the thorough preparation of help and support. Moreover, they still were not sure which were friends or declared foes, an important question to those who must deal with unexpected and sudden matters. The Turks and Turkish Greeks, who were faithful to Rocafort, remained so stunned and aghast after the deed that they were unable to take any resolution. The Almugavars were divided; most of them loved him, but others hated him. All the gentility and the nobility, as the most offended parties, were among those who had fervently sought his perdition.

The night that Rocafort was captured was full of turmoil and suspicion. Then in the morning it seemed calmer because they learned that Rocafort and his brother were alive. When it appeared to Thibaut that the army was off guard and more secure, one night with great secrecy he embarked with the two Rocaforts in his galleys and set sail for Negroponte, deceiving all our Company. In the morning when they saw that the galleys had departed and that Thibaut had taken the brothers, all became very angry, saying that even though Rocafort had such base habits, he was their captain, and that they did not find it right to surrender him to his enemies, who would mock him and our nation and put him to a vile and insulting death that would disgrace everyone. They said that if Rocafort had merited it, the army should have punished him at their own hands instead of placing him in those of his greatest enemies.

With this talk, spirits became more and more enflamed, stirring Rocafort's intimate friends to the point that the Turks and Almugavars took up arms against those who had taken a principal part in his capture, pursuing them into their lodges with incredible fury and passion. They killed those who they came upon, without a soldier or knight daring to resist them. Such were the inclination and affection of the soldiers toward Rocafort that his evils and base dealings with his friends were never able to erase it, nor on this occasion could they be calmed until they had avenged him and satisfied themselves at their pleasure. In this insurrection or mutiny fourteen officers most widely known as Rocafort's enemies were left dead, as well as many other people among their followers and servants who had tried at the beginning to resist. It was a remarkable fact that our men, situated in the midst of their enemies, underwent civil war continuously for three years, shedding more blood than they had in all the other wars with foreigners. And, although civil wars usually do not occur when battles are going on with aliens, it did so happen with the Catalans, who were attacking the enemy and killing one another at the same time.

Thibaut arrived with the two captive Rocafort brothers at Naples, where he delivered them to King Robert, their mortal enemy. The source of this enmity was Berenguer de Rocafort's unwillingness to surrender some castles in Calabria[1] that belonged to Robert, under the terms of the peace made among all the kings, until the King satisfied the balance of their wages to him and his men. Kings regard as an insult and great impudence a demand of them by violent means for payment for services; therefore, although Rocafort was by then satisfied, Robert always nurtured his resentment of this insult. He then ordered that the two brothers be taken to the castle at the city of Aversa, locked up in a dark prison, and left there without being given anything to eat until they died.

Berenguer de Rocafort was the most fortunate and valiant captain that there had been in many ages, and the most worthy of praise if his vices had not increased at the same pace as his prosperity. He had served the King, Don Pedro, and his sons, Don Jaime and Don Fadrique, as captain. Then, with new plans, he had joined Roger in Asia, where he had gone with no small forces. At the death of Corbarán de Alet he became Seneschal, field marshal, and general of the army. After Roger's death and the imprisonment of Berenguer, he governed for a period of five years without competitor, destroying many cities and provinces during this time. He won three battles with a very unequal number of men, one of them against an Emperor of the Orient; maintained a war during this time in the center of the enemy provinces; and finally crossed from Gallipoli to Cassandria with his army, burning and destroying all that opposed him. He was never beaten, not even in small skirmishes. He triumphed over all his enemies, always conqueror in all civil and foreign wars. But the end of all this good fortune was a grievous imprisonment and a wretched death, although, in the opinion of all, it was a very just punishment from heaven for the innocent blood of his friends that he had spilled, as well as of many others who had died unjustly at his hands.

Gisbert de Rocafort shared the same fate as his brother, although, according to what can be gathered from the historians of those times, he had not proceeded as dissolutely. He was, however, participant and companion in many of his crimes, especially in the murder of Berenguer. Perhaps he was less noticed because he did not have his brother's position; vices are observed more in those of greater fortune. About who these knights were, or from what family they came of the many in Catalonia with that surname, Muntaner is silent. It is the same case with many others who went on this great enterprise, whose names he did not even mention. This was surely a noteworthy error or oversight, and an occasion of grave harm to the noble houses still existing today in these kingdoms who had ancestors in this most distinguished expedition.[2]

REFERENCES

1. The Rocaforts had fought for King Fadrique of Sicily against Prince Robert of Calabria, who had been sent as lieutenant in 1299 by his father, King Charles II of the House of Anjou, in the struggle over the rule of Sicily. In the same year Robert lost a great land battle at Falconaria, followed by the siege of Messina that ended in August of 1302. The two rivals agreed on the treaty of Caltabellota during the next year, by which Robert would retain the mainland part of the kingdom as King of Naples and Fadrique the island as King of Trinacria, the ancient name of the island of Sicily, for his life time. But some of Fadrique's supporters refused to relinquish the property they held in the heel-and-toe region of Calabria after the settlement. Among these was the Aragonese fortress at Le Castella in the old olive groves on the Ionian coast near Isola di Capo Rizzuto and the Sila and Le Serre Mountains.

2. Among these is the house of Moncada. The family name does appear frequently in subsequent histories of the expedition. Matteo de Moncada served as Vicar General of Athens and Neopatras (1359-1367), ruling on behalf of the Duke from the House of Aragon. His son, Guillermo Ramón de Moncada, held the title of Count of Augusta and was active in the politics of the Aragonese crown at the end of the fourteenth century. (Setton, p. 100.)

BOOK FIVE

THE CATALANS ELECT GOVERNORS AND OFFER TO SERVE
THE DUKE OF ATHENS WHEN HE SOLICITS THEM

AFTER THE WRETCHED affair of Rocafort and those
who followed him, the Company remained not only without a
chief, but also without persons capable of such responsibility. The
government of a people so varied, accustomed to obeying famous
captains and growing old under their command, hardly could be
turned over to one who was not equal to his predecessors in valor
and nobility of blood. Roger de Flor was the man who first had
governed them, a leader, as was said, very remarkable among all
the captains of his time. Then had come Berenguer de Entenza,
illustrious for his blood and deeds, followed by Rocafort, famous
for his victories. In addition to these, there had been many knights
and captains of renown who could have occupied the post, but
they had all perished through the cruelty of Rocafort, who had
always sought their ruin as rivals and competitors. There is no
argument, good or bad, that a man will heed when he has at
stake a great position and he cares not whether the means he uses
to acquire and keep it are good or evil, provided that he is successful in his intent.

The Council met to elect a chief and, considering their lack of
leaders, they decided to name two knights, a chieftain, and an
Almugavar, all four to govern the camp together, under the
council of twelve. They were occupied with this problem of leadership for some time in Cassandria, where they received ambassadors
from Count Gautier of Brienne, who had succeeded to the Duchy
of Athens after the death of its Duke,[1] the last descendant of
Bohemond,[2] who had left the state to the Count, his first cousin,
because he lacked successors. Roger Deslaur, a Catalan knight and

native of Roussillon who served the Count, brought this message. He offered them the treaty on the part of his lord, which provided that if they should come to his service he would give them wages for six months in advance and the same advantages that they had had in the employ of Emperor Andronicus. But it was questionable that they would be able to go to serve him unless he gave them a fleet in which to reach him, because the journey seemed impossible by land, since they had to cross so many provinces, almost all hostile, full of broad rivers and rugged mountains, nearly all unknown to them. In spite of all these difficulties, all the agreements were signed against the time when they might be able to serve him.

Our men spent the following winter in some need of provisions, so that, as the time passed, they talked of abandoning Cassandria and attacking Thessalonica, the capital of the provinces, where the major enemy forces were. The Catalans and Aragonese were certain that if they won this city, they would be able to found their empire in it with much security and to acquire the greatest riches of the Orient, because Irene, the wife of Andronicus, and María,[3] the wife' of his son, Michael, resided there with all their court.

These counsels were not as hidden from Emperor Andronicus as they thought, and he undertook at once to make ready, because he knew that the Catalans had the courage for undertakings so great and seemingly impossible. He sent experienced captains to Macedonia to raise men for the defense of the principal cities. He ordered that the harvests of all fields be collected inside them, in order to insure against the harm that would be caused by a lack of provisions, as well as to leave the land in such a condition that the enemy could not maintain himself with what was left on it. He also commanded that a wall be raised from Christople to the adjacent mountain to impede the Catalans on their return to Thrace. With these plans it seemed to the Emperor that he could finish off the Catalans without having to meet them face to face, which he never wished to venture, because he believed it impossible to conquer them with force and violence. These efforts of Andronicus came near to turning out well if the valor of our men had not made them vain and unprofitable.

REFERENCES

1. Gautier de Brienne, fifth of that name, succeeded his cousin, Guy II de la Roche in the early summer of 1309. He was the son of Isabelle de la Roche-Bruyeres and Hugues de Brienne, the Count of Lecce in Calabria and Bailie of the Duchy of Athens from 1291-1294.

2. The Norman prince, eldest son of Robert Guiscard, who followed his father on the first crusade into Byzantium. He took the oath of allegiance to the Eastern Emperor, Alexius I Comnenus, to return control of any places he might conquer that had previously been ruled by the Empire. He captured Antioch, then quarreled with Raymond, Count of Toulouse and Viscount of Provence, for its possession. Ignoring his oath, he assumed rule of the capital, but had to defend himself against the Turks. The Emir, Malik Ghazi, captured Bohemond, but returned him to the crusaders for ransom. He then left Antioch to his nephew, Tancred, and went to war against Alexius, who defeated him in 1108.

3. María or Xene of Armenia, the wife of the Byzantine co-Emperor, Michael IX Palaeologus, was in Thessalonica with her husband's stepmother and her children, Andronicus, Manuel, Theodora, and Anna. Before her marriage, her husband had discussed with the House of Aragon the possibility of taking as wife the Princess Yolanda, sister of Jaime II the Just and Fadrique II of Sicily in 1296, but the plan miscarried.

Sixty-First Chapter

THE ARMY LEAVES CASSANDRIA AND MOVES TO THESSALY

OUR MEN LEFT Cassandria, moving in all their strength back toward Thessalonica, which they expected to find as unprepared for defense as a city so great and populous could be. But it was very different from what they thought: for the city was on its guard, with plenty of provisions and warriors. They tried to attack it with a direct assault, but the two Empresses within, attended by the most valiant captains of the Empire, kept the city free. The Catalans, recognizing such a gallant defense, abandoned the enterprise and lodged in the settlements near by, from which they raided the land in search of sustenance. But when they found it empty of people and cattle, they suspected the enemy's plan, which they had not foreseen.

They then attempted to leave, because eight thousand men, not counting their captives, horses, and baggage, were a great number to sustain and live on what the enemy had left of the harvest. Realizing then their inevitable ruin if they were delayed, they determined to return to Thrace by the same road that they had taken to come. But, when a prisoner warned them that the pass at Christople had been closed by a wall and enough people to defend it, they almost regarded themselves as lost. They believed that the Macedonians, Thracians, Illyrians, Acarnanians, the people of Thessaly, and all the neighboring inhabitants were also behind this preparation and would join their forces to attack them or at least would prevent their search for provisions, without which they would inevitably perish. Their extreme need, as always happens, made them resolve to cross all the province of Macedonia and to enter Thessaly, whose people lived without fear of their swords, because they believed that Macedonia and the forces inside it were impregnable walls that would prevent the Catalans from harming them.

Scarcely had they taken this counsel than they put it into execution, so that Andronicus could not oppose it. Thus, they left Thessalonica, gathering together all their forces with incredible diligence, so that the enemy could not impede them at the entrance to the mountains. They traveled through enemy towns, taking from them only the provisions that they needed because the fear of danger was greater than their greed, which they did not delay to satisfy. On the third day they arrived at the banks of the River Peneus that runs between Mounts Olympus and Ossa and waters that very pleasant valley called Tempe, so celebrated in antiquity. In the farm houses and villages on the shores of this river they lodged, where, invited by comfort and the mildness of the climate, they spent the rigor of the winter.

The opportunity to make an easy, safe departure for Thessaly, with abundant supplies that they found in this land, little plundered before by military people, gave them the opportunity for this respite. This was the Tempe Valley so esteemed by the ancients, both for the mildness and gentleness of its air as well as for the religion and spirits that they believed resided in the forests, groves, and river, which they deemed a paradise and a suitable dwelling place for their gods.

When the Greeks learned the road that the Catalans had taken, they were unsure that they might not return and did not wish to anger them. But the invaders were traveling so rapidly that even if their enemies had wished to pursue them, they could not have caught up with them. The Greeks were left with new fears of these people whose energy and valor exceeded all their forces and plans.

Sixty-Second Chapter

THE CATALAN COMPANY GOES DOWN INTO THESSALY,
AGREES TO LEAVE THIS PROVINCE,
AND MOVES ON TO ACHAEA

WHEN SPRING CAME,[1] the army left the valley and went down to Thessaly, without encountering an enemy to oppose them, so that they were free to force most of the peoples who lived on the plain to pay tribute to them. This province was at that time subject to a ruler of little capacity, who was married to Irene, the illegitimate daughter of Emperor Andronicus.[2] He was in discord with his father-in-law because he would not recognize the obedience that he owed to the Empire. At this time, the Eastern monarchy of the Greeks was in its last decline, for most of the subject rulers would not recognize its hegemony. They saw it to be powerless, and hence without rights; for submission is given only to the powerful. In the same way, the Empire of the Romans in the West has come to be only a vain title of its past grandeur, since Italy, France, Spain, and England, which at one time rendered tribute to it and accepted its laws, today see themselves free, since its power has declined, and with that was lost its right to rule; the Goths and other nations from the north reduced it to this misery.

When the ruler of Thessaly learned that these forces now in his state were superior to his, he was able, with the help of good counsel and loyal ministers that he had, to achieve what others had not been able to do with arms: to persuade the Catalans with grants and appeals to leave his state. Thus, with a courteous embassy, after having fortified several cities and defense-works (so that this too might be yet another occasion to persuade the Catalans not to give up a sure thing for a doubtful one), he offered them needed supplies and dependable guides to lead them to Achaea or wherever they might wish. At the same time, he gave them a large sum of money. When one's power is very inferior, using money to win protection from the oppression that is suffered cannot be considered cowardice or disgrace. The commanders and counselors of the army met, and, in consideration of the difficulties and dangers that could occur if they remained in the province, judged as useful and necessary the agreement to depart and move on, for the farther they went to the south, the closer they would be to help from Sicily and Spain. They answered the envoys that they would accept the pact, at which the negotiations were concluded. The ruler then delivered the money and food, and the Catalans punctually departed on the day that they had offered to leave. With this, Thessaly was left free of grave damages by its own intelligent measures, and the Catalans were also spared losses, because war is harmful to all, and often the winner differs only in name from the loser.

The road that our people took was through the mountainous part of the province of Thessaly, called the Vlachia, part of which they were forced to cross. Zurita, when he reported the route of this army, was badly mistaken in saying that the land they passed through was called Valachea. He did not know that there was a province named Vlachia, although he drew the information from Muntaner, who does call it Blachea. Zurita, unfamiliar with this name, corrected Muntaner, calling the land Valachea because of the similarity of the names, but the Catalans did not come within a hundred leagues of Valachea. It should be called "The Vlachia," which, according to Nicétas[3] at the end of his history, is the mountainous land of Thessaly, which falls well within the route that the Catalans took and is named as Muntaner says. Its natives are called Vlacos, a warlike people who had had the eastern Emperors under their power for many years, and even today uphold their name and valor among the Turks. Since then they (the Vlacos) have subdued this barbarous and powerful people. Muntaner is hard put to it to find adequate words of praise for the effort that was expended on this passage through Vlachia, which was with arms always in hand and fighting all the way, such was the resistance that they found in the inhabitants. I understand that one of the greatest accomplishments of this expedition was opening a way through this region, so full of valiant people, veteran warriors.

Finally they came through it at heavy cost, to the universal admiration of those who knew the danger, with the help of their good and faithful guides from Thessaly. They crossed the strait called Thermopylae,[4] celebrated for the three hundred Spartans who died with Leonidas, defending the pass against Xerxes and for the liberty of Greece. From there they went down to the shore of the River Cephisus that flows down from Mount Parnassus[5] and runs toward the east, passing between the people to the north that the ancients called the Opuntian Locrians and the Epicnemidian Locrians and on the south, Achaea and Boeotia. This river reaches Lebadea and Haliartus, where it forks, loses its name, and becomes the Aesopus and the Ismenus. The Aesopus flows down through the center of the province of Attica until it enters the sea; the Ismenus joins the Aulide and discharges into the Euboean Sea, which is called the Negroponte today. In these bordering districts of the Locrians, the Catalans established their camp for the fall and winter, consulting about what to do the following spring.

REFERENCES

1. 1309.

2. John II Angelus Ducas, whose title was Sebastocrator in the Byzantine hierarchy, was married to Andronicus's illegitimate daughter, Irene. John of Thessaly, or of Neopatras as the Latins called the area, was the grandson of the Sebastocrator, John

I the Sickly, and had been a ward of Duke Guy II de la Roche of Athens since his grandfather's death. Though still very young, he did not choose to continue as ward of Guy's successor, Gautier de Brienne.

3. Nicetas Choniates, or Akominatos, was a Byzantine historian and high functionary of the Empire in the twelfth and thirteenth centuries. His history in twenty-one books covers the period from John II Comnenus to Baldwin, 1118 to 1206. (Gili Gaya, p. 333.)

4. The "hot gates" is a narrow pass along the eastern coast of Greece between Mount Oeta and the Gulf of Lamia, now a rocky plain six miles from the sea. In 480 B.C. a small Greek force under King Leonidas of the Spartans held back Xerxes and his huge Persian army there for three days.

5. This double peak in the Parnassus range just north of Delphi was then well wooded with myrtle, laurel, and olive trees below and firs higher up. The snow-covered summit figures in the legends of the gods, especially Apollo, the Muses, and Dionysus, to whom it was sacred.

Sixty-Third Chapter

THE DUKE OF ATHENS RECEIVES THE CATALANS

WHEN THE DUKE of Athens learned that the army of the Catalans had passed over the mountains and crossed the Vlachia, he urgently sent his envoys to the chiefs of the Company, fearing that other neighboring rulers would receive them into their service. Since it was an army of so much renown, everyone tried to win its favor. The Duke, therefore, made great offers of payment and advantageous salaries, reminding them of the word that they had given him when he sent Roger Deslaur to them at Cassandria, that they would come to serve him.[1] When the Catalans heard the embassy from the Duke, his friendship seemed more useful to them than that of the other rulers in the vicinity. Consequently, they concluded the treaty with him, under the same terms as they had when they served Emperor Andronicus.

With this new support, the Duke launched a campaign to retrieve what his enemies had occupied of his state. The nearest and most powerful rivals were Angelo, the ruler of the Vlacos, and Emperor Andronicus, who, as a Greek ruler, hated the Latin name and desired to expel from his state the Duke and the rest of the

Frenchmen who followed him. The Despot of Larta, called Andracia by the ancients, also was threatening him with his arms. Against these three enemies, who were powerful even when divided, the Duke initiated war. He was so fortunate in it that he not only checked the fury and rigor of his enemies and defended his state, but also won back thirty strongholds that they had seized. Ultimately, peace was negotiated and concluded with all of them, very advantageously, however, for the Duke.

None of the events of this war that the Catalans waged against the enemies of the Duke are reported in detail by any historian, but only in general terms of their major events.[2] Nor does there exist any memoir or work from which could be drawn anything that would illustrate these incidents, that were surely very remarkable because the enemies they overcame were powerful in number and courage. It is a great misfortune of our nation that such memorable deeds as these, which could perpetuate our fame in future centuries, are buried in silence.

REFERENCES

1. Roger Deslaur, a private Catalan from the province of Roussillon, was engaged by John of Thessaly to deal with the Catalan Company in the spring of 1310.
2. With the help of the Catalans, Gautier captured more than thirty strongholds in Phthiotis and the Gulf of Pagasae, forcing the Emperor and his ally, Anna, the Despoina of Epirus, to sue for peace within six months. (Setton, p. 8.)

Sixty-Fourth Chapter

THE DUKE UNGRATEFULLY DISMISSES THE CATALANS WHO
HAD SERVED HIM AND REFUSES TO PAY THEM, SO THAT
BOTH SIDES PREPARE THEMSELVES FOR WAR

WHEN THE DUKE realized that he was absolute master in a peaceful state, he did not undertake to fulfill his word to pay our men what he had offered when he had called them into his service. On the contrary, treating them with little respect, he schemed for their ruin: behavior that seems impossible, forgetting such recent and remarkable benefits as the restoration of his state and the checking of such powerful enemies. This change and alteration was strangely surprising to the Catalans and Aragonese, who had expected to live in honor and comfort from his hand from then on, especially since the Duke had been raised in Sicily at the castle of Augusta, showed affection for the Catalans, and spoke their tongue as if he had been a native and it were his own.[1] They were left amazed to find him so changed when more pledges and obligations became due.

The plot that the Duke had devised to free himself of the inconvenience that soldiers could cause in his peaceful state was as follows: he chose from the army two hundred mounted soldiers, those of major service and abilities, and three hundred infantrymen, among whom he divided some properties, modest enough, throughout all his state. These men were left very happy, and the others, too, who expected that the Duke would use the same liberality with them. But when the time came that they believed their hopes would be fulfilled, the Duke ordered them instead to leave his state within a short period, threatening to treat them as rebels and enemies if they did not obey him.

Our men, although they were confused and disturbed by this blow that was so unforeseen, replied to him with their customary valor and determination that they would obey with much pleasure once he had paid them the salary that he owed them, since they had served him so well. He must also pay them the wages for six months in advance that he had offered them when they came to his service, so that they could acquire vessels with this money in which they could return to their homeland safely, though poorly paid. The Duke replied to this demand with so much anger and such ingratitude for their past services that he ordered them out of his presence and out of his land. He said that he neither owed them anything nor wished to pay them what they had so shamelessly demanded, and that they should prepare for their departure immediately if they did not wish to see themselves dead or captured. This answer obliged our men to determine that they would die before leaving his land without receiving entire satisfaction from him. They gave him to know of their resolution, at the same time overpowering some important positions, where the people, although forced to do so, were paying tribute for their support.

When the Duke learned that the Catalans intended to defend themselves, he called large gatherings of people, both natives and foreigners, to throw them out of his state by force, which he could have accomplished with less expense, danger, and display of his ingratitude if he had sent them off with the wages that they had so well merited. In the end he was resolved to expel them forcibly, for which he collected a very powerful army, to which our limited strength was quite unequal. The Athenians, Thebans, Plataeans, Locrians, Tokens, Megarians, and eight hundred French knights reached about sixty-four hundred horsemen and eight thousand infantrymen, although Muntaner claims that there were many more. But in this case, I have chosen to follow Nicephorus, who writes diffusely enough and should have had more information, since he found himself nearer than Muntaner, who was not present on this expedition. But the Greek is more neutral when he writes of the affairs of foreigners, instead of those of his own nation. The two hundred knights and three hundred foot soldiers to whom the Duke had given the properties that were mentioned, seeing the danger of their comrades, believed that the same harshness would also be executed upon themselves afterward. They went to the Duke and told him that they understood he had gathered an army to go against their companions and friends. If this was true, they were renouncing the properties that he had given them, because they deemed it a better lot to die defending their own people than to enjoy riches in peace while the rest were perishing. The Duke, confident of his forces that were so superior to ours, answered them in words so abusive and full of a thousand outrages and affronts that this reply alone would have obliged them to seek vengeance, even if they had not come fully resolved to leave his service. The words of all men should be very measured, but more so those of rulers, because discourtesy can expect nothing but hatred and more often the desire for the pursuit of satisfaction and vengeance. Insolent speech causes just indignation even in the most humble. Courtesy is a bond with which hearts are bound; when used with enemies, it is often the means to soften their hearts in the midst of the greatest impulses of their fury.

After this incident, the five hundred went out to join the rest of the Catalans and Aragonese, warning them of the Duke's final resolution. Nicephorus says that the ruler was so proud and arrogant, seeing so many and such brilliant men under his hand, that his plans grew greater than to destroy the Catalans. This he planned to do as merely incidental to his plot to enter the provinces of the Empire, carrying a cruel and bloody war even as far as Constantinople. But God stopped all these plans at their beginning; for overweening confidence in oneself never succeeds.

REFERENCES

1. Gautier de Brienne had been held a prisoner of the Catalans during his childhood ten years before, as a hostage against his father, Hugues de Brienne, in the stronghold of Gagliano near Syracuse, when the Catalans were fighting for King Fadrique against Robert of Calabria over the rule of the southern part of the Italian boot. (Miller, p. 224.)

Sixty-Fifth Chapter

THE DEFEAT AND DEATH OF THE DUKE OF ATHENS, AFTER
WHICH THE CATALANS COME TO POWER IN THOSE
STATES AND CEASE WANDERING

W HEN THE CATALANS and Aragonese learned that the Duke was marching with all his following against their camp, they did what they had often been forced to do by necessity, which was to rely upon their valor alone. They decided to go out to meet him, although they had to fight with such inequality. Among all three nations, thirty-five hundred horsemen and four thousand foot soldiers made up the Company when they left their quarters to receive the Duke. On the first day they pitched their camp in some pastures, through which a very large irrigation canal crossed, offering them a stratagem and plan important for the ruin of the enemy. The grass of the meadow grew a span[1] high, enough to cover the ground surface. They flooded all the nearby fields, where they judged that the enemy cavalry would make its first attacks. For their own men they left some areas dry, so that when it was necessary they could go out to skirmish on firm, dry ground. The plan succeeded well, because the next day[2] the Duke came out with all the army, so powerful that he was careless in observing the stratagems of the enemy. It seemed to him that the splendor of his arms and regalia alone should suffice to humiliate his enemies.

When he discovered the Catalans, he marshalled his squadrons, sending forward the cavalry in which he had the greatest confidence and taking the vanguard in person with a troop of two hundred French cavalry, the most outstanding of the province. While the Duke was making ready for the battle, our men sought to do the same, mixing the squadrons and troops of the Turks and Turkish Greeks among the Catalans. But these soldiers stood aside, saying that they did not choose to fight, because they believed it impossible that the Duke would come against the Catalans, by whom he had been so well served. They suspected that it must be a trap in which they were to be destroyed as people of a different religion. The Catalans and Aragonese were not disturbed by this resolution of the Turks, although because of the shortness of time they were unable to undeceive them. Nor did they seek to decline the battle; on the contrary, they set out with more courage to skirmish with and bait the foe so that he might the more readily come looking for his own death.[3] The Duke with the first troop of the vanguard rushed to close with a squadron of infantry that was on the other side of the submerged fields, the cavalry furiously pushing forward without noticing that it was in the midst of the marsh. At the same time the Almugavars, swift moving and unencumbered, with darts and swords fell upon those who, weighted down with iron, were wallowing with their horses in the mud and slime.

The rest of the troops came up to help the Duke and fell into the same danger. The Duke, as one who was better known, was among the first to die at the hands of those he had scorned and abused with insulting words a short time before.[4] This is the usual end of the arrogant and overweening, who ordinarily come to perish where they believed that they must triumph.

When the Duke and those of his troop were dead, the rest of the field was left in fear and confusion, now attacked on all sides by the Catalans and Aragonese. The Turks and Turkish Greeks, whose suspicions had been allayed when they saw that our men were cutting down the Duke's troops, went out to reinforce them and gave fulfillment to their victory. Many important men had died with the Duke; of the seven hundred knights who had entered the battle only two were left alive.[5] One of these was Bonifacio da Verona[6] and the other was Roger Deslaur, the knight from Roussillon, well known to the Catalans because he had often come on embassy from the Duke to our captains when they were living at Cassandria. The battle was very terrible and bloody, with the pursuit and slaughter lasting longer than the conquering had. When they had seen that the Duke was dead and the first troops of the cavalry mired down, the soldiers of the rest of the enemy army fell into great disorder, so that it was easy to rout them.

After having won such a remarkable victory, the Company went forward, within a few days overpowering the city of Thebes and then Athens, with the forces of the Duke's state surrendering to them without waiting for a siege, because all of their defense had been lost in the battle.[7] After this, our Catalans and Aragonese were left the lords of that state and province at the end of thirteen years of war. Therewith they brought all their wandering to an end and established their residence, enjoying the property and the women of the vanquished: for when they realized that they were masters of everything without opposition, most of the soldiers married the richer and more prominent persons of the province, founding in it a new state and lordship. Our Kings of Aragon greatly valued this state, since it had been won, not with their own forces nor the common property of their kingdoms, but instead by private men who were their subjects. It is great good fortune for princes to have such vassals, so that the labor, expense, and danger go to the subjects' accounts, while the fruits of the victories, the conquest of kingdoms, the glory of having acquired them and their command and government are for the ruler in whose state they were born.

The Catalans were so lacking in prominent persons and knights who could govern them that they asked Bonifacio da Verona, one of the two knights who were left alive after the battle, to be their captain. But it seemed to Bonifacio that he would have the same authority over them that Thibaut had had, so that he would not accept what they offered him. I find certainly two strange things in this matter: the first, that the Catalans would cast their eyes upon a foreigner and their prisoner to be their captain; and, second, that he did not wish to be it. Disappointed in their will, they made Roger Deslaur the captain and gave to him as his wife the widow of the lord of Salona, a rich and eminent woman.[8] The state was governed for some time by this captain.

REFERENCES

1. Measure of eight to ten inches, approximately the width of a man's hand with the fingers extended. Later historians believe that the grass grew after the plain between Livadia (Lebadea) and Skripou, the Copiac basin, was flooded in the interim before the Franks arrived.

2. Monday, March 15, 1311, on the south bank of the Cephissus River, near the village of Kapraina (Chaeronea to the ancients), located in the northern part of the Boeotian province west of where the river widens into the Copais Lacus.

3. Muntaner reports the incredible number of 24,000 foot soldiers collected by Gautier. When the Catalans saw his huge force, they sent messengers to the Duke, offering to return his castles and go away if he chose to make peace with them. But he demanded unconditional surrender instead, which they refused. They did not have the choice of retreat, either, since a strong Greek force, under the general, Chandrenos, was at their rear in Thessaly. (Setton, p. 10.)

4. Five days before his death, the Duke made his will, in which he asked to be buried in the monastery of Daphne with other de la Roche relatives. (Setton, p. 10.) Many years after the battle, Duke Gautier's head was borne on a black-draped funeral galley to Brindisi in southern Italy and then to Lecce, the home of his ancestors, just south on the coast line of the Italian heel. There it was buried in 1348 under a marble monument next to the altar in the Church of Santa Croce. (Miller, p. 228-29.)

5. Actually several others survived, including Jean de Noyers de Maisy, the Frankish nobleman who had taken Prince Fernando prisoner, and who had died in 1326, and Gautier's brother-in-law, Niccolo I Sanudo, who was the son of Duke Guglielmo I of the Archipelago, and who lived until 1341. Probably others were preserved to

hold for ransom, such as Antonine le Flamenc, the lord of Carditza in Boeotia, when they were known to be rich.

6. The Catalans revered Bonifacio because of his remarkable history. He was the grandson of King Guglielmo I of Thessalonica, of the dynasty founded by the crusade leader, Bonifacio of Montferrat, but his generation was poor; he was the youngest of three brothers who owned one castle together. He managed, however, always to be well dressed and elegant of bearing. When Guy de la Roche, Duke of Athens, chose Bonifacio among other great nobles to do him the service of dubbing him knight, the young man borrowed money to provide one hundred wax candles, decorated with his own arms, for the ceremony. In return, the Duke gave him a gift of money and his cousin, Agnes de Cicon, daughter of a baron of Negroponte, as wife. When Guy died, Bonifacio served as bailie of the estate in the interim before the ascension of Gautier de Brienne. Later he recaptured the former Byzantine fortresses of Karystos, Larmena, and Metropyle, becoming one of the most important Lombard lords in Negroponte by 1296. (Miller, pp. 193-94.)

7. All of the Duchy of Athens was taken from the Burgundians except the cities of Argos and Nauplia on the Peloponnesus, which were held for the Briennes for a time by Gautier de Foucherolles. The Company made its headquarters at Livadia and other Boeotian castles, where the Greek natives admitted the Catalans to the strongholds. In return they received the rights and privileges of Franks, except that of marriage to Catholic women. The Catalans destroyed the great castle of Saint Omer, where Prince Fernando had been held prisoner. (Setton, p. 13.) In another of the huge castles, at Livadia (Lebadea) was preserved the head of Saint George, patron saint of the Catalans, as well as the English. This treasured relic became the center of bargaining in 1354 between King Pedro IV of Aragon and Pope Clement VI in an attempt to have the Church's ban of excommunication against the Catalan Company removed. The Catalans kept the head.

8. This lady was the widow of Thomas III d'Autremencourt, sometimes referred to as Stromoncourt, the lord of Salona and Marshal of Achaea. He was the chief vassal of Duke Guy of Athens and one of the most prominent men of Romania. Salona, called La Sola by the Catalans, was the ancient city of Amphissa in the Parnassus region of Corinth.

Sixty-Sixth Chapter

THE TURKS WISH TO RETURN TO THEIR HOMELAND, LEAVE
THE SERVICE OF THE CATALANS, AND GO BACK TO
GALLIPOLI BY THE SAME ROAD THEY CAME

WHEN THE TURKS and Turkish Greeks saw that their comrades, the Catalans and Aragonese, had ended their wandering and were resolved to found their seat and lineage in that state, they chose to return to their homeland. They determined to separate themselves from our Company, even though the Catalans proposed to them various pacts so that they would remain, offering them villas and places where they could live tranquilly and participate equally with them in the rewards for their victories. But nothing sufficed to detain them, because, they said, it was now time to return to their country and see their friends and kindred. Now that they found themselves with so much riches and prosperity as they had, they especially wished to make their native land the center of their repose.[1]

With this decision the Turks and Turkish Greeks parted amicably from our Company to return to their homeland. They took the same route over which they had come when they traveled with the Catalans from Gallipoli. They crossed all of Thrace, without the resistance of any person, wrecking and destroying all the provinces they passed through with great inhumanity. The Turkish Greeks with their captain, Meleco, were Christians, but more in word than in deed. He did not choose to undertake a new treaty to return to the service of Andronicus, either because he doubted that they would accept him, or that if they did accept, he feared that they would kill them even after giving them assurances. They knew that the Greeks and their ruler, Andronicus, were deeply resentful of the battle that the Catalans had won at Apros. They had been the first to abandon Michael, having subsequently left the imperial banners of Andronicus, whom they were serving, and had joined his greatest enemies, the Catalans and Aragonese. For seven years they had continually destroyed the Empire with them, causes enough to fear that in any reconciliation they might make, such great offenses would never be forgotten.

Although Meleco despaired of taking that opportunity, luck opened another way for him that he could follow easily. The prince of Serbia offered him a good reception, with the condition that he would not bear or use arms except when the ruler desired it. Meleco accepted and he and his men remained in Serbia in a calm and quiet life, very different from what they had before they came there.

Kalel, the captain of the Turks, who came to the number of thirteen hundred horsemen and eight hundred infantry, went to

Macedonia, where he determined to settle until they could safely return to their own country. Within the province in the meanwhile they did so much damage that the inhabitants were forced, because they did not have the strength to drive them out, to arrive at some agreement that would oblige them to leave. It seemed most convenient for both sides for Kalel to abandon the province if the natives would assure him the pass at Christople and give him ships to cross the strait. Without these two aids, or lacking either of them, his return to their country of Anatolia was impossible. The Turks knew little of navigation, since, as long as they still had provinces to win on the mainland, they had no interest in those on the other side of the sea. Kalel, therefore, could not rely on those of his nation for ships. The pass at Christople was impossible to get through because of the wall that had been constructed in it after our men had come through.

The Greeks advised Emperor Andronicus of the pacts under which the Turks had given their word to leave the province. They emphasized the danger and risk involved in detaining them and what all Macedonia would suffer if the Turks despaired of getting through the pass and found that the way to their country was closed to them. They could attack Thessalonica or undertake some similar enterprise to which their desperation would force them. Recalling how dearly his contempt for the Catalans had cost him, he was quickly moved to take a decision and accept their terms, offering the Turks free passage through Christople and ships to cross the narrow strait of the Hellespont. In order that no one could annoy them, he sent a guard of three thousand horsemen to them under the famous captain called Senancrip Stratopedarch,[2] one of the principal dignitaries of that Empire. With these men, Kalel and the rest of the Turks went through the pass of Christople and traveled on almost to Gallipoli, where they had been told that they would be given embarkation.

REFERENCES

1. When the Turks decided to return to Anatolia, refusing the three or four strong-

holds that they had been offered, the Catalans gave them the weapons and horses that had been taken in the battle of the Cephissus. (Setton, p. 14.)

2. The Stratopedarcha was the prefect of the militia, according to Nicephorus in Book IV. (Rosell, p. 60.)

Sixty-Seventh Chapter

THE GREEKS BREAK THE WORD PROMISED TO THE TURKS,
WHO DISCOVER THE TREACHERY, TAKE A
CASTLE, AND FORTIFY IT

As THEY AWAITED the ships, Senancrip's captains and men observed the great riches that the Turks were carrying, which were spoils from their own provinces. To them it seemed great cowardice to allow those barbarians, who were so few, to return to their own country with these goods. They decided to break the royal word and security, judging that action as less unworthy than to suffer so much disgrace. They agreed on how and when they would attack them, deciding that it should be at night, the appropriate time for people not being on their guard. They did not discuss the matter with enough secrecy, so that the Turks received news of what was being plotted against them, in such great offense to reason and justice themselves, as well as to the universal law of nations which provides for the inviolability of good faith, even when promised to the enemy himself.

The Turks rose up that night and occupied the nearest castle that was available to them, putting themselves on defense with the determination to die revenged. When Senancrip and his captains discovered what had occurred, there was great confusion among them about whether it was better to attack or to advise the Emperor of what was happening. The latter opinion prevailed; they then informed him. But, although the message was sent immediately and went rapidly, Andronicus delayed in his decision: a fault very common to rulers and most pernicious, since the occasion passes while the solution is withheld, arriving when it is no longer possible to profit by it. And moreover it is even more dangerous when the matter is of major importance, as are those having to do with war, when small mistakes become the causes of the loss of kingdoms and monarchies. To delay in the choice of options to follow is worse than to carry out that which is regarded as less appropriate. In this case it was obvious how much more important it was for Andronicus either to command that they should at once fight the Turks or give them ships to cross the strait. Whichever of these two courses that he should take, which were the choices about which he was in doubt and uncertainty, it would have been more appropriate than postponing the decision in order to give the Turks time to receive help or to fortify and prepare themselves, as they did.

The Turks, disillusioned because the Greeks had not kept their word, became desperate men, making a great effort to warn the people of their own nation on the other side of the strait. Their countrymen, learning of the danger in which Kalel and his men found themselves and the vast riches that they had, came over to their aid in great multitudes, making many voyages in small vessels. When they saw that there were now so many of them together, they not only undertook to defend themselves, but also began to raid the land, with which they were well acquainted.

Sixty-Eighth Chapter

THE TURKS CONQUER MICHAEL AND DO
GREAT DAMAGE IN THRACE

WHEN EMPEROR ANDRONICUS, fearing that those few enemies were gaining strength, finally decided to finish them off at once, his resolution almost cost him the life of his son,

Michael Palaeologus. Michael undertook the expedition in person
with the men of war that he had and a great multitude of peasants,
who were drawn more by greed for spoils than by a desire to fight.
They were all sure that when the Turks saw Emperor Michael and
the pomp and vanity of his courtiers, they would surrender. The
Greeks were so negligent that they went in pursuit of the Turks
as if it were a hunting trip, without putting their squadrons in
order and forgetting all points of the ordinary conduct of war,
either in ignorance or because any preparation against so few people seemed useless to them. But the Turks, having no other recourse than to fight or die meanly, left their women, children, and
property with enough men for their defense inside their fortifications and went out to confront their enemies with seven hundred
horsemen.

Emperor Michael came up very imprudently, expecting to find
the Turks not out in the field, but instead defending the small
space of land that they had fortified. When they discovered the
troop of seven hundred riders that had come out to meet them,
there was so much disturbance among the Greeks and disorder in
the peasants that their ranks broke before they were attacked. The
troop of the seven hundred Turkish cavalry closed in on the side
where they saw the colors and the royal standard of Emperor
Michael, who was neither in a secure area nor surrounded by the
defense that he should have had. By this time the peasants had
already turned tail and abandoned the post with which they had
been charged. Many soldiers in whom Michael had had some confidence thereupon did likewise, so that in a moment he found himself defeated without fight.

The standard was lost. Even though with shouts and pleas
Michael tried to stop those who were fleeing, he was either not
heard or ignored. When he finally realized that he was alone and
pressed by the Turks, he turned the reins of his horse, full of tears
and anguish, and fled with the rest. His enemies pursued him, and
if some honorable captains and soldiers had not turned to face and
engage the Turks, he would doubtless have been overtaken. But
the Turks were detained by those few who had resisted them and

left off the pursuit. They put all their strength into defeating those who were defending themselves, whom they finished off in a short time, thus bringing their victory to a successful close.

They sacked Michael's tents and lodges, finding much money and jewels of great value in the one which had been his lodging. Among them was an imperial crown with very fine stones of inestimable price. This came into the hands of Kalel, who put it on his head, joking about the imperial dignity and insulting in words the man who had lost it with so much dishonor. One of the causes for Michael's rout was that he was fighting men to whom he had broken his word; since keeping one's word is required by the universal law of nations, and we are obliged to do so by all divine and human laws, God permits such events as the barbarian triumph over the Christians in punishment for such execrable evil. The Greeks should have remembered what it had cost them a few years before to break faith with the Catalans, for if the Catalans and Aragonese had found a ruler who had encouraged them, they might well have taken over the Greek Empire in their resentment. After this victory so unexpectedly won, the proud and emboldened Turks raided all through the province of Thrace, wrecking and destroying what they could. For a period of two years Andronicus could not stay them and the natives had such fear of them that they no longer went out to till the land.

Sixty-Ninth Chapter

PHILES PALAEOLOGUS CONQUERS THE TURKS,
LEAVING ALL OF THEM DEAD OR CAPTIVE

W HILE THE EMPEROR was attempting to procure foreign militia to raise an army because he could not form one of his own, a kinsman of his, Philes Palaeologus, a man until then regarded as timid, who wanted only to stay quietly at home, asked him for his permission and power to assemble the men he would need, offering to take charge of this mission himself. Andronicus recognized the man's excellence, believing that he must be sent from God to remedy so many damages, and determined to put him in charge of the war. He left Philes to his own methods, because he was sure that his own sins were the cause of so many evils, since a great army had not been enough to conquer a small number of Turks. Therefore, he put his only hope in Philes's goodness, giving him money, arms, horses, and the men that he wanted.

Before he went out into the field, Philes required that everyone should confess, since it was impossible to achieve any good outcome in any other way. He distributed most of the money in charity for the poor and to the monasteries so that they would be in continuous prayer: general help for all troubles with which to appease the wrath and earn the mercy of God. When he had done this, he sent through many regions to search out the enemy. Then he received information that Kalel with twelve hundred horse had raided the fields of Bessia, where they had done much looting. With this news, Philes traveled for three days out of the villages surrounding Constantinople and pitched camp along the river that is called Xerogypso by the natives. And at the end of two days that he was there, warning reached him near midnight that the Turks were close, laden with great spoils.

Philes prepared himself for the battle; when the sun came up, both sides were revealed clearly and distinctly. In great haste the Turks placed their carts around the captives and loot, made their usual prayer, as Gregoras reports, and threw dust on their heads. When the fighting began, Philes attacked the enemy. The commandant of the right wing, having killed two Turks with his own hands, then was wounded in a foot, so that he had to leave the battle. This so demoralized the men fighting on that side that they would have dispersed if Philes had not encouraged and detained them with his valor. They fought for a long time, but the victory inclined toward Philes's side, and the Turks fled, routed and conquered, with many of them dead in battle. The Greeks followed in pursuit until the Turks reached a castle where they had fortified themselves. Philes pressed his victory, and a few days later besieged them.

When the Emperor heard of the success of the expedition, he sent some Genoese galleys to guard the strait so that no one could come to the aid of the besieged. The Turks realized that their situation was desperate, with all routes for their rescue closed, and determined to leave the castle at night to die like men. Two thousand Bulgar horsemen and many Genoese came to join Philes, whereby the siege was tightened. Even though they saw that Philes was now more powerful, the Turks did not alter their resolution; on the contrary, with renewed courage and spirit they went out at night and attacked the lodges of the camp, but were beaten back and driven out with great losses. The next night they returned to try their fortune again, attacking the tents and lodges of the Bulgars, whence they came out very badly mauled.

As a last resort they resolved to abandon the castle and go back toward the sea, where the galleys of the Genoese were, among whom they hoped to find some mercy, since they had not offended them. The night was very dark, so that many of the Turks who were attempting to go toward the sea fell into the hands of the Greeks, who killed them without pity. The rest reached the water's edge. Nicephorus says that the Genoese killed and captured many. Muntaner adds that this was done under pledge that they would carry them to Anatolia without harming them, but that when they were taken on board the galleys, the Genoese threw them into chains and killed them. However it happened, these Turks, comrades of the Catalans and Aragonese, were finished off, after having harassed the Empire alone for nearly three years as they retreated along the five hundred miles or a little less, that there are between Athens and Gallipoli.[1] Even though there were so few of them, Andronicus had to make use of the Bulgars and Latins to destroy them. Even so, it was taken for a miracle that God had worked through the means of Philes, for when they had seen Michael ruined and conquered, the Greeks believed that there were not now enough human forces to resist the Turks, and that they would have to apply to divine ones instead.

REFERENCES

1. Apparently the Genoese conspired with Andronicus to capture most of the Turkish leaders by this ruse. About half of them were killed and the rest sold at slave markets in Italy. Muntaner lamented the end of his Turkish comrades "and how much it was to their misfortune that they separated from the Company." (Setton, p. 14.)

Seventieth Chapter

OF SOME EVENTS OF THE CATALANS AND
ARAGONESE IN ATHENS

THE CATALANS AND Aragonese, now firm and secure in the provinces of Athens and Boeotia, were governed for some time by Roger Deslaur, as we have said before. But a little later,[1] either as a result of Roger's death or because they had grown tired of his government and had dismissed him, they sent envoys to the King, Don Fadrique. Though they had received but scorn and insult from him, they still had heartfelt affection for him and petitioned him to do them the service of sending a ruler and lord to govern them. With this embassy the King was mollified for his past resentment of their refusal to accept his nephew, the Infante, Don Fernando, in his name. Since Rocafort, who he was sure had been the source of this counsel, was dead, and Providence was now offering him the same opportunity that he had sought then, he did not pursue his anger. It is my understanding, however, that he would not have kept alive his displeasure at the risk of losing such a good occasion to advance his son with an estate so grand.

The King, Don Fadrique, took counsel about the person he should send to the Catalans, deciding then to name his second son, the Infante, Manfred, as ruler and lord of those states, and as such the envoys swore fealty to him in the name of all the Company. But since Manfred was still very young, his father, the King, did not choose for him to go then. Instead he sent Berenguer Estañol,[2] a man of great courage and prudence, to govern them in his name until the Infante should be of age. The envoys were content with this appointment, since they had also authority from the Company to accept him. Berenguer Estañol joined them with his galleys and returned to Athens, where he was well received, since the Catalans and Aragonese now saw themselves under the protection of their natural rulers. This they would have sought before if Rocafort had not prevented those honorable intentions for his private interests.

Berenguer Estañol having arrived to take charge of the government of our people, undertook then a war with the rulers bordering their state, now with one and then another, which he deemed a suitable measure to establish his rule in the land, since it was traditional for the Catalans to be always occupied in some foreign combat in order to avoid the civil and domestic dissentions that idleness customarily awoke in their fierce temperaments. The Catalans of Athens very prudently accepted this plan as a principal means of their security. They had on one side Emperor Andronicus, with whom they were rarely at peace; on another, the ruler of the Morea; and on the other two, the Despot of Larta and the Lord of Vlachia. While they fought with one, they called truce with the others, preserving themselves in this way for many years with so much reputation in the East that I have read of them in the history of Cantacuzene, that was brought to light by Father Pontani,[3] that that same John Cantacuzene refused to leave the side of Andronicus, the grandson, and go out from Constantinople to govern a province: he gave for his excuse that the province was next to the Catalans, so that he could not reach it without many men of war. This explanation seemed adequate and they accepted it. And in an anecdote that Zurita includes, he tells about a Dominican friar[4] who was encouraging the King of France to undertake the conquest of the Holy Land: the cleric pointed out that the Catalans had already opened the way and that it would be important to the expedition to have them on his side and to urge them to go along on the enterprise.

While Berenguer Estañol lived and was chief and captain in Athens, the Catalans had continual wars, not with all at one time, but with first one and then another, without ever any leisure for their arms. When Estañol died, they again asked the King, Don Fadrique, for a governor and leader to command them for the Infante, Manfred. Don Fadrique sought to give them a distinguished person; consequently, he ordered his son, the Infante Don Alfonso,[5] to depart from Catalonia with ten galleys and sent him, very well accompanied, to govern the state for his brother, Manfred. The pleasure that the Catalans and Aragonese took in receiving a pledge of the royal House of Aragon among them was noteworthy.

But Alfonso did not govern very long for his brother, Manfred, who died a short time afterward. Don Fadrique then sent to tell the Company to accept as their prince and lord Alfonso himself, who was ruling them. With this decision, the Catalans and Aragonese were all left very content, considering that their state was now secure because their prince resided with them. They took great care in his marriage, so that his lordship would be preserved in his sons and descendants. They gave to him as wife the daughter and only heir of Bonifacio da Verona, whom they had loved and honored greatly as long as he lived, and after his death they had wished to perpetuate the government and command of their state in his descendants.[6] This lady had a third part of the island of Negroponte and thirteen castles on the mainland of the Duchy of Athens. The Infante, Don Alfonso, had many sons of her, and she became one of the most distinguished women of her time. Zurita, however, does not agree on this with Muntaner, whom I am following.

At this point we come to the end of the expedition of our Catalans and Aragonese, until such time as we have extensive and dependable information about what happened during the one hundred and fifty years that they held power in that state.[7]

REFERENCES

1. In 1312, Deslaur was no longer *marescalcus et rector universitatis,* or Marshal and Rector of the Company. (Setton, p. 15.)

2. Estañol was a knight from Ampurias, who governed as Vicar General for four years until he died in 1316. He was replaced by Guillermo Thomasi, temporary Captain and Viceregent of the Company. The little prince, Manfred, was ten when Thomasi arrived; he died from a fall from his horse at Trapani in 1317, and was

buried in the Dominican Church. He was succeeded as absentee Duke of Athens by his younger brother, Guillermo II of Aragon. When the latter died in 1338, he left the duchy in his will to his younger brother, Juan II, Marquis of Randazzo. Juan ruled for only a decade, dying of the Black Death of Europe in 1348. (Setton, p. 16-17.) None of the Aragonese Dukes ever saw the Acropolis. There were three more official Dukes of the Sicilian House of Aragon: Fadrique I of Randazzo (1348-1355); Fadrique III the Simple of Sicily (1355-1377); and María of Sicily (1377-1379?). They were followed by two more Dukes and many subsequent claimants in the fourteenth and fifteenth centuries from the House of Aragon in Catalonia.

3. The work cited is the *Historiarum libri IV ex interpretatione Jacobi Pontani*, published in Paris in 1645. Cantacuzene's history was thus the first work to be published by Colbert, the famous printing house of the Louvre, under the patronage of Louis XIV for the great series of Byzantine historians that is now called the Paris Corpus. The work begins with the accession of Andronicus III in 1320 and ends a few years after the author's own abdication. John VI Cantacuzene was the Emperor of the Byzantine state, succeeding the Palaeologus dynasty, from 1341 to 1354. After the fall of Constantinople to the Turks in 1453, John's descendants were a Phanariote family that became promient in Rumanian history, entering the service of the Turks and rising in the Ottoman Empire. In Moncada's time, the five sons of Andronic Cantacuzene (1553-1600) were rulers in Moldavia and Wallachia.

4. In Chapter XI of Book VI, he reports that a cleric of the order of Saint Dominic had composed a Latin discourse in 1332, from which Zurita translates some paragraphs. The friar is exhorting the King of France, Philippe of Valois, to undertake a crusade to the Holy Land. (Gili Gaya, p. 361.)

5. King Fadrique's illegitimate son, Alfonso Fadrique, was sent to govern for his younger half brothers as Vicar General, arriving in Piraeus with ten galleys full of assorted adventurers. He remained as actual ruler of the territory for about fourteen years (1317-1330), styling himself "President of the fortunate army of the Franks in the Duchy of Athens." It was a period of energetic expansion for the Catalans, who took several castles on the Island of Negroponte and then moved into Thessaly after the death of Duke John II Angelus Ducas in 1318. Alfonso Fadrique was retired as Count of Malta and Gozzo in 1331 and died seven years later. He was replaced as Vicar General by Nicholas Lancia in 1338, after a brief interim service by the Marshal, Odo de Nouvelles. A subsequent Count of Malta and Gozzo, Niccolo Acciajuoli, was a distinguished Florentine banker and courtier who had been Grand Seneschal to the Kingdom of Sicily under the boy king, Luis, Fadrique's grandson. His family, whose name is derived from *acciaio* or steel, brought about the end of the Catalan control of Athens ultimately in 1388. The Acciajuolis gathered their fortune from twelfth-century steel foundries, moving into banking, finance, and other kinds of power in Florence. (Setton, p. 68.)

6. Marulla da Verona brought also titles to the island of Aegina and the fortress towns of Zeitaunion (or Lamia) and Gardiki in Thessaly with her marriage in 1317, although she did have a brother, Tomas. Among the many children she bore before her death in 1326 were Pedro Fadrique, Juan Fadrique, Jaime Fadrique, Bonifacio Fadrique, and Simona, who married Giorgio II Ghisi, Venetian noble of Negroponte.

7. A note appearing at the end of the Barcelona manuscript says: "I have seen no other memoirs, only a fragmentary page on which there is . . ." (Gili Gaya, p. 363.) We now, however, have the *larga y verdadera noticia* that Moncada awaited, with the works of Antoni Rubió i Lluch and Kenneth M. Setton's *Catalan Domination of Athens 1311-1388*.

APPENDIX

I

When Moncada was thirty-six years old, he was in the prime of his career as a diplomat in the service of the king, Felipe IV of Castile. Under the title of Count of Osona, which he bore as the first son of Gastón de Moncada, he traveled frequently, discharging a variety of missions for the government. One of these was a secret embassy on behalf of his sovereign to Catalonia, where a new viceroy had recently been appointed. The Catalans were refusing to accept their designated ruler, Bishop Juan Sentís, until the king had first pledged to uphold through him the traditional customs of that princedom. Catalonia had been guaranteed certain privileges of usage inherent in its own laws ever since the Castilian monarchs had come into possession of the region many years before.

Because of some harsh excesses of his predecessor, the new Bishop of Barcelona was being denied the oath of allegiance by his subjects. It was a delicate situation that King Felipe confided to Moncada, trusting his tact and discretion — as well as his fidelity, since the Count himself belonged to the proud and ancient Aragonese-Catalan nobility that continued to be restive under foreign domination. We know that he deftly reconciled the opponents, to the great satisfaction of the king and his advisors in the Supreme Council. They rewarded him by naming him ambassador to Germany, replacing the prestigious Count de Oñate of the family that had contributed much to the exploration of the North American continent. The appointment was made in June of 1623 in Vienna, but for unrecorded reasons Moncada did not reach there to assume his position until July of the following year.

King Felipe's letter of instructions to him, which remained secret until discovered and published by Cayetano Rosell y López in 1852, reveals the relationship of the monarch and his courtier. The original document, now in Codice H 35, folio 168, of the Biblioteca Nacional at Madrid, is as follows:

WHAT THE KING DESIRES THAT YOU, DON FRANCISCO DE
MONCADA, COUNT OF OSONA, SHOULD DO IN CATALONIA:

You have been informed in detail about all that has happened
in regard to his oath to the Bishop of Barcelona, whom I have
named as Viceroy of Catalonia, and about the resistance that has
arisen there. Although my people declare that these measures were
born of the love they bear for me and of their desire to see me in
that Princedom, which I believe, there has, nevertheless, been so
much excess that it would be just to proceed to the punishment of
the guilty without waiting for more instances. But wishing to use
the most gentle methods with vassals who have been so loyal to
me and that I love and value so much, and having been requested
by the Count of Olivares, my Lord Chamberlain and Royal Master
of Horse, to suspend any harsh measures until we see what results
an investigation carried out by you can achieve, I have agreed to
this procedure. Therefore, I charge you to leave immediately for
the city of Barcelona without any delay. Proceed on your way with
the greatest diligence possible, with the appearance of going about
business for our House, but without indicating in any manner that
I have sent you or that the journey has been undertaken on my
orders.

When you have arrived, you shall meet with the Bishop of Barcelona with the greatest dissimulation possible. You shall tell him
what you are doing; charging him, too, with secrecy, give him my
letter of authorization that you are carrying. Inform yourself of all
the particulars to be taken into account in order to further your
purpose. When you have gone into the business thoroughly and
found out the state of affairs, you shall proceed to the best disposition of the problem that your prudence and devotion to my service,
and your knowledge of matters and feelings there, finds most
suitable.

In our view, it is a matter of prime importance firmly to establish the nobility of the Princedom and of its towns and cities, as
well as other persons who have opposed the resistance that has

occurred, telling them, if you deem it necessary, that I have found myself well served by their zeal and good intentions shown on this occasion, and anything else that you think to the purpose. Give the Count of Olivares's letters that you carry in this regard to the persons who seem appropriate to you.

Then you will try (after you have ascertained who are the persons fit for what we are attempting and who are not inclined toward us in the matter) to bring them around by whatever means you find convenient. Tell them in particular that there is little justice in their protests, and that what has been ordered was done in conformity to their privileges and is most proper to my service and to the good government of the princedom, which has always been my major concern; without my desiring, in any case, to restrict the observance of their privileges.

When this is done, unless it seems better to you to apply your first effort to those already inclined toward us without delaying for the second effort, you may deliver the letters you carry from the Count of Olivares for the city of Barcelona and the representatives of the Princedom, explaining fully in his behalf his desire that this matter be settled through his good offices, both because of its importance to my service as well as for the good of the Princedom and the city of Barcelona. Offer them in the Count's name, that if they agree to his written proposal, he will take special care that I carry out their wishes to their satisfaction, and that not only in present but in future matters as well, he will be charged with representing them to me and winning my support for them.

Although I have considered sending someone from the Council of Aragon to deal with punishment for the guilty, I have decided against it for the reasons that I have written at the beginning. It will be advisable, however, that this word be unofficially circulated there, without it being attributed to you or any officer of mine, and that you avail yourself of it, either confirming it, if you think it advantageous to do so, or stating that it has no basis, if this should seem more suitable.

When you have arrived and observed the state of affairs, inform me about it by express mail, being careful to dispatch your letter in all secrecy. During the course of negotiation, you will do the same in regard to what can be expected from it, and when it is finished, concerning the results, arranging to get the word here as quickly as possible, since you understand how important it is not to lose a moment of time, so that in accordance with your report, I may take the most appropriate resolution. As to anything else that may occur, I leave you to deal with it, relying on your prudence to follow the route that you regard most suitable. With that I remain assured of a good outcome.

I, the King
Madrid, December 30, 1622

II

Samuel Gil y Gaya's prologue to the CLASICOS CASTELLANOS *edition of the* EXPEDICION, *published by Espasa-Calpe, S. A., of Madrid in 1941, remains the most authoritative study of the work yet undertaken. The complete essay appears below.*

PROLOGUE

The information about Moncada that his biographers have transmitted to us has its origin in the *Cataluña ilustrada* of his contemporary, Esteban de Corbera, who left a manuscript of this work, later to be augmented and published by Fray José Gómez de Porres as *Continuación de Cataluña ilustrada de Corbera,* printed in Naples by Antonio Gramignani in 1678. Folios 8, 434, and 435 are concerned with Moncada. Nicolás Antonio, who knew Corbera's manuscript, as he states in an essay on "Stephanus de Corbera" in the *Biblioteca hispana nova,* collected and amplified these facts for that work in 1672. All biographical works since then have been based on these two sources, most of them limited to reproducing what Corbera and Nicolás Antonio wrote, without adding on their own more than a few details, generally of little importance, to illuminate the life of the author of the *Expedición.* The works of the scholar Vicente Jimeno, author of *Escritores del*

reino de Valencia (Volume I, pages 326-7), which was published
at Valencia in 1747, and of Fray José Rodríguez, whose *Biblioteca valentina* was printed by Joseph Thomas Lucas in Valencia
in 1747 (page 142), were used by Eugenio de Ochoa, who wrote
the prologue for an edition of the book that we are now reissuing.
It was published in Paris in 1840 by Baudrey as Volume 18 of the
colección de autores españoles, in *Tesoro de historiadores españoles.* According to Foulché-Delbosc in *Revue hispanique* of 1919
(Volume XLV, page 353), this Paris edition is a reprint of the
Madrid edition of 1805, the prologue of which was totally re-
produced by Jaime Tío in another edition printed in Barcelona
in 1842.

All these precursors are referred to by don Cayetano Rosell in
the section of his prologue to *Historiadores de sucesos particulares*
that he devotes to Moncada; and although he does add some interesting details that he succeeded in verifying, the life of our
author remains merely sketched in a vague and statistical form:
dates, positions he held, favors that he received at court. The facts
do not suffice for us to appreciate the distinctive aspects of Francisco de Moncada's personality, much less to see how his life is
reflected in his work, which is always the literary critic's primary
interest in biography. In this prologue we are forced to present to
the reader, with the aid of facts both published and unedited that
we have succeeded in collecting, the most characteristic traits of
this fine aristocrat of politics, military affairs, and style.

The family of the Moncadas, whose name is joined to the
earliest enterprises of the Catalan Reconquest, possessed in the sixteenth century, in addition to their ancestry and wealth, all the
prestige that legend had attached to the history of those men who
had fought tenaciously against the infidel Moor in dark and distant
centuries. Writers and prelates had embossed the nobility of their
illustrious surname with titles redolent of sanctity and wisdom.
The French and Sicilian aristocracies were related to branches of
the Moncada family, which reflects in their respective countries the
glory and influence of the Spanish Moncadas, so esteemed by the
kings of the House of Austria. Felipe II had named Francisco de

Moncada, the grandfather of our author, Marquis of Aytona. Don Gastón de Moncada received the charges, among others, of Viceroy of Aragon and Cerdeña and Ambassador to Rome. Of Gastón's marriage to Catalina de Moncada, baroness of Callosa, was born in Valencia their first child, Francisco de Moncada, baptized the 29th of December in 1586. (The birth is also attested in a *Consulta sobre las encomiendas procedentes de órdenes militares en el reino de Aragón,* available in the Biblioteca Nacional in Ms. No. 2336, folio 130, which was ordered by Moncada's grandson, Miguel, for the purpose of proving that many of his ancestors had been born in Valencia, thereby bequeathing him the right to some estates of the Order of Calatrava in Valencia.)

The villa of Aytona had been ceded in fief to Guillén de Moncada by Jaime I the Conqueror, as a dowry for his vassal's wife, Constanza, who was the natural daughter of the king of Aragon, Pedro II. Guillén, who had been lord of Aytona until then, was established as a count by Charles I and as a marquis by Felipe II, as recorded in the royal decree of October 1, 1581. This title, with all the óthers of the House of Moncada, now belongs to the dukes of Medinaceli. Further on we shall see that the desire to exalt their own was one of the principal motives that gave impulse for the narration of that famous expedition on which so many of the Entenzas and Sicilian Moncadas were distinguished.

About his youth we are left with few concrete facts. Alberto Mireo in chapter 387, page 256, of *Scriptor* tells us of the precocity of his talent and the inclination that he showed for classical studies from the first years of his education. All his writings that are left to us — prepared or at least planned for the greater part before he reached the age of thirty-five — effectively reveal a spirit formed from childhood by knowledge of the Greek and Latin classics, although there may be some exaggeration in Mireo's praise.

The political and military missions of his father, on which Don Francisco almost always accompanied him, were an excellent apprenticeship in war and the knowledge of man that later served him in his confrontation with the thorny difficulties that he was to overcome in Flanders and Vienna, much to the satisfaction of

Felipe IV and the Count-Duke of Olivares. Escolano says that the first son of Gastón de Moncada "served from childhood on the voyages that took place by sea"; some documents also tell us that he served the king from his tenderest years in the galleys commanded by the Marquis of Santa Cruz. This explains why he was preferentially designated to naval commands in the Flanders campaigns, in which he was revealed to be very experienced. Only to please the king would he accept missions with the army, as he made clear to King Felipe IV in letters we shall discuss further on.

At least by 1610 he was married to Margarita de Castro y Cervellón, daughter and heiress of the baron of La Laguna, whose titles passed in this way to the Moncada family. (We base this as the latest possible date, on Escolano's work, which reports that the first son of the House of Moncada "is married to the daughter of the baron of La Laguna." It was printed in 1611, but the prologue is dated 1610.) Margarita was the marquise of La Puebla, viscountess of Illa, baroness of La Laguna, lady of Alfajarán y Hoz and of the Houses of Cervellón and Despés, according to Paz y Meliá's *Archivo y biblioteca de la Casa de Medinaceli*, Volume I, page 392. After marrying, Moncada lived at court at his father's side, until the advent of Felipe IV.

The ascertained dates of his works lead us to assume that the major literary activity of our author was completed between his marriage and 1623, when the *Expedición* was printed and he was named Ambassador to Germany. In May of 1618 he wrote the second of his letters in Latin to Pedro de Marca, who published them together with his "Genealogía de la Casa de Moncada" in *Histoire du Béarn* in Paris in 1640. Esteban de Corbera tells us that before 1623 he saw a study by Moncada titled *Antigüedad del Santuario de Monserrate,* which was not printed and today is lost. The *Expedición,* unpublished until 1623, was written at least in its first form by 1620, the date of the dedication to his uncle, Juan Moncada, the archbishop of Tarragona. The only work that perhaps was not composed in that period is the *Vida de Boecio.* Its title page: "Vida/ de/ Annizio Man/ lio Torquato/ Severino Boecio/ escritta por/ don Francisco de/ Moncada, marqués de

Aytona, con/ de de Ossona, visconde de Cabrera/ y Bas, gran Senescal de los/ Reynos de Aragón./ Que fué/ Embajador de Alemania, General de la/ Armada de Dunkerke, Gobernador/ y Cappn. General de los Payses Vajos/ y de Borgonna, del consejo de estado/ de su Majestad, y Mayordomo May/ or del sereníssimo sennor In/ fante doɴ Fernando de glo/ riosa memoria./ Franco-fvrti/ Apud Gasparum Rotelium." The licenses bear the date of 1642. The book was printed six years after his death, though this date cannot be established beyond question.

On the basis that the *Expedición* reveals a well-formed writer, Rosell supposes that Moncada must have written more works than have come to our notice. It is possible; but the fact is that no other works are alluded to other than those already mentioned in the books of bibliographers that would certainly have known of the then living Count of Osona, a title borne by the elder sons of the House of Moncada.

From the moment that he was named Ambassador to Germany, we see his energy so absorbed in diplomatic business that he was no longer able to dedicate himself to the pleasant and serene life of letters, that hidden aspiration of his spirit that palpitates with such subtle emotion behind the courtly euphemisms of his letters to the king, demanding relief from the charges that weary him, so that he can return to Spain.

His intervention in politics began in 1622. The king confided in him a secret mission to Catalonia where he was directed to pacify the dissidents who would not accept as Viceroy Bishop Juan Sentís until Felipe IV should first pledge to honor the privileges of that princedom, according to traditional usages. It was the beginning of that disaffection that later exploded into the war of Catalonia. Moncada skillfully carried out his commission and calmed the disturbances to the great satisfaction of the king and the Supreme Council. Before he returned to Barcelona, he was named Ambassador to Germany as a substitute for the Count of Oñate. The appointment was dated June, 1623, according to Julián Paz, *Archivo general de Simancas*, Catalogue II, Vienna, 1913, page 267. But for motives of which we are ignorant, he deferred his trip and did not arrive in Vienna until July of the following year.

From the moment of his arrival at the Imperial court, we can follow the life of Moncada step by step, using as a basis the correspondence that was exchanged between him, the king, and his ministers, of which originals or copies are preserved in several archives and libraries of Europe. We have utilized principally the copies contained in five manuscript volumes of our National Library. Here is the list of papers referring to the Marquis of Aytona that have come to our attention and will be cited subsequently:

Registro de las cartas que escribió el Marqués de Aytona a Su Majestad estando sirviendo la embaxada de Alemania, Volume II, covering the years 1627-9 from January 6, 1627, to December 18, 1629.

Cartas y papeles de Su Magd. para el marqués de Aytona, su embaxador en Alemania, sobre el negocio y rompimiento de Mantua y Monferrato, 1628. Listed by Gayangos in the Spanish manuscripts of the British Museum, volume III, work 417.

Cartas y correspondiencia con el Rey y ministerio sobre la embaxada de Alemania, 1624-33, Biblioteca Nacional of Madrid, manuscript 1433-37.

Papeles relativos a su embajada en Alemania, Julián Paz, *Archivo general de Simancas*, Catalogue II.

Correspondencia de don Francisco de Moncada con Felipe IV, 1634, Archives des anciens gouvernements des Pays-Bas, Brussels, 1906, Volume I, page 42.

Correspondencia del cardenal-infante don Fernando con el Marqués de Aytona, esperando la llegada de Su Alteza, August, 1633 to September 1634 (*idem id.*).

Correspondencia con la infanta Isabel Clara cuando el Marqués estaba en Viena, 1627-28 (*idem id.*, page 45).

Acte de ce qui s'est passé sur le fait de gouvernement politique des Pays-Bas après le decès de madame Isabel et auquel fut commis le seigneur marquis d'Aytona, December 1, 1633.

Commission du gouvernement général des Pays-Bas et de Bour-
gogne pour le marquis d'Aytona, jusques à ce que y arrive l'infant
Ferdinand, December 19, 1633, in Morel-Fatío, *Catalogue des*
Manuscrits espagnols et portugais, Bibliothèque Nationale, Paris,
page 130.

The letters of Moncada, still unpublished, are models of concise
clarity and elegance; besides constituting valuable documents in
the history of the international relations of Spain, they also put us
in contact with the spirit of their author much more than can his
works written for a literary end.

As soon as he took charge of his embassy, he began to intervene
effectively in the negotiations for peace among the German states.
He tried to placate the Duke of Bavaria, who was complaining
that Felipe IV had not helped him to attain the honor of Palatine
Elector. He was forced to win over to the side of the House of
Austria the inconstant Electors of Saxony and Mentz. He attended
the Diet of Hungary, where the Archduke Ferdinand was pro-
claimed and crowned king of that state. He captured the Emperor's
confidence to the point that he sometimes seemed to be the axis of
Imperial politics in Vienna, rather than merely the ambassador of
Felipe IV. The letters that report on these German affairs are in-
cluded in Volumes I, II, and III of the manuscripts in the National
Library of Spain, dated from July 18, 1624, to October 25, 1629.
On several occasions the Count-Duke expresses the approval of the
Spanish Court of the direction that Moncada was able to give to
the negotiations in Germany.

In spite of his diplomatic successes and the esteem that he enjoyed on the part of the Caesarian majesty, Moncada was not content with the kind of life to which his responsibilities obliged him.
He felt homesick for Spain, where he would be able to devote himself completely to his favorite family and literary concerns. The
economic problems to whose immediate solution Felipe IV's ministers had to attend delayed the remittance of funds that Moncada
required for the raising of German and Italian troops, as he had
been ordered, for the defense of several Flemish cities under attack

by the Dutch. Because of this his negotiations went very slowly; on more than one occasion he had to advance his own money to carry out the orders he had received. All these reasons obliged him to beg courteously for his relief in March of 1628. In spite of his reiterated supplications, the Spanish court delayed its answer. He writes,". . . I find myself completely disconsolate, realizing myself so lacking in means with which to aid the service of your Majesty and myself that I cannot but point out to Your Majesty that anyone else who might occupy this post would leave you better served," on August 23, 1628, in a letter collected in Volume II, folio 87. Finally, the Marquis of Mirabel was named his substitute in November and Moncada was granted the permission he had asked to return to Spain. Nevertheless, the replacement did not go for the time being to Vienna, so that Moncada had to remain there until the end of the following year, vainly expressing his impatience in most of his letters. He points out to the king that his father had died in 1625, making the necessity of his return to Spain more urgent. He says that he had inherited the possessions of the family estate with the title of Marquis of Aytona; if the king did not hurry his replacement, the House of Moncada would be ruined and with it Felipe would lose the loyal services that the marquises, his ancestors, had lent to the crown.

But the king needed the intelligence and energy of the new Marquis of Aytona to untangle the exceedingly complicated matters in Flanders. His aunt, Princess Isabel Clara, who was weak and surrounded by ambitious people, asked Felipe IV for a capable counsellor to help her deal with the pressing situation of the Low Countries, daily more difficult under the attacks of the Hollanders, supported by all the enemies of the House of Austria. On May 29, 1629, the king posted to Moncada his appointment as Ambassador Extraordinary to his aunt's court, but in a later letter charged him "until the business in which you are currently so involved and about which you are so well-informed is adequately settled, I deem it necessary and hence order you to remain in that court." The marquis expressed his thanks for the new honor offered to him, and resigned himself to await the order for departure for Brussels, although he first requested leave to visit Catalonia to arrange the affairs of his House. But he did not receive leave, however, because matters in Flanders became critical and required his immediate presence.

After turning over to Jacques Bruneau, the new resident in Vienna, the files of the Embassy, Moncada received orders to leave for Milan to take charge of the government there himself. We do not know the causes that motivated the Monarch's changed decision; perhaps it was at the instance of the marquis himself. But when he arrived in Italy, he received a counter order to leave without losing a moment for Flanders, which he reached on the 11th of November of the same year. King Felipe IV greatly appreciated the promptness with which he was obeyed on this occasion; when Moncada died, he valued this sacrifice as one of the greatest proofs of loyalty that he had received.

A few days after his arrival in Flanders, he begged the king again to retain him there only a short time, so that he could make use of the leave he had been granted to go to Spain and attend to the affairs of his House. The language of his first letters from Flanders, severe enough in comparison to the courteous circumspection with which we have seen him express himself up to that point, indicates clearly his discontent with the new post he now occupied. He did not lack reasons for it: he suspected that the princess feared her nephew might become excessively involved in her domestic affairs, and believed that she had not well received his appointment as chief officer of her court. Therefore, he requested the king to consider whether his services would be more useful in some other place. In addition, the inferior ministers dealt directly with the princess without the knowledge of the Spanish Ambassadors, and Moncada ultimately found himself forced to pay his own expenses because the king did not provide funds with the necessary punctuality.

In a final effort to remedy the chaos in the Low Countries, Felipe IV ordered that the Marquis of Aytona be recognized as supreme commander after his aunt, and counselled her to take no resolution without consulting him. His talent and personal charm, however, did more to bring him into the confidence of Isabel Clara within a short time than did the royal exhortations. He also earned the respect of all the Spanish and Flemish ministers; after a few months he was the indispensable man for all.

In March of 1630 he was given the interim command of the Armada, and definitely confirmed in it in February, 1631. The army was at the charge of the Marquis of Santa Cruz. It is surprising what a clear vision Moncada had of the present and future domination of Spain in Flanders; in most of his letters to King Felipe in 1631-32, he tells him quite directly that these provinces will inevitably be lost, no matter what efforts the Spanish might make to hold them. Foremost among these letters is the one dated March 6, 1631, for its literary beauty and precise description of the dangers in international terms to the House of Austria.

These years were ones of incessant activity for him. He saw to military operations as diligently as he was permitted by means, always scarce and tardy, sent from Spain. He maintained correspondence with the Spanish ambassadors in Italy and Germany in an effort to keep up the spirits of friends and allies of the decadent House of Austria. He intervened in the flight of the queen mother from France and arranged to offer help and encouragement to the Duke of Orleans in his frustrated rebellion against Richelieu. But, in spite of the glory and general admiration that he enjoyed in his post, he had never felt more keenly his desire to abandon the brilliant and active life that his loyalty to his monarch imposed upon him. To his constant petitions for relief came answers such as this insensitive passage in a letter from Felipe dated October 4, 1632 (to be found in Volume V, folio 73): "In one of your letters you ask me for permission to come here, and this at a time when your presence is so much needed there; I believe that you should have thought better of it." We must recognize in him the dignity of a superior spirit that felt an intimate disdain for the present glory that surrounded him and always desired to descend from the high place where his talents and nobility had put him. The judgment of his contemporaries and the brief pause that the period of his command in the descending process of Spanish power in the

Low Countries represent exclude the possibility that we are dealing with a pusillanimous man, concerned only with abandoning
a charge superior to his abilities.

In November, 1632, he was named *mayordomo mayor* to the
Prince-Cardinal Ferdinand, whose journey to Flanders within a
short time was announced. By order of the king, Moncada left the
command of the Navy and assumed in exchange the direction of
the Army. The Marquis expressed his gratitude for both orders
"because in service to Your Majesty I esteem what is given me as
much as what is being taken from me," and further adds, "I regard it as an honor, as I should, to continue serving Your Majesty;
I have no choice but to sacrifice my obedience to Your Majesty."

The death of Princess Isabel Clara placed the general government of the Low Countries, by Felipe IV's decision, in the hands
of Moncada. He then reorganized the Army, attracted some dissidents to the Spanish cause, and won two victories against enemy
troops. In 1635, after having staved off for some time the inevitable downfall of Spanish rule in those provinces, he died on the
field of Goch, a settlement in the Duchy of Cleves, without having
realized his hope for a quiet life of which he had dreamed so
often since leaving Spain never to return. Felipe IV expressed to
Moncada's children, Guillén Ramón and Catalina, the profound
sorrow occasioned him by the loss of such a loyal vassal at the
moment when his services were most needed. His letter of con-
dolence is recorded by Gómez de Porres on page 435: "The death
of the Marquis of Aytona has caused me great sorrow and just
grief, since I have lost in him a minister of so many gifts that I
do not know another who equals him; and I am obliged to suffer
his loss more because he accepted the responsibility of serving
me in Flanders when everyone else declined to do so, and because
he abandoned completely for my service his children and property,
concerning himself only with serving me with fidelity, unselfish-
ness, and love. I am therefore obliged to show my gratitude for
this with a generous hand, since I wish the world to know that
I prize one who knows how to serve as the Marquis did, may God
have mercy upon him."

Seven years after his death the *Vida de Severino Boecio,* which had circulated in manuscript among the numerous admirers of the Marquis of Aytona, was printed in Frankfort. We cannot explain the composition of this work as a mere pastime of an erudite man simply because classical citations that were ostentatious displays of learning among many of his contemporaries are rather scarce. The true meaning of this book, so brief and so simple, for a man like Moncada who lived amid brilliant surroundings and grandeurs with which he could not, in his heart, identify himself, may perhaps be explained by a secret affinity that he had formed in his reading between his spirit and the image of Boethius, admirable for his serenity in adversity, and who had found in thought, not the refuge of the weak and the tired, but instead a stronger inner world, indifferent to either the applause or censure of men. Moncada was certainly never persecuted himself; his glory and power grew without cease. But in spite of that, we can perceive in his life and writing a lightly disdainful gesture, a certain elegant skepticism about his own successes and about the Royal Majesty itself, which he had so totally served.

*   *   *

Although the *Expedición* was not printed for the first time until 1623, it was already written, in any event, in 1620, according to the date of the author's dedication to his uncle, don Juan de Moncada the Archbishop of Tarragona. The library of the Royal Academy of Belles Lettres at Barcelona preserves a manuscript of an authentic version before the edition that we can call "official." This manuscript, published by Foulché-Delbosc in the *Revue Hispanique* (Volume XLV, 1919, pages 349-509), is briefly described in the review, *Estudio* (XXIX, 1920, pages 221-2) in an article signed by M. C. B. It bears the title, *Empresas y victorias alcanzadas por el valor de pocos catalanes y aragoneses contra los imperios de turcos y griegos,* and is a primary form of the work that, when compared to the text of the first edition, clearly shows us its subsequent additions, and, at the same time, Moncada's stylistic techniques.

Some errors in the text of 1623 led Rosell to believe that the *Expedición* was published without receiving the author's final touches. On the contrary, a comparison of both versions presents convincing evidence of the painstaking care with which Moncada corrected his work before deciding to print it. The edition is not only an orderly amplification of the manuscript, but also an effort at embellishment of the style, with a search for the most elegant turn of speech, the most precise word, almost always achieved.

Moncada's corrections of his first version are more numerous and careful at the beginning of the book. As we go forward with the reading, the two versions become more and more alike, until they come to be almost exactly the same in the last chapters. The author, therefore, revised his book carefully. If we were not satisfied by the comparison suggested, we would be convinced by the marginal notes added to the manuscript of Barcelona by Moncada himself, indicating the appropriateness of adding or deleting something from the text, suggestions that were subsequently followed in the edition of 1623.

Consequently, the *Expedición*, according to Foulché-Delbosc, has passed through three successive phases: first, the manuscript; then, the self-criticism made by the author in the marginal notes on rereading it, and finally the printed text.

Nevertheless, the suggestions of Rosell and others about some editorial errors have some foundation. The book was printed when the author was already in Vienna. In his absence the copyists changed some words, especially proper names, and thus they were printed without Moncada being able to correct them. The editor warned of this in the following prologue:

FROM THE PRINTER TO THE READER: Although in the correction of this book the care that my obligation and its importance require has been shown, some mistakes may remain that we call *errata*. What printed work is entirely free of them? Perfection is very rare in frail humanity. The greatest diligence still results in omissions; it is impossible to catch everything. Those errors that do not change the true sense of the subject are less important. To err in the proper names of persons and places is the major inconvenience, because it is to fail in a matter which requires the most accuracy and verification. This cannot be helped, however, without the principal author of the work. The blame for the faults, where they exist, falls to the clerks whose carelessness perverts the fidelity of the original in their transcription; it is easy to change letters and consequently names. This complaint has always been common about the confusion that such negligence causes in histories, since hardly any has escaped this danger. It may be that in this way some names have been changed or perverted, such as Trene for Irene, Gregorio for George, and others in like manner. They are accidents that seem excusable because they happen so easily. It has been impossible to prevent them. The author, whose duty it was to correct such errors, was absent and the copy of his work was corrupt. Only his authority and censure could have repaired it. In general, I am confident the damage will be negligible. May the curious reader be indulgent and await corrections in the next edition.

The mistakes are for the most part unimportant and do not suffice to convict the author of slovenliness, as one of his critics has done.

Patriotism and the desire to honor the memory of the Moncadas who participated so brilliantly in the Catalan-Aragonese dominion of Athens moved our author to study the ancient Catalan chronicles and to compare them to the accounts of Byzantine historians who wrote shortly after the deeds of the *Expedición*. He saw contradictions among them and decided to write a narrative of those events that would be impartial and based on critical study of his sources. He was aided by the *Chronicles* of Muntaner and Desclot, the *Memoires* of Berenguer de Entenza, and the chapters dedicated to the expedition by Zurita in his *Anales de Aragón*, and the works of the Greek historians, Pachymeres, Gregoras, Chalcocondyle, Cantacuzene, and several others. Two articles by the Catalan scholar, Antoni Rubió i Lluch, examine these sources: *"Estudios sobre los historiadores griegos acerca de las expediciones catalanes a Oriente"* in the *Revista de Ciencias Históricas* of Barcelona (Volume III, 1881, pages 57-70) and *"La expedición y dominación de los catalanes en Oriente juzgadas por los griegos,"* in *Memorias de la Real Academia de Buenas Letras* of Barcelona (Volume IV, 1887, pages 5-123).

We have left to the notes that accompany the text we are publishing the evaluation of the degree to which each of these sources was utilized. That examination would lengthen this prologue beyond the limits that we intend. It is enough to indicate here that Moncada follows almost always chapters 194-243 in Muntaner's *Chronicle* with regard to the order of the narrative, diverging from it only when necessary to go into episodes on which there is disagreement among the historians or he wishes to present personal critical judgment in regard to the deeds he is describing. Gibbon errs when he says that Moncada "never cites his authorities" on page 365 of Fitzmaurice-Kelly's *History of Spanish Literature* (1914). On the contrary, the frequency with which he names the authors that he follows is most unusual in historians of the seventeenth century.

The author did not live to realize his undertaking entirely. He interrupts his history at the moment when the Catalans secure their domination of the Duchy of Athens, announcing his intention to continue the work when "we have full and true information about what happened in the space of one hundred fifty years that they held that state." We have already shown in the preceding biographical notes that diplomatic affairs and the Flanders wars occupied him until his death, before he could write the second part of his work. But it has been continued more recently in the numerous and scholarly researches of Rubió i Lluch: *Catalunya a Grecia. Estudis històrics i literaris* (Barcelona, 1906); *La lengua y la cultura catalanes en Grecia en el siglo XIV*, Volume II of the *Homenaje a Menéndez y Pelayo*; *Atenes en temps del catalans* (Volume I of *Anuari del l'Institut d'Estudis Catalans* of 1907); *Els governs de Matheu de Moncada i Roger de Lluria en la Grecia catalana*, Volume IV of the *Anuari* for 1912; *"La població dels ducats catalans de Grecia"* in the *Boletín de la Academia de Buenas Letras de Barcelona* (Volume IV of 1907-8); and *"Significació de l'elogi de l'Acropólis d'Atenes pel rei Pere el Cerimoniós"* in Volume III of the *Homenaje* (1925). Thanks to his research, we begin to have "the full and true information" that Moncada needed when he left his history interrupted.

In spite of his extensive classical culture, Moncada did not undertake the history as a mere dilettante humanist, in the mode that Italian historiography of the Renaissance had imposed on all Europe, but rather as a man of action who could see the past behind the present, and his narrative is an intensely dramatic actualization of the Aragonese and Catalan deeds in the Byzantine Empire.

No study has yet been undertaken of our historians of the Golden Age that would permit us to fix with any exactitude the significance of Moncada in classic Spanish historiography. E. Fueter's *History of Modern Historiography* is limited to telling us that the *Expedición* is no more than a superficial arrangement, with humanistic rhetoric, of chapters 194-243 of Ramón Muntaner's *Crónica*, with some additions taken from Zurita and the Byzantine historians, and places it in the class of memoirs and military monographs along with the works of Mármol, Mendoza, Melo, and others. He states, besides, that the novelistic nature of the material was what invited Moncada to choose it, because it lent itself to the purpose of singing a hymn to Aragonese valor.

All these critics have spoken to some degree of the Latinistic rhetoric of our historians of the sixteenth and seventeenth centuries. But when the attempt is to define its extent in specific terms, it is usually claimed that all of them deliberately imitate Tacitus, Titus Livy, Cicero, Sallust, as if no important differences existed among these Latin writers. It is curious to observe that in our manuals of literary history Moncada is accused of imitating each one of them, and even all four of the authors mentioned. This rhetoricism which, defined only in this vague and general manner, has come to be almost a cliché in the criticism of all Renaissance historiography, has, nevertheless, shades sufficiently differentiated to separate periods and authors.

The first phase of humanism in history, represented in Italy by Petrarch and in Spain by Marineo Sículo, Vaseo, Garibay, Sepúlveda, and, in part, Mariana, is characterized by the eagerness to produce in the historical account an esthetic effect like that of a tragedy or poem, according to the Ciceronian definition of history

as *opus oratorium maximum* [the greatest work of orators]. Their
works, generally written in Latin, undertake to imitate Titus Livy,
in whom they admired not only the richness of his language, but
also his preference for matters that lend themselves to esthetic
and declamatory development. Machiavelli and Guicciardini in-
augurated in Italy the new school of the Renaissance, more realistic and less poetic. In our country this second phase does not
appear so differentiated as in Italy; instead, it was formed little by
little in a slow evolutionary process without a fixed dividing line.
But it is mainly perceptible in the historians of particular events,
such as Moncada and Hurtado de Mendoza, whom the concrete
nature of their material and the contemporary view of reality
obliged to look at facts more or less critically, and generally to
subject their purely formal and limited rhetoricism to the language
of concise, yet conceptual, diction of Sallust and Tacitus. History
was still valued primarily as literature, but with real foundations
established with a certain critical sense, and with the literary ele-
ment limited to ornamental effects achieved by dint of meticulous
and classical expression. Only the historians of the Indies—except
Gómara and Solís—wrote completely naturally, imitating the Roman historians in no way.

Some critics have wanted to make Hurtado de Mendoza the model that Moncada proposed to follow in the *Expedición* and have
even painted analogies between its prologue and the one that heads
the *Historia de la guerra de Granada*. After attentively reading
both prologues, we believe that such similarities do not exist, unless those referred to are some general ideas about the purposes
of history that are to be found as well in all contemporaries. Read,
for example, the prologues of Melo and Gómara, and you will see
clearly that what one has here are concepts common to all classical historians. Nevertheless, the possibility is not excluded that
Moncada may have known the manuscript of the *Guerra de Granada* before composing the work we are now discussing. But even
if the alleged imitation did exist, the difference between the temperaments of the two authors would have produced a divergent
development of their respective materials, however similar they

may have been basically. In Mendoza description predominates: color, the movements of armies coming and going in conflict. Besides the desire to glorify some chieftains of his family, it appears that he narrates the uprising of the Moors of Granada merely in order to present the reader with a series of interesting and vivid episodes that took place in an area that he well knew. Moncada is more reflective and more interested in political affairs, the conclusions that a man of government can draw from the events he reports. His accounts are sometimes concluded with very brief reflections, with which he does not pointlessly interrupt the liveliness of the action, but which are compact in content and always profound, revealing in their author the great knowledge of men that allowed him to observe with such clarity the politics of his own time. When discussing the factions that formed in the victorious army, he reports that the party of Berenguer de Entenza was the smaller but consisted of the more important persons, because "those in the minority are usually the better." In another chapter when the Catalans are besieged at Gallipoli, the chiefs deliberate over the decision they should take. Among the proposals that are presented, the least reasonable one prevails, only because the most powerful general supported it. Moncada adds this simple comment: "Governing depends more upon will than on reason."

This aristocratic feeling for the attraction that strong individuals exercise, when applied to his art as a narrator, is responsible for the fact that rather than lingering in the description of great masses of troops in combat or describing a countryside he could have experienced only in a reflective manner, he concentrates the interest on the principal chieftains, whose moral physiognomy appears caught in extraordinary relief. Roger de Flor, Entenza, Jiménez de Arenós live intensely in his pages. The figure of Rocafort, so repulsive, seems endowed with a profoundly dynamic quality that converts him into the most important actor of the *Expedición*. Without him the Company might have dissolved, enticed by the courtly flattery of Emperor Andronicus.

In this book Moncada has left us the account of a great chivalrous adventure that arose in one of the fullest moments of Aragonese history, when, the Reconquest already having been terminated from the Balearic Islands to Valencia, Aragon, triumphant in Italy, spread throughout the Mediterranean its intense vitality.

The marvelous deeds of the Company came to be for Spain a splendid compensation for its almost complete lack of participation in the crusades to the East.

The historical theme of the *Expedición* had its medieval version in poetic fiction: *Tirant lo Blanch* is the story of the chivalric deeds of Roger de Flor. The Romantic sensibility was also moved by the prodigies of valor in those adventures. García Gutiérrez and numerous Catalan writers of the past century have been abundantly inspired by the book that we are now republishing.

SAMUEL GIL Y GAYA

BIBLIOGRAPHY

OTHER WORKS BY MONCADA

Vida de Anicio Manlio Torcuato Severino Boecio. Frankfort: Gaspar Rotelio, 1642. Preserved among the manuscripts of the Biblioteca Nacional in Madrid, Códice Cc. 85.

Antigüedad del Sanctuario de Monserrate. Not extant.

Genealogía de la casa de Moncada. Paris: Pedro de Marca, 1640. Printed in the folio, *Histoire du Béarne,* which also contains two of Moncada's Latin letters.

EDITIONS OF THE CHRONICLE

Empresas y victorias alcancadas por el valor de pocos catalanes y aragoneses contra los imperios de turcos y griegos. 1618?

Manuscript in the Real Academia de Bellas Letras in Barcelona. Published by Foulché-Delbosc, Revue Hispanique, Tomo XLV (1191), 349-509.

Barcelona: Lorenzo Deu, 1623 (quarto).

The title page of this first edition, of which a copy is preserved in the Biblioteca Nacional at Madrid (MS. No. 17760 of the archive for the seventeenth century) offers this information: "Espedición/ de los catalanes y aragoneses/ contra turcos y griegos/ Dirigida a don Ivan de Moncada/ Arçobispo de Tarragona/ por don Francisco de Moncada/ conde de Osona, su sobrino./ Año 1623. Barcelona, Lorenço Deu. 4 fols. + 184 fols., nums, + 4 fols. Portada grabada por Io[an] Batista, platero de Tarragona, con los escudos de Aragón y de la casa de Moncada."

Madrid: Antonio Sancha, 1777 (octavo). Reprinted in 1805.

Paris: C. J. Trouvé et Cie., 1828. Translated to French by the Count of Chamfeu.

Paris: 1840. Printed in Baudry, *Colección de autores españoles,* Tomo XVIII. Introduction by Eugenio de Ochoa.

Barcelona: Juan Oliveres, 1842. Printed in *Tesoro de autores ilustres,* Vol. 3. Prologue and notes by Jaime Tío. Reprinted in 1864 and 1875.

Madrid: Imprenta y Estereotipía de M. Rivadeneyra, 1852. In Cayetano Rosell y López, *Biblioteca de autores españoles desde la formación del lenguaje hasta nuestros días*, Tomo X: *Historiadores de sucesos particulares*, Vol. I.

Madrid, Barcelona: 1853. Printed in *Las glorias nacionales*, Tomo IV.

Madrid: 1860. Printed in *Obras históricas*, Tomo II.

Madrid: Librería, Imprenta, y Biblioteca Militar, 1882.

Paris: Casa Editorial Hispanoamericana, 1912. Printed with *La novela de Roger de Flor* and other works.

Madrid: Ediciones de *La Lectura*, 1924. *Clásicos Castellanos*, edited by Samuel Gil y Gaya.

Madrid: Espasa-Calpe, S. A., 1941. *Clásicos Castellanos*. Prologue and notes by Samuel Gil y Gaya.

Buenos Aires: 1948.

REFERENCE SOURCES

Desclot, Bernardo, *Chronicle of the Reign of King Pedro III of Aragón*. Translated by F. L. Critchlow. Princeton, New Jersey: Princeton University Press, 1928-34.

Lowe, Alfonso, *The Catalan Vengeance*. Routledge and Kegan Paul: London and Boston, 1972.

Miller, William, *The Latins in the Levant: A History of Frankish Greece (1204-1566)*. Cambridge, England: Speculum Historiale, 1964 edition.

Muntaner, Ramón, *The Chronicle of Muntaner*. Translated by Lady Goodenough. London: The Hakluyt Society, 1920-21, 2 vol.

Nicolaur d'Olwer, L., *L'expansió de Catalunya en la Mediterránia Oriental*. Barcelona: 1926.

Ostrogorsky, George, *History of the Byzantine State*. Translated by Joan Hussey. New Brunswick, New Jersey: Rutgers University Press, 1957.

Peers, E. Allison, *Catalonia Infelix*. London: Methuen and Company, Ltd., 1937.

Rubió i Lluch, Antoni, *La expedición y dominación de los catalanes en oriente juzgados por los griegos.* In *Memorias de la Real Academia de Buenas Letras* (4 and 5). Barcelona: 1883.

Setton, Kenneth M. *The Catalan Domination of Athens, 1311-1388.* Cambridge, Massachusetts: The Medieval Academy of America, 1948.

Schlumberger, G. *Expédition des Almugavars ou routiers Catalans en Orient de l'an 1302 à l'an 1311.* Paris: 1902.

Shneidman, J. Lee. *The Rise of the Aragonese-Catalan Empire: 1200-1350.* New York: New York University Press, 1970. Volumes I and II.

GENERAL HISTORICAL BACKGROUND

Altamira y Crevea, *A History of Spanish Civilization.* Translated by P. Volkov. New York: Richard R. Smith, Inc., 1930.

Ballesteros y Beretta, Antonio. *Historia de España y su influencia en la historia universal,* Tomo III. Barcelona: Casa Editorial de P. Salvat, 1922.

Head, Constance, "Manuel Palaiologos: The Traveling Emperor," *Mankind,* Vol. 4, No. 3 (1973).

Kantorowicz, Ernst, *Frederick the Second, 1194-1250.* Translated by E. O. Lorimer. New York: Richard R. Smith, Inc., 1931.

Thompson, James Westfall. *History of Historical Writing.* New York: The Macmillan Company, 1942, 2 vol.

Wood, Charles T. *The French Apanages and the Capetian Monarchy, 1224-1328.* Cambridge, Massachusetts: Harvard University Press, 1966.

INDEX

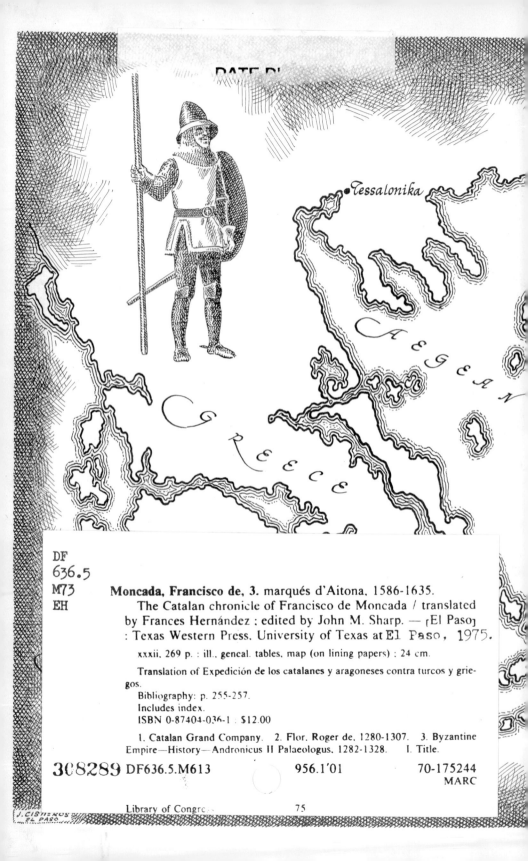